D1474965

Comparative
Judicial Review
and Public Policy

Recent Titles in Contributions in Political Science

Comparative Judicial Review and Public Policy

Edited by Donald W. Jackson
and C. Neal Tate

Prepared under the auspices of the Policy Studies Organization
STUART S. NAGEL, Publications Coordinator

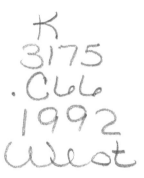

Contributions in Political Science, Number 306

GREENWOOD PRESS

Westport, Connecticut • London

Library of Congress Cataloging-in-Publication Data

Comparative judicial review and public policy / edited by Donald W.
  Jackson and C. Neal Tate.
        p.   cm. — (Contributions in political science, ISSN 0147–1066
  ; no. 306)
    Includes bibliographical references and index.
    ISBN 0–313–28615–9
    1. Judicial review.   2. Political questions and judicial power.
  I. Jackson, Donald Wilson, 1938–   . II. Tate, C. Neal (Chester
  Neal), 1943–   . III. Series.
  K3175.C66   1992
  347′.012—dc20
  [342.712]   92–12511

British Library Cataloguing in Publication Data is available.

Library of Congress Catalog Card Number: 92–12511
ISBN: 0–313–28615–9
ISSN: 0147–1066

First published in 1992

Greenwood Press, 88 Post Road West, Westport, CT 06881
An imprint of Greenwood Publishing Group, Inc.

Printed in the United States of America

The paper used in this book complies with the
Permanent Paper Standard issued by the National
Information Standards Organization (Z39.48–1984).

10 9 8 7 6 5 4 3 2 1

To John Marshall,
who certainly wrought far more than he knew
at the creation of Judicial Review

Contents

Acknowledgments

The editors and the Policy Studies Organization are thankful for the generous support provided for the preparation and publication of this book by the Brown Foundation and Texas Christian University. Thanks are due also to the Research Committee on Comparative Judicial Studies of the International Political Science Association, at whose various meetings, particularly its August 1989 conference at the University of Lund in Sweden (hosted graciously by Professor Torbjörn Vallinder), where discussions and papers were presented from which this book has emanated. We also want to express our thanks and acknowledge the dedicated work and care of Marilyn Eudaly and Carmelita Shepelwich in preparing this manuscript for publication.

Part I

Comparative Judicial Review and Public Policy

1

Comparative Judicial Review and Public Policy: Concepts and Overview

C. Neal Tate

> The authority of a court to declare laws and official acts unconstitutional is a practice which sheds a strong light on the interplay of law and politics. It is a judicial act which gives to judges so obvious a share in policy-making that where it prevails there is little room left for the pretense that judges only apply the law.
>
> (Ehrmann, 1976: 138)

That judicial review is relevant to public policy making should be no surprise. For example, at this writing, the legislature in my home state of Texas has recently completed its fourth straight session (one regular, three special) dedicated completely or heavily to an effort to alter state policy to fund public education more equitably. Clearly, legislators have done so not because they wish to; their behavior has consistently suggested that they would very much prefer to avoid the issue, and they face budgetary strictures that make the task extraordinarily unpalatable. Rather, they are doing so because they have been ordered to by state courts that have held existing funding arrangements unconstitutional. All along, legislators have done so under the threat that if they fail to come up with a new, satisfactory funding policy, a reallocation of state funds from richer to poorer school districts will be ordered by a special master already appointed by the district judge supervising their work. That judge has already once found wanting a statute they passed to solve the problem, and many knowledgeable legislative observers expect that the same fate awaits the law resulting from their latest effort.

This involvement of the state's judiciary in Texas' education funding policy through the exercise of judicial review is by no means unique. Currently, various

of the state's governing authorities are also under state or federal judicial mandates to alter existing public policy concerning prisons, the election of state
judges, and the districting of city council seats in Dallas. What is true for Texas
is also true for many other American states and localities, and for the nation as
a whole.

What is less widely recognized by political scientists and policy analysts,
journalists, politicians, and others concerned with the making and content of
public policy, is that equally dramatic examples of the public consequences of
the exercise of judicial review are easy to find outside the United States, a nation
that is frequently thought to be unique because of the strong policy role played
by its courts through judicial review. This symposium provides perspectives that
should help students of judicial review and public policy revise their assumption
of its exceptional and American character, and establish a more accurate picture
of its worldwide significance. Before turning to a review of some of the evidence
relevant to that purpose, however, the subject of this book needs some
clarification.

TYPES OF JUDICIAL REVIEW

From the U.S.-centered perspective, the meaning of judicial review is well-
understood: It refers to the ability of a court to determine the acceptability of a
given law or other official action on grounds of compatibility with *constitutional*
forms. This form of judicial review is the primary focus of most of the chapters
in this book, as it probably is for the public law field as a whole. But in fact
there are more shades of meaning to "judicial review," if one considers its use
around the world. To comprehend how the authors in this symposium have used
the term it is important to spell out the variety of practices that can be labeled
judicial review. Several aspects of judicial review are relevant when one examines
judicial review in comparative perspective. I will discuss the differences between
the constitutional and administrative, direct and indirect, *a priori* and *a posteriori*,
abstract and concrete, and all courts and constitutional court review. In addition,
I will introduce the concept of the coerciveness of judicial review.

Constitutional and Administrative Review

One of the first necessary clarifications concerns the identification of judicial
review with constitutional review. It is this identification that, above all, con-
tributes to the tendency to see judicial review as a policy device of most relevance
in the United States. It is certainly true, as David Danelski, Peter Russell, and
Mary Volcansek all document in their chapters in this volume, that the nineteenth-
century United States Supreme Court should receive credit for the modern for-
mulation of the practice that assigns to courts the power to declare laws and
other government actions unconstitutional. But, as Russell notes in the case of

Canada and the Commonwealth, the judicial review of administrative actions has been in existence for much longer.[1]

Administrative judicial review occurs when the courts consider whether the actions of government agencies (other than the courts) are legally appropriate and proper or represent an abuse of discretion beyond what the law allows. Relevant laws, including constitutions, may provide a definition of what is appropriate exercise of bureaucratic discretion. For example, the Philippine Constitution of 1987 speaks of the courts' ability to correct "grave" abuses of discretion. Whether constitutional or not, such definitions would need to be interpreted in the context of other statutes or rules specifying the duties of agencies. But, as written, they provide few limits on what judges may choose to regard as an appropriate or inappropriate exercise of discretion.

What I understand to be the conventional judgment sees constitutional review as the more important, more dramatic means through which judges make policy. But, as Maurice Sunkin demonstrates in analyzing requests for leave to appeal the decisions of administrative agencies in Great Britain, one could certainly argue that administrative judicial review is the more significant policy institution, from the point of view of the ordinary citizen trying to navigate the government bureaucracy in search of a service, a benefit, or redress for a complaint.

Direct and Indirect Review

One classic work on judicial review (McWhinney, 1969: 13) distinguishes between direct and indirect judicial review. Direct review is identical to constitutional review as defined above. E. McWhinney defines indirect review as occurring

where a court, either not having the power to annul or override enactments of the legislature as "unconstitutional" or else simply choosing not to exert that power in the instant case, says, in effect, in the process of interpretation of a statute, that the legislature may or may not have the claimed legislative power, but it has not, in the language it has used in the enactment in question, employed that power.

One might be hard-pressed to draw a sharp boundary line between indirect and administrative judicial review, since legislative enactments depend inevitably on administration. But the distinction McWhinney makes is important to one wishing to view the policy significance of judicial review from a comparative perspective because it draws attention to the fact that courts need not exercise constitutional review to alter even the formal enactments of other policy-making institutions. When courts are exercising indirect judicial review they conclude typically that "Parliament could not have intended" the result that is being rejected because that result would be inconsistent with some other clear intention of Parliament, common law principles, or the provisions of well-accepted legal principles. Such judicial pronouncements go well beyond the typical administrative review finding that an agency official has committed a grave abuse of discretion that must be overturned.[2]

As McWhinney notes, the fact that a nation has formal constitutional judicial review does not prevent its judges from exercising indirect judicial review. In fact, both the canons of legal construction as well as political realities impress upon courts the desirability of avoiding constitutional review unless absolutely necessary. This means that in practice the differences in the exercise of judicial review between courts possessing and those not possessing constitutional review should depend upon its existence less than is sometimes assumed by analysts who place great emphasis on constitutional review,[3] and more upon other factors, perhaps legal or political cultures and traditions and the personal characteristics and preferences of judges.

Martin Edelman's chapter on the Israeli Supreme Court describes its search for a formula to protect rights and affect regime policies in the absence of constitutional judicial review or, indeed, of a written constitution. It suggests both the possibilities for the exercise of indirect judicial review and the importance of self-imposed views of what it is proper or possible for judges to do in challenging legislative supremacy through judicial review.

A Priori/A Posteriori and Abstract/Concrete Review

Two further basic distinctions that are important in the comparative context stress whether the constitutionality of a law or official action is determined before or after it takes effect, and whether a declaration of unconstitutionality can be made only in the context of a specific legal dispute. In the American federal context, judicial review occurs exclusively after the law or action has been promulgated or taken effect (*a posteriori*) and only as a result of the involvement of litigants in a concrete case or controversy. But in many nations, especially those of Western Europe, judicial review may take place also or even exclusively in advance of the promulgation or effectivity of the law or action (*a priori*) and may also be exercised in the abstract, in the absence of an actual case or controversy stimulating its exercise.[4]

A court that can engage in *a priori* and abstract review would appear to have maximum potential for policy influence using constitutional review. After all, such a court could outlaw a statute or regulation before it ever began to be implemented, and on the basis of a hypothetical constitutional argument about its effect. Alec Stone's analysis of the development of abstract review in Western Europe confirms that the combination is a powerful one. On the other hand, one must remember that the most restrictive combination, *a posteriori* concrete review, has hardly relegated the U.S. Supreme Court to a minor policy role. As usual, it is apparent that other factors also must influence how courts use judicial review to develop their policy roles. One of these surely is whether judicial review is in principle available for exercise by all courts or only by a designated constitutional court.

All Courts and Constitutional Court Review

Another distinction important to understanding judicial review, at least in its constitutional form, has to do with the extensiveness of the practice. The United States employs what one might call an all courts model. Any court may exercise judicial review, and a declaration of unconstitutionality on the part of a lower court judge need not be approved by any higher authority to be effective. But in many nations, judicial review may be exercised only by a specially designated court. This may be referred to as the constitutional court model.

The policy influence of the judiciary must surely be maximized when a nation employs the all courts model. The example of the current policy situation in Texas used to introduce this chapter illustrates how important the policy making of lower courts can be when the all courts model is in place. Restricting the power to declare legislation and regulations unconstitutional to a constitutional court might increase the breadth of the typical constitutional questions posed to the courts, but it also sharply reduces the number of occasions and range of policy issues on which courts can be invited (or can invite themselves) to exercise judicial review.

On the other hand, one should remember that constitutional review is not the only form of judicial review available to courts. Indirect and administrative review are always available to all courts in the hierarchy. The extent to which they are actually exercised by courts across the judicial structure probably will be increased where all courts constitutional review does exist. But we do not know what other factors may influence nonconstitutional courts to more or less assertiveness in their exercise of judicial review.

Coerciveness of Review

William Kitchin's chapter (also see Kitchin, 1990) suggests that nations differ in what he calls the coerciveness of judicial review. His point is an important one even if events in the (former) Soviet Union have now overtaken his particular analysis. At one extreme, courts exercising judicial review have the authority to require other litigants and, more importantly, government officials to act constitutionally or to cease acting unconstitutionally.[5] Kitchin calls this coercive judicial review. At the other extreme, the ability of courts to declare official laws or actions void on grounds of unconstitutionality may be very limited or restricted. In between, the opinions of the courts regarding constitutionality may be advisory, but not mandatory or coercive in their effects.

To some extent, Kitchin's conceptualization overlaps with the categories already introduced: judiciaries lacking constitutional judicial review are "restricted," while those having constitutionally based judicial review are "coercive" or "advisory," at least in principle. But by calling our attention to whether judicial review as exercised is only advisory or in fact mandatory, Kitchin expands our ability to understand the policy significance of judicial review around the world. Thus, coerciveness of review may be one more useful addition to our cornucopia of concepts.

The contemporary world of judicial review contains examples of political systems illustrating the types of judicial review just outlined. The American model requires that judicial review be concrete and *a posteriori*, but it is exercised via a mandatory or coercive order by all judges. Abstract, *a priori*, coercive review by a constitutional court occurs in France. Indirect and administrative judicial review occur wherever judicial systems are independent enough to exercise any policy role.

ORIGINS OF JUDICIAL REVIEW

The origins of constitutional judicial review are varied. The chapters in this volume illustrate this variety with examples of judicial review systems that are indigenously developed and externally imposed, ancient and very modern, still largely imminent (as was the case in the "reforming" Soviet Union), and debatably under development (in Israel). In reviewing the well-documented case of the inclusion of judicial review into the postwar Japanese constitution and comparing that case with the more obscure American adoption, Danelski has demonstrated how closely connected judicial review is with the development and, indeed, the manufacture of democratic government. Volcansek shows how the Italian institution was crafted with both American and European experiences in mind to acknowledge the realities of postwar Italian politics, including especially the continued domination of the judicial hierarchy by career judges with fascist backgrounds.

Russell's account of the origins of Canadian judicial review paints a picture of a judiciary initially diffident toward its exercise as a result of its British origins, colonial practice and objectives, and the requirements of a precarious federalism. Despite those origins, judicial review now has been pushed to the center of the policy process because of the inability of other political decision-makers to cope with the most contentious of the issues arising from that very federalism—constitutional developments that both deliberately and as a matter of functional necessity magnify its use in determining crucial policy issues, and the influence of the model prevailing below its southern border.

Stone's analysis describes the origins and spread of abstract judicial review in Europe. Significantly, a perceived need to provide a mechanism to protect the fundamental rights of citizens, a reaction to fascism or militaristic authoritarianism, was a prime factor leading to the (re)creation of constitutional courts in Austria, Germany, Spain, and, by inference, Greece, Italy, Portugal, and, perhaps, the European Community. My research indicates that faith in the efficacy of judicial review as a bulwark against authoritarianism also underlay the inclusion in the 1987 Philippine constitution of what must be one of the world's most expansive grants of judicial review authority.

Kitchin analyzes the bases for and the early experience with judicial review in the Soviet Union, in effect being "present at the creation" (before events so overtook reforms that the Union entirely collapsed). Edelman recounts the struggle of Israel to establish a written constitution with judicial review and explains the political and religious factors promoting and opposing its establishment. He shows us a political system "before the creation," and helps us understand why the institution of judicial review can be resisted in an otherwise largely liberal state.

JUDICIAL REVIEW AROUND THE WORLD

The use of constitutional judicial review to make sometimes very dramatic public policy is not an American monopoly, but is increasingly characteristic of judiciaries around the world. In Canada, the Supreme Court has been thrown, probably initially unwillingly, into the thick of the thorniest disputes about the nature and future of the Canadian Confederation as a result of the adoption of the Charter of Rights of 1982. By deciding against the cultural sovereignty of Quebec and in favor of minority (in this case, English) language rights in several cases, it is being given credit, at least by some critics, for driving one more nail into the coffin of Canadian national unity.[6] The nature of the growth of judicial review in Canada leads Russell to conclude his chapter by arguing that

with the addition of Charter [of Rights] review to federalism review and with a reasonably activist judiciary sustained by a public still relatively naive and unrealistic about judicial power, . . . the importance of judicial review in Canada at the present time equals if it does not exceed its importance in the United States.

Volcansek's chapter echoes Russell's conclusion when she begins by noting that "in practice, European courts have been noticeably more aggressive in asserting their authority of judicial review than have their brethren in the United States." Further, her review of the development and use of judicial review in Italy concludes that the practice has become "stable," and that, in adapting judicial review to the Italian context, the Constitutional Court has achieved a legitimacy that shapes the actions of other political actors and "the potential to use it to profoundly influence the nation's life." This is so even though Italy arguably lacks most of the preconditions sometimes assumed to be necessary for the effective exercise of judicial review.

Also focusing on the European context, Stone's analysis makes clear the tremendous policy impact and still greater potential inhering in abstract judicial review, a practice that has spread across Europe since 1950 precisely in those nations that traditionally abhorred American-style judicial review. Stone argues that much public policy in France, Germany, Austria, and Spain has become "juridicized" as a result of the work of the constitutional courts in those countries, and that, when exercising their powers of abstract review, these courts can usefully be thought of as "third legislative chambers."

That judicial review might have become newly relevant as a result of the legal/constitutional changes occurring in the then reforming (and by now, former) Soviet Union is the clear implication of Kitchin's analysis. Following a useful conceptual scheme for classifying the practice of judicial review by national judiciaries, Kitchin suggests that judicial review in the Soviet Union (as it was then) had already become the "independent-advisory" type. While this kind of judicial review is not likely to be associated with the most dramatic and intrusive judicial policy initiatives, Kitchin notes that it would nevertheless have been a significant change from the USSR's previous "dependent-restricted" model. He also demonstrates that there were already (at the time of his writing) some impressive instances of the exercise of judicial review by the then recently established Committee on Constitutional Oversight. In its first finding of unconstitutionality, the Committee overturned a politically sensitive public order decree of President Gorbachev. Later, the Committee's agreement even to consider the constitutionality of the USSR's system of residency permits led to the immediate abolition by the Council of Ministers of many of the most restrictive and burdensome rules that were then a part of the system, before the Committee had an opportunity to rule against them.

While it is certainly far too early to be sanguine about the progress of political reform in the "Commonwealth of Independent States" that has largely replaced the Soviet Union, much less about the future of the leaders promoting change, it does appear that constitutional democracy and judicial review have a chance of becoming more powerful tools in the hands of a new set of important "Commonwealth" or "State" policymakers, possibly to include constitutional judges.

The discussion so far has shown that the relevance of judicial review to public policy making extends well beyond the boundaries of the United States to Canada and the European continent, even to so previously unlikely a political system as that of the (former) Soviet Union. Given that, it should hardly be surprising to find that judicial review also has been an important public policy influence outside the industrialized West.

In the Philippines, as Tate's chapter shows, the Supreme Court has had a long history of involvement in important policy questions through the mechanism of judicial review. Indeed, one might conclude that the Court had on more than one occasion the opportunity to shape the very nature of the constitutional regime. Thus in the early 1970s, the Supreme Court validated 14 years of subsequent dictatorship by Ferdinand Marcos when it could not bring itself to declare ineffective a new constitution guaranteeing one-person rule by the incumbent president, even though it invalidated the ratification procedures Marcos had concocted to adopt the constitution. Later, the same court helped ease the dictator from power when it refused to invalidate his calling of the "snap" presidential election that led to his downfall, after he had realized that calling the election was a strategic mistake.[7]

It is difficult to imagine how a court might assert more dramatic control over the policy process than that asserted by the Supreme Court of India, the keystone institution in what Carl Baar's chapter identifies as "the world's most active judiciary." In the 1970s, the Indian Supreme Court ruled unconstitutional legally adopted amendments to the Indian constitution, amendments adopted specifically to circumvent the judiciary's persistent frustration of the prime minister and Parliament when they had adopted ordinary statutes. It did so on the grounds that the new amendments violated the constitution's "basic structure" (see Mirchandani, 1977).

Despite these examples, not all nations have experienced a dramatic expansion of policy making through judicial review. Nils Stjernquist's account of the development of formal judicial review in Sweden maintains that it has not become an important policy tool there, even though it is now formally enshrined in the national constitution. In part, this is because Stjernquist excepts from his negative conclusion the review of a law in advance of its enactment, *a priori* judicial review. Common in Europe, such review in advance has in fact always been a part of the Swedish governmental heritage. Stjernquist attributes the unimportance of *a posteriori* judicial review in the American tradition to a number of factors, but speculates that it may nevertheless become more relevant to the Swedes as a result of greater European cooperation and the requirements of supranational European courts and judges.

If one turns attention to indirect and administrative judicial review, the universe of examples that might be cited to exemplify its policy role expands greatly to include virtually every nation in which the judiciary has any independent role in public law. It is not feasible to field a full set of illustrations here. But looking at the chapters in this volume that treat judiciaries lacking constitutional judicial review, one can see, from Edelman's account, how the Israeli Supreme Court has used indirect judicial review to affect policies central to the partisan interests of the ruling parties, while Sunkin's analysis intends to show us the nature and some of the consequences of administrative judicial review in the United Kingdom. One also suspects that, had Stjernquist considered the exercise of indirect and, especially, administrative review in Sweden, he might have painted a somewhat different picture of the policy role of the Swedish judiciary.

JUDICIAL REVIEW, JUDICIAL ACTIVISM, JUDICIAL RESTRAINT

Of course there are many critics of the policy activism revealed by these kinds of exercises of the power of judicial review. Typically, the critics argue that judges should refrain from such actions in deference to the original intention of the framers of whatever constitution they are interpreting or to the actions of the allegedly more democratic policy institutions, legislatures, and elected executives. So deeply entrenched are these views that they are capable of being shared by critics of all ideological persuasions. Typically, who is currently expressing these views is determined by the perceived direction of the judiciary's model policy making or the interests the judiciary is perceived to serve. It is rare for those who are concerned about judicial activism to recognize that it is a phenomenon that can be characteristic of both liberal and conservative viewpoints.[8] The history of the American judiciary, and especially of the U.S. Supreme Court, could well be structured according to which political ideologues are currently criticizing the judiciary for ignoring original intent, the intent of Congress, and the like. Current debate about the role of the Canadian Supreme Court and its exercise of judicial review under the Charter of Rights suggests that such an analytical viewpoint applies in Canada as well (see the discussion in Morton, Russell, and Withey, 1990).

Why this continuing argument over the activist exercise of judicial review? Most frequently, the answer is that critics want the courts to follow a different line of policy making. But in a rigorous logical exercise, Donald Jackson's contribution to this volume suggests the insurmountable practical and theoretical difficulties with arguments that judges *can* or, given the prevailing normative assumptions of democracy, always *should* be guided by the intent of constitutional framers, legislators, or other lawmakers. Jackson's analysis is persuasive even if one grants that the critics believe their arguments (e.g., Moos, 1991), and are not merely distressed because the courts are not making the kinds of public policies they would prefer.

Arguments over the desirability of the policies made by judges are inevitable and, in a democratic society, no doubt constructive. But given the difficulties that surround even well-intentioned efforts to avoid policy making through the exercise of judicial review, we need to continue to expand our understanding of this ever more important policy tool. This book is offered as a contribution to such an increased understanding.

WHAT IS MISSING?

Though much is covered in this book, much remains to be learned about the policy significance of judicial review. Missing, for the most part, are the systematic empirical analyses of the exercise of judicial review within and across national political systems that are needed to test the adequacy and generality of the plausible conclusions offered in its chapters. Missing also are sufficient analyses of the prevalence and significance of judicial review outside the context of Europe and North America. Future research should address these foci to further enhance our knowledge of the policy significance of judicial review.

NOTES

1. It is also true that precursor versions of constitutional judicial review can be found in ancient Greece and Rome (Becker, 1970: 205–06).

2. I stress again that judicial review does not occur only when courts find the actions of other policymakers or government agents unacceptable. Indirect and administrative review occur just as surely when courts say that "Parliament surely intended" a challenged result or that the administrator's challenged decision was not a grave abuse of discretion.

3. See the influential *Comparative Politics: System, Process and Policy* (Almond and Powell, 1978: 240–41), for example.

4. *A priori* concrete review would appear to be logically impossible.

5. This does not mean that judges have the control of the means of coercion that would be necessary literally to force executives to act as they dictate. It implies only that the rule and expectations are that executives must comply with the order of a court exercising judicial review.

6. See the table of cases nullified and the discussion in Morton, Russell, and Withey (1990: 14–17), for example.

7. These two cases illustrate that a court's exercise of judicial review to validate executive actions can have consequences that are just as important to the course of public policy making as decisions that invalidate such actions.

8. Even political scientists, who should have sufficient familiarity with the history of the U.S. Supreme Court to know better, seem to fall into this trap. For a rare example of an editorialist for a conservative newspaper who seems to have come to a realization that judicial activism is not a liberal monopoly, see Moos (1991).

REFERENCES

Almond, G. A., and Powell, G. B. (1978). *Comparative politics: System, process and policy*. Boston: Little, Brown.

Becker, T. L. (1970). *Comparative judicial politics: The political functioning of courts*. Chicago: Rand McNally.

Ehrmann, H. W. (1976). *Comparative legal cultures*. Englewood Cliffs, N.J.: Prentice-Hall.

Kitchin, W. (1990). The implications for judicial review of the current legal reforms in the Soviet Union. In Donald W. Jackson and C. Neal Tate, eds., Symposium on judicial review and public policy in comparative perspective. *Policy Studies Journal* 19: 96–105.

McWhinney, E. (1969). *Judicial review in the English-speaking world*, 4th ed. Toronto: University of Toronto Press.

Mirchandani, G. C. (1977). *Subverting the constitution in India*. Columbia, Mo.: South Asia Books.

Moos, B. (1991). Despite change in court, judicial restraint still lacking. *Dallas Morning News* (May 31), p. A23.

Morton, F. L., Russell, P. H. and Withey, M. J. (1990). The Supreme Court's first 100 charter of rights decisions: A statistical analysis. Occasional Papers Series, Research Study 6.1, Research Unit for Socio-Legal Studies, University of Calgary.

Part II

Establishing Judicial Review as a Policy Tool

2

Documenting the Establishment of Judicial Review: Japan and the United States

David J. Danelski

In trying to ascertain the origins of judicial review in the United States and Japan, one is struck by the difference in data for each country. For the United States, the data are fragmentary, unclear, and cover almost 200 years of history. For Japan, the data are detailed, clear, and cover a single year—the first year of the American occupation of Japan. The Japanese data not only show precise origins of judicial review in Japan; they show with clarity the nature, purpose, and premises of the institution. They also suggest hypotheses about the origins of judicial review in the United States. That is not surprising, for the Americans who proposed that judicial review be a part of the Japanese Constitution drew heavily on their own understanding of American constitutional history and experience.

The analysis that follows is both historical and comparative. Unlike the usual historical analysis, however, it begins with the establishment of judicial review in Japan in 1946 and works backward to the institution's ultimate origins in the United States and England. Three concepts organize the analysis—the idea, the purpose, and the premises of judicial review.

JUDICIAL REVIEW IN JAPAN IN 1946

Although Japanese courts under the Meiji constitution never had power to declare legislation unconstitutional, legal scholars in Japan were familiar with the idea of judicial review. In fact, they were aware of two ideas of judicial review, one American and the other European.[1] The difference between the two was that the former permitted determinations of constitutionality by ordinary courts in concrete cases and the latter permitted abstract as well as concrete review but only by a special constitutional court.

In late 1945, there were three Japanese positions on judicial review. The official cabinet constitutional investigative committee, headed by Minister of State Joji Matsumoto, took the position that there was no need for judicial review in the Japanese constitution (Tanaka, 1976: 687). Another official committee, headed by Prince Fumimaro Konoe, did not reach any clear conclusion on judicial review, for its work was aborted when the Allies charged Konoe with war crimes; but Professor Soichi Sasaki, who worked closely with Konoe, submitted to the emperor an outline of a constitution that mentioned judicial review (Naito, 1961, I: 81–82). It is almost certain that Sasaki had in mind the European version of the institution. Finally, one political party and at least one private group proposed judicial review without specifying its form (Sato, 1962, I: 607–608, 684–685).

The first important event leading to the establishment of judicial review in Japan occurred on January 11, 1946, when Lt. Col. Milo E. Rowell, a military lawyer on General MacArthur's staff, analyzed a constitution proposed by a Japanese private group. "There is no provision," Rowell wrote in a memo that day, "directly authorizing the courts to declare acts of the Diet and orders of Cabinet unconstitutional. In order to thoroughly safeguard individuals from abuses by the majority it is desirable to place this power in the courts." In summarizing the provisions he thought were necessary, Rowell said there had to be a provision that the constitution was the supreme law of the land and a provision granting to the courts "the power to declare legislation unconstitutional subject to review by the Diet which can reverse on a two-thirds vote of both houses." This novel idea of judicial review was consistent with a 1946 U.S. policy statement on constitutional reform (SWNCC–228), which provided that no organ of government could have "more than a temporary veto over legislative measures approved by the legislative body."[2] At the time Rowell wrote his memo, he had not yet seen the policy statement. When later asked about his January 11 memo, Rowell said he did not require adoption of the American idea of judicial review because it would have been too startling for the Japanese. Besides, he added, he thought that his proposal was a nice compromise in the distribution of legislative and judicial powers (Rowell, 1976).

Early in February 1946, General Douglas MacArthur, the Supreme Commander of the Allied Powers in Japan, decided that the Japanese government's attempt to revise the Meiji constitution to strengthen democracy in Japan, as required by the Potsdam Declaration, was a failure. Therefore, he asked the Government Section of his Headquarters to draft a constitution for submission to the Japanese. On February 3, Rowell and two other military officers, Col. Charles L. Kades and Comdr. Alfred R. Hussey, as the steering committee of the drafting operation, met in a Tokyo hotel to discuss the outline of the draft constitution. When the meeting ended, Hussey (1946) wrote in a pocket notebook: "Kades, Rowell, Hussey (at Dai Ichi Hotel). Steering Committee—not to be disturbed—Quotation from Gettysburg Address—Limited right of review by Court *absolute* on Bill of Rights. Unicameral legislature." The modification of Rowell's original notion of judicial review was probably Hussey's idea, for

Kades had doubts about granting the Supreme Court any power of judicial review. Years later Kades (1976) recalled that when they had discussed judicial review, he had said that the American Supreme Court might appropriately have this power because it operates in a federal system and seeks to maintain a balance of state and national power, but Japan has had a unitary system of government, and for that reason its Supreme Court did not need the power. At that point, Hussey or Rowell—Kades did not remember which one—pointed out that the American Supreme Court was not only the balance wheel of federalism but also the protector of the Bill of Rights. Because the Japanese Supreme Court was also to have that function, it needed the power to declare unconstitutional laws that violated individual rights. Kades recalled that he had agreed.

The idea of judicial review expressed in the steering committee meeting would remain intact throughout the drafting process. But Kades's doubts about judicial review for the Japanese lingered. He feared the Supreme Court might become a judicial oligarchy. Rowell thought that was unlikely, for in all cases, except those concerning individual rights, the Supreme Court's decisions would be subject to review by the Diet.

Ten days after Rowell, Kades, and Hussey first met at the Dai Ichi Hotel to discuss drafting a constitution for Japan, these three officers, joined by Brig. Gen. Courtney Whitney, presented a draft constitution to Foreign Minister Shigeru Yoshita at his home. Less than a month later, the Japanese and Americans reached agreement on the content of the constitution. The Americans made few concessions in the negotiations, but they did agree to a major change in the article authorizing judicial review. The concession occurred during around-the-clock negotiations on March 4 and 5, 1946. Although the Japanese had retained the article in their draft, they did not know what to make of the provision and asked the Americans why they had proposed such an unusual type of judicial review. One of the Japanese negotiators, Tatsuo Sato (1946), recorded the exchange between the Americans and Japanese in these words:

[The Americans] were a little embarrassed and asked in return why our draft adopted these points. We answered that because this provision was important, we could not eliminate it, but we did want to inquire about it. They then asked us which institution was better as the final arbiter of constitutionality. We answered the Court would be from a separation of powers viewpoint. They accepted our opinion, and the first three sentences of the provision were revised and the rest of it was eliminated.

Hussey's notes (1946) show the same exchange as follows:

Hussey: Is there objection in the way we phrased it [?]

Japanese: Chapt. III [the Bill of Rights in the draft] is so important that decision should be generally [by the] Diet.

Hussey: We feel protection of fundamental rights [is] so important that [the] S.C. [Supreme

Court] should have [the] power—you permit a weakening of prot[ection] for indiv[iduals] if you give Diet power of review over judicial decisions.

Japanese: Safer to give it to Diet.

At that point Hussey wrote: "Sudden reversal on J[apanese] part—[they] want [the] S.C. to have final review in all cases." Obviously there was some miscommunication early in the exchange, for the Japanese and American reports of it are inconsistent, but there was no miscommunication about the Japanese request for the Supreme Court to have final review in all cases. The Americans agreed, and the provision authorizing judicial review—Article 81 of the Japanese constitution—was then revised to read as follows: "The Supreme Court is the court of last resort with power to determine the constitutionality of any law, order, regulation or official act." Was the provision a statement of the American or European idea of judicial review? Japanese constitutional scholars disagreed on the answer, and the Japanese Supreme Court finally settled the matter by deciding that Article 81 reflected essentially the American idea of judicial review (Tanaka, 1976: 687).

The source of the Japanese understanding of the American idea of judicial review was Chief Justice John Marshall's opinion in *Marbury v. Madison* (1803).[3] The idea he had expressed was simple: Courts have the right to declare unconstitutional legislative acts void. The idea was not, of course, original with Marshall. Alexander Hamilton had discussed it at length earlier in *The Federalist*, and some of the Framers at the Constitutional Convention at Philadelphia in 1787 had supported it. "The Framers," wrote Berger (1969: 23), "did not pluck the concept [of judicial review] from the void. It harked back to [Chief Justice Edward] Coke's 1610 statement in *[Dr.] Bonham's Case:* 'when an Act of Parliament is against common right and reason . . . the common law will control it and adjudge such act to be void.' "

Whether Coke's dictum in *Dr. Bonham's Case* was the initial expression of the idea of judicial review has been the subject of controversy. Corwin (1914: 28–29) wrote that "it would be the height of absurdity to suppose that [Coke's dictum] spelled out anything like judicial review." Corwin's position was that Coke's words clearly indicated his belief

that principles of "common right and reason," being part of the Common Law, were cognizable by judges while interpreting acts of Parliament. For the rest, however, they must be read along with Coke's characterization of Parliament as the "Supreme Court" of the realm. Being a court, Parliament was necessarily bound by the law, even as it declared and elaborated it; but being the *highest* court, its interpretations of the law necessarily bound all other courts. As he plainly indicated [later], both by his *words*, in his Institutes, and *practically*, by his connection with the framing of the Petition of Right, Coke regarded Parliament itself as the *final* interpreter of the law by which both it, the King, and the judges were bound.

American colonists, however, had a different view of Coke's dictum in *Dr. Bonham's Case*; they saw it as authorizing judicial review much as we understand it today. In arguing against the writs of assistance in Boston in 1761, James Otis relied on Coke's dictum in *Dr. Bonham's Case*. "As to Acts of Parliament," said Otis (quoted in Mott, 1926: 126), "an Act against the Constitution is void; an Act against natural Equity is void; and if an Act of Parliament should be made in the very words of this Petition, it would be void. The Executive Courts must pass such Acts into disuse."[4] Other American lawyers made similar arguments in opposing the Stamp Act soon thereafter. "Our friends of liberty," Massachusetts Lieutenant Governor Huchinson wrote in 1765 (quoted in Plucknett, 1926: 63), "take advantage of a maxim they found in Lord Coke that an Act of Parliament against Magna Carta or the peculiar rights of Englishmen is *ipso facto* void."

Corwin may have been correct that Coke did not intend his dictum in *Dr. Bonham's Case* as a statement of judicial review as we now understand the idea, but that dictum, as interpreted by Otis and other eighteenth-century Americans, was the ultimate source of the idea of judicial review in the United States.[5]

PROTECTION OF INDIVIDUAL RIGHTS

The principal purpose of judicial review in Japan was the protection of individual rights. That purpose stemmed from the following provision in the Potsdam Declaration (SCAP, 1949, II: 413): "The Japanese government shall remove all obstacles to the revival and strengthening of democratic tendencies among the Japanese people. Freedom of speech, of religion, and of thought, as well as respect for the fundamental human rights, shall be established." Although Washington policymakers required the guarantee of individual rights in any Japanese constitutional reform, they did not require judicial review. Nonetheless, Americans in Japan naturally thought of judicial review as a means to protect individual rights. Soon after the Japanese surrender, when George Atcheson, Jr., an American career diplomat who was MacArthur's political advisor, met with Prince Konoe to discuss constitutional reform, he listed several basic criticisms of the Meiji constitution (Atcheson, 1945), one of which was lack of a provision stating that the "judiciary should protect the rights of the people against the Government." Later, Rowell stated the same idea, and at the first meeting of the steering committee, Rowell, Kades, and Hussey agreed that judicial review should be absolute in all cases involving individual rights, indicating judicial review's principal purpose. In the negotiations between the Americans and Japanese concerning the judicial review provision in March 1946, Hussey reiterated that individual rights were so important that the Supreme Court should protect them with an absolute power of judicial review, and the Japanese agreed.

A strong argument can also be made for the proposition that in the late eighteenth century the principal purpose of judicial review in the United States was also the protection of individual rights. Marshall provides support for the proposition (*Marbury*, p. 163; Haskins and Johnson, 1981; 90). Every individual whose rights have been violated, wrote Marshall, has recourse to the judiciary for protection, for that is "the very essence of civil liberty." Hamilton et al. (1969: 522–524) also provide support for the proposition. Unless courts possess the power of judicial review, Hamilton wrote in *Federalist* No. 78, "all the reservations of particular rights or privileges would amount to nothing." Judges, he added, require independence because they must "guard the Constitution and the rights of individuals." The most direct statement on the subject is Madison's (1789, I: 439) in the debate concerning the adoption of the Bill of Rights:

If [individual rights] are incorporated into the Constitution, independent tribunals of justices will consider themselves in a peculiar manner the guardians of these rights; they will be an impenetrable bulwark against every assumption of power in the Legislature or Executive; they will be naturally led to resist every encroachment upon rights expressly stipulated for in the Constitution by the declaration of rights.

PREMISES FOR JUDICIAL REVIEW IN JAPAN

The Japanese Constitution clearly states four premises necessary for judicial review: (1) the rule of law—the idea that the constitution is the supreme law and that no one is above the law; (2) the constitution is law in the sense that it can be judicially enforced; (3) the determination of constitutionality is solely a judicial function; and (4) judicial independence.

Articles 98 and 99 of the Japanese constitution clearly reflect the rule of law. "This Constitution," states Article 98, "shall be the supreme law of the nation and no law, ordinance, imperial rescript or other act of government, or part thereof, contrary to the provisions hereof, shall have legal force or validity." And to emphasize that no one is above the law and the constitution, Article 99 provides that all public officials, including the Emperor, have "the obligation to respect and uphold the Constitution." Finally, Article 81 articulates the second and third premises in these words: "The Supreme Court is the Court of last resort with the power to determine the constitutionality of any law, order, regulation or official act." Article 76 insures judicial independence by providing: "All judges shall be independent in the exercise of their conscience and shall be bound only by this Constitution."

Although the United States Constitution states these premises less clearly, the premises are discernible. By placing sovereignty in the people and making the Constitution the "supreme law of the Land," the Framers made it binding on all units of government; thus they provided for the rule of law. They gave the courts the government's entire judicial power and directed some of its provisions specifically to judges for enforcement—for example, trial by jury and standards of proof in treason trials. Thus they accepted the premise that the Constitution is law enforceable by judges whose function it is to determine and apply that law. Finally, they accepted the premise of judicial independence. Indeed, they sought to guarantee it by separating judicial power from the legislative and executive powers, by guaranteeing judicial tenure during good behavior, and by prohibiting the diminution of judicial salaries. These premises were crucial for judicial review.

In the first part of the *Marbury* opinion (p. 163), Marshall explicitly stated the first premise when he wrote that "the government of the United States has been emphatically termed a government of laws, and not of men. It will certainly cease to deserve this high appellation, if the laws furnish no remedy for the violation of a vested legal right." According to Haskins and Johnson (1981: 195), Marshall emphasized the rule of law in *Marbury* because "many middle-of-the road Federalists, including the Supreme Court judges, genuinely feared that Jefferson would assert that, as the elected representative of the people, he was not accountable to the law but was above it." Later in the opinion (pp. 177–178), Marshall stressed that the Constitution was "superior, paramount law, unchangeable by ordinary means." From that premise, Marshall argued: "If . . . the constitution is superior to any ordinary act of the legislature, the constitution, and not such ordinary act, must govern the case to which they both apply."

Hamilton (pp. 522–523) argued that the second premise followed from the first and that the first premise was a fact. "A constitution is, in fact," he wrote, "and must be regarded by the judges as, a fundamental law. It therefore belongs to them to ascertain its meaning, as well as the meaning of any particular act proceeding from the legislative body." Marshall (p. 177) made a similar argument in *Marbury* when he wrote: "It is emphatically the province and duty of the judicial department to say what the law is. Those who apply the rule to particular cases, must of necessity expound and interpret that rule. If two laws conflict with each other, the courts must decide on the operation of each."

Hamilton and Marshall not only used the third premise that the determination of constitutionality is essentially a judicial function; they attempted to explain why judges have this function. Hamilton (p. 523) based his argument on popular sovereignty. The judges' power to declare acts of the legislature unconstitutional, he explained, does not

by any means suppose a superiority of the judicial to the legislative power. It only supposes that the power of the people is superior to both; and that where the will of the legislature, declared in its statutes, stands in opposition to that of the people, declared in the Constitution, the judges ought to be governed by the latter rather than the former.

Marshall (p. 178) agreed with Hamilton's explanation and added in *Marbury* that the determination of constitutionality is the "very essence of judicial duty."

Hamilton particularly stressed the judicial independence premise. He argued (pp. 521–525) that judicial independence is essential to a limited constitution. The kind of limitations he had in mind were the prohibition of bills of attainder and *ex-post-facto* laws. "Limitations of this kind," he declared, "can be preserved in practice no other way than through the medium of courts of justice, whose duty it must be to declare all acts contrary to the manifest tenor of the Constitution void." Hamilton (p. 525) was aware that judges would have to possess an "uncommon portion of fortitude" to fulfill their function as "guardians of the Constitution," particularly "where legislative invasions of it had been instigated by the major voice of the community." That is precisely why he believed judicial independence was a necessary condition for judicial review.

The premises underlying judicial review go back at least to the time when Sir Edward Coke expressed them in his heated exchange with James I at Hampton Court on November 10, 1608. Coke told James that the fundamental law binding all persons, even the king, was the common law (premise one), which was enforceable in courts (premise two). According to Coke, judges knew this fundamental law by virtue of their legal expertise, which they gained through long study and experience. Thus, they were, Coke maintained, the sole interpreters and declarers of the law (premise three). Although Coke did not at that time speak of judicial independence (premise four), he exhibited it in his exchange with the king. James had been offended by Coke's statement that only judges could determine the law. "Then the king should be under the law, which was treason to affirm," James shouted. Coke, showing independence as well as courage, answered: "The king should be under no man, but he is under God and the Law."[6]

SUMMARY

The ultimate origins of judicial review in the United States and Japan were in early seventeenth-century England. Coke first expressed the premises for judicial review in his dispute with James I at Hampton Court in 1608. Two years later, in *Dr. Bonham's Case*, Coke expressed the idea that judges might declare void acts of Parliament contrary to the common law. Whether Coke's dictum was legally sound or whether Coke intended it in the sense as we know it today is less important than how others later understood the dictum. Otis and other Americans interpreted it as expressing the idea that judges could hold unconstitutional legislative acts void and thereby protect individual rights, and that interpretation continued right up to the Supreme Court's decision in *Marbury*.

The delegates to the Philadelphia Constitutional Convention in 1787, though aware of the idea of judicial review, did not provide for it in the Constitution. Whether or not it was their intent to do so remains a question for which there is no clear answer. But it is clear that the Framers accepted the premises of judicial review. Relying on those premises, Hamilton argued for judicial review in the *The Federalist* in 1788, and Marshall, making essentially the same arguments, established the institution in *Marbury* in 1803. Between those dates, judicial review gained increasing support in the states and nation, and the Bill of Rights was added to the Constitution, thus increasing support for judicial review, an instrument to protect the guarantees in the Bill of Rights.

In 1946 the Americans and Japanese together established judicial review in

Japan. The Americans took judicial review for granted. The Japanese had to be persuaded, but they were familiar with the idea of judicial review and accepted it. As a result, Article 81 became a part of the Japanese constitution. A series of milestones mark the road to judicial review's establishment in Tokyo in 1946: Hampton Court (1608), London (1610), Boston (1761), Philadelphia (1787), and Washington (1803). Historical and comparative analysis of the events relating to judicial review that occurred at those places and times not only reveals more clearly the institution's origins; it also provides a deeper understanding of the institution's nature, purpose, and premises.

NOTES

1. Japanese law faculties covered judicial review in their courses on Anglo-American law and European law. Professor Kenzo Takayanaki, an Anglo-American specialist who taught at Tokyo University, wrote a series of articles on American judicial review in the 1920s and 1930s. The articles were published as a book entitled *Judicial Supremacy* in 1948 (Tanaka, 1976: 686). Professor Soichi Sasaki, who taught at Kyoto University, wrote about and advocated the European version of judicial review, particularly the type of review provided for in the Austrian Constitution of 1920 (Ishimine, 1974: 53–54).

2. SWNCC–228 had been written by the State-War-Navy Coordinating Subcommittee for the Far East. The statement's title was "Reform of the Japanese Government System." Its last revision was on January 7, 1946. One of the constitutional reforms it required was the guarantee of individual rights, but it did not state precisely how those rights were to be guaranteed. It mentioned both American and British practices but indicated no preference. It supported judicial independence, but judicial independence characterized both the American and British judiciaries. It spoke approvingly of "the judicially-enforced Constitution" in the United States, which suggested judicial review, but it also spoke approvingly of the British governmental system, which did not have judicial review. The Japanese government, then, apparently was free to choose either model provided it did not contravene other provisions of SWNCC–228. If it adopted judicial review as practiced in the United States, it might have contravened SWNCC's requirement that no other organ of government could have more than a "temporary veto over legislative measures approved by the legislative body." The most plausible construction of SWNCC–228 was that it permitted limited judicial review—that is, Japanese courts could be empowered to declare legislation unconstitutional if the Diet could reverse such decisions.

3. The American idea of judicial review at the time of *Marbury v. Madison* was narrower than it is today. As Nelson (1972: 1172) wrote:

> Judicial review [in Marshall's time] was thought, in sum, only to give the people—a single cohesive and indivisible body politic—protection against faithless legislators who betrayed the trust placed in them, and not to give judges authority to make law by resolving disputes between interest groups into which the people and their legislative representatives were divided.

The Japanese Supreme Court has also taken a narrow view of judicial review. The following quotation, provided by Ishimine (1974: 142), of former Chief Justice Yokota's view is illustrative:

To declare a statute unconstitutional is the gravest and most delicate duty of the courts. In the light of the principle of separation of powers, the judiciary must pay decent respect to the legislative branch and presume every statute as constitutional. In view of this, it is urged that all judges of our country would realize and approve the rule of the clear case; that is to say, a statute can be declared unconstitutional only in a clear case. If every judge of our country handles a case with such understanding, any hasty decision of unconstitutionality would be avoided.

Charles Kades also had a narrow view of the Japanese Supreme Court's power of judicial review. He told me in an interview in 1976:

What I had in mind was something on the order of the Supreme Court of the United States but with not as great power. I was afraid there would be a judicial oligarchy in Japan if we gave the Supreme Court of Japan the same power as the Supreme Court of the United States. . . . So I was always trying to chip away at the powers that Rowell was conferring on the Court.

4. John Adams, who observed Otis's argument, later recalled (Quincy, 1969: 521–529) that Otis

seems also to have had in mind the equally familiar *dictum* of Lord *Hobart*—'Even an Act of Parliament made against natural equity, as to make a man a judge in his own case, is void in itself' . . . (*Day v. Savage*, Hobart 85: 1614). Lord Holt is reported to have said, 'What my Lord Coke says in *Dr. Bonham's Case* . . . is far from any extravagancy . . . ' The law was laid down in the same way, on the authority of the above cases, in Bacon's Abridgment, first published in 1735; in Viner's Abridgment, published 1741–51 (from which Otis quoted it); and in Comyn's Digest, published 1762–67, but written more than 20 years before. And there are older authorities to the same effect. So that at the time of Otis's agreement his position appeared to be supported by some of the highest authorities in the English law.

5. At the time American colonists were invoking Coke to protect their rights against what they saw as British oppression, the idea of judicial review was at best weak in England, for the "Glorious Revolution" in 1688 had established Parliamentary supremacy. But paradoxically, as Cappelletti (1971: 39) has written, "the 'Glorious revolution' not only did not hinder, but rather it supported the development of the new doctrine of judicial review in the colonies," for the colonial charters often provided that the laws enacted by the colonies to be "reasonable" and "not contrary to the laws of the Kingdom of England." Thus, "in numerous cases the Privy Council of the King held that the Colonial law could not stand if they were opposed to the Colonial Charters or to the laws of the Kingdom." Later, state constitutions replaced the colonial charters, which John Adams (Quincy, 1969: 529) saw as important to the rise of judicial review in the United States.

The reduction of the fundamental principles of government in the United States to the form of written constitutions established by the people themselves, and beyond the control of their representatives, necessarily obliged the judicial department, in case of a conflict between provision and a legislative act, to obey the Constitution as the fundamental law and disregard the statute. This duty was recognized, and unconstitutional acts set aside, by courts of justice, even before the adoption of the Constitution of the United States.

6. Coke's dispute with James I was over the question of whether the King had the power to decide cases himself or only through his courts. Coke (*Prohibitions del Roy*, 1608: 64–65) said to James: "The King in his own person cannot judge any case . . .

[T]his ought to be determined and adjudged in some court of justice, according to the law and custom of England.'' James said that since law was founded on reason, could not he and others also know the law? To which Coke responded:

> [T]rue it was that God had endowed his Majesty with excellent science, and great endowments of nature; but his Majesty was not learned in the laws of his Realm of England, and causes which concern the life, or inheritance, or goods, or fortunes of his subjects are not to be decided by natural reason but by the artificial reason and judgment of law, which law is an act that requires long study and experience, before that a man can attain to the cognizance of it; and that Law was the golden met wand and measure to try causes of the subjects which protecteth his Majesty in safety and peace.

REFERENCES

Atcheson, G., Jr. (1945). ''Memorandum of conversation with Prince Konoe on October 8, 1945.'' RG 331, SCAP, GS, Central Files Branch, Misc. Files and Reports, Box 2229D. Suitland, MD.: National Records Center.

Berger, R. (1969). *Congress v. the Supreme Court*. Cambridge, Mass.: Harvard University Press.

Cappelletti, M. (1971). *Judicial review in a contemporary world*. New York: Macmillan.

Corwin, E. S. (1914). *The doctrine of judicial review*. Princeton, N.J.: Princeton University Press.

Dr. Bonham's Case (1610). 8 Co. Rep. 113b.

Hamilton, A., Jay, J. and Madison, J. (1969) (orig. pub. 1788). *The federalist or the new constitution*. New York: Modern Library.

Haskins, G., and Johnson, H. A. (1981). *Foundations of power: John Marshall: 1801– 15: History of the Supreme Court of the United States*, Vol. II. New York: Macmillan.

Hussey, A. R. (1946). *Notebook*. File 25–A, February 3. Alfred R. Hussey Papers. Ann Arbor: University of Michigan.

———. (1946). *Notes*. File 26-E, March 4–5. Alfred R. Hussey Papers. Ann Arbor: University of Michigan.

Ishimine, K. (1974). A comparative study of judicial review under the American and Japanese constitutional law. J.S.D. Dissertation, Cornell University.

Kades, C. L. (1976). Interview by David J. Danelski, June 16.

Madison, J. (1789). *Annals of Congress*, 1st Sess.

Marbury v. Madison. (1803). 1 Cranch 137.

Mott, R. L. (1926). *Due process of law*. Indianapolis: Bobbs Merrill.

Naito, Y. (1961). *A history of the reform of the judiciary after the end of the war: Compiled by an official who was involved in the process* (in Japanese), 5 vols. Tokyo: Legal Training and Research Institute.

Nelson, W. E. (1972). ''Changing conceptions of judicial review: The evolution of constitutional theory in the states, 1790–1860.'' *University of Pennsylvania Law Review*, 120: 1166–1185.

Plucknett, T.F.T. (1926). ''Bonham's Case and Judicial Review.'' *Harvard Law Review* 40: 36–70.

Prohibitions del Roy (1608). 7 Co. Rep. 64.

Quincy, J., Jr. (1969) (orig. pub. 1865). *Reports of cases argued and adjudged in the*

Superior Court of Judicature of the Province of Massachusetts Bay between 1761 and 1772. New York: Russell & Russell.

Rowell, M. E. (1946). Memorandum for chief of staff, January 11. Milo E. Rowell Papers. Palo Alto, Calif.: Hoover Institution for the Study of War and Peace.

———. (1976) Interview by David J. Danelski, March 10.

Sato, T. (1946) Memorandum on the process of negotiations at GHQ on March 4 and 5, 1946. Toshiro Irie Papers. Tokyo: Constitutional and Political Materials Section, Diet Library.

———. (1962). *A history of the drafting of the Japanese Constitution* (in Japanese), 2 vols. Tokyo: Yuhikaku.

SCAP, Government Section (1949). *Political reorientation of Japan*, 2 vols. Washington, D.C.: U.S. Printing Office.

SWNCC–228. (1946) Reform of the Japanese government system, January 7. Milo E. Rowell Papers. Palo Alto, Calif.: Hoover Institution for the Study of War and Peace.

Tanaka, H. (1976). *The Japanese legal system*. Tokyo: University of Tokyo Press.

3

The Growth of Canadian Judicial Review and the Commonwealth and American Experiences

Peter H. Russell

To an English common law lawyer, judicial review refers primarily to judicial review of administrative actions. For many centuries and long before the advent of written constitutions, English judges heard cases challenging the legality of actions taken by agencies of the state. In the seventeenth century "common lawyers joined in alliance with the parliamentarians" to remove an executive-controlled Star Chamber and vest judicial control of administrative actions in the common law courts (de Smith, 1973). Review by the "ordinary tribunals" of the lawfulness of acts and decisions of bodies and officials subordinate to Parliament is one of the three ingredients of what A. V. Dicey (1961) defined as "the rule of law." This is an essential part of Canada's legal inheritance— something it shares with other countries whose legal systems have English foundations.

Nowadays when political scientists and constitutional lawyers talk about judicial review it is not this older, more generic use of the term they have in mind. In these circles judicial review refers to the practice of courts measuring legislation against the requirements of a written constitution and striking down legislation that, in the judges' opinion, offends the constitution. In countries with written constitutions this narrower but politically more significant notion of judicial review—primarily American in its origin—has eclipsed the more generic English conception.

While judicial review in this American sense will be the focus of this chapter, it is important to point out that constitutional review in Canada and in other countries with similar legal roots may owe a good deal to the older English practice. The key rationale for judicial control of administrative actions is maintaining the supremacy of the law made by parliament and the courts over subordinate state agencies. Similarly, the logical justification for judicial review of legislation is maintaining the supremacy of the constitution, the state's highest law, over all other organs of public power. The success of the English common law judges in monopolizing the power of enforcing legal limits on government power paved the way for judges of the ordinary courts in Canada, and in other common law countries that adopted written constitutions, to exercise the function of enforcing constitutional limits on legislatures.

THE ORIGINS OF JUDICIAL REVIEW IN CANADA

Judicial review of legislation in the Canadian case has an imperial root. This is true of all countries that, like Canada and the United States, have a British colonial background. Colonial legislatures in the British Empire were limited by statutes enacted by the Imperial Parliament and in some cases by Royal Charters and Governors' Commissions. First, the Committee on Trade and Plantations and subsequently the Judicial Committee of the Privy Council, as the highest court in the empire, reviewed the validity of colonial legislation. This power was exercised with respect to the American colonies before the Revolution (McGovney, 1944). Although it is not clear whether any of the courts in what is now Canada invalidated legislation before Confederation, B. Strayer (1983) assures us that Canadian judges at the time of Confederation would have been prepared to strike down colonial statutes exceeding the legislative powers conferred on the colonial assemblies.

In marked contrast to the revolutionary beginning of the United States, the founding of Canada in 1867 did not sever the imperial tie. Although the terms of Canada's constitution were negotiated by Canadian politicians in Canada, the constitution itself, the British North America Act (BNA Act), was an act of the Imperial Parliament in Westminster. Two years before Confederation, the supremacy of imperial statutes had been clarified by the Colonial Laws Validity Act, which provided that colonial laws would be void if they conflicted with applicable imperial statutes. While the Statute of Westminster in 1931 removed this shackle from ordinary legislation in Canada, the BNA Act continued to be protected by the Colonial Laws Validity Act. Thus, in strict law, judicial review in Canada rested on an imperial foundation right down to 1982 when the Canada Act transferred custody of the constitution to Canada and completely severed Canada's legal subordination to the Imperial Parliament.

But this, it must be emphasized, was strictly the formal legal situation. Conceptually and philosophically, in their thinking about judicial review and in their justification of it, Canadians had moved away from an imperial rationale long before 1982.

At the time of Confederation there was some recognition that the federal nature of the constitution gave rise to the need for a judicial arbiter. The "Fathers of Confederation" did not talk about "judicial review" but several of them acknowledged that jurisdictional disputes between the two levels of government could be settled by the courts. Some were certainly aware of the role the U.S.

Supreme Court had played in interpreting that country's constitution. Jennifer Smith (1983) suggests that copies of Story's *Commentaries on the Constitution of the United States* must have been available to the framers of the Canadian Constitution and claims that among them "no one had any illusions about the significance of judicial review."

Smith has probably overstated the Canadian founding fathers' appreciation of judicial review. If they had understood it as well as she suggests, surely they would have been much more concerned with the design and establishment of a Canadian Supreme Court. Instead, they were content simply to give the federal parliament the power to establish a General Court of Appeal at some indefinite time in the future, leaving constitutional adjudication to the local courts with an appeal to the Judicial Committee of the Privy Council.

This underappreciation of judicial review at the time of Canada's founding should be contrasted with the situation that pertained at Australia's founding some 30 years later. Australia's founders were deeply aware of the American experience with judicial review, recognized its importance in shaping the country's constitutional future, resisted (unsuccessfully) the imperial Judicial Committee's exercise of this function, and in their constitution made provision for a national supreme court—the High Court of Australia—with the primary responsibility for judicial review (Galligan, 1987).

At the time of Canada's Confederation there was not a widely shared constitutional philosophy that demanded judicial review as an essential condition of liberal, constitutional government. There is no indication that many Canadians in 1867 were inclined to look on their written constitution—the BNA Act—as a higher law setting limits on all legislatures. John Marshall's rationale for judicial review in *Marbury v. Madison* would not have struck a very responsive chord among the Canadian political elite of that day. To enforce the Constitution the Fathers of Confederation were inclined to rely on executive devices modeled on imperial government as much as, if not more than, judicial review. The federal government was given a power of veto over provincial legislation similar to the imperial government's power of veto over dominion legislation. Infringements of the minority school rights enshrined in section 93 were to be appealed to the federal cabinet, not the judiciary. It would be a long time, and not until a fundamental mutation had taken place in Canada's constitutional culture, that the written constitution would be regarded as a supreme law to be interpreted and enforced exclusively by the courts.

CANADIAN FEDERALISM

The first chapter of this mutation occurred in the three decades following Confederation. During these years the Canadian polity, in theory and in practice, moved decisively toward classical federalism. The movement was generated by aggressive provinces, led by Ontario and Quebec, resisting federal encroachments, insisting on a wide interpretation of their own powers, and, by the 1880s, pressing for constitutional changes to strengthen provincial rights (Vipond, 1985). This provincial rights movement was responded to sympathetically by the Judicial Committee of the Privy Council as the final arbiter of Canadian constitutional disputes. In a series of decisions in the 1880s and 1890s, the Judicial Committee cut down the scope of the broad federal powers over peace, order and good government, and trade and commerce to make room for a fair measure of "provincial autonomy" (MacDonald, 1951). In the 1892 *Maritime Bank* case, the Judicial Committee enunciated a doctrine of dual sovereignty and explained the purpose of Canada's constitution in terms of classical federalism:

The object of the (BNA) Act was neither to weld the provinces into one, nor to subordinate provincial governments to a central authority, but to create a federal government in which they should all be represented, entrusted with the exclusive administration of affairs in which they had a common interest, each province retaining its independence and autonomy (Russell et al., 1989: 52).

There has been much speculation on what inspired the Judicial Committee to espouse this approach to Canada's constitution. In part, as Ivor Jennings (1937) has suggested, it may have been a sense of judicial restraint. During these early years when aggressive provincial legislatures were generating most of the constitutional challenges, an imperial supreme court in an era of liberal imperialism, unlike a nation-building supreme court, may have been inclined to minimize its involvement in Canadian affairs by finding grounds for upholding provincial legislation. It is also possible that the senior British judiciary of that day envisaged themselves establishing the Judicial Committee as a dispassionate judicial umpire for the federal commonwealth they saw emerging from the empire, and felt that in such a role they should be sensitive to the claims of local minorities, such as the French Canadians in Quebec, against the claims of national majorities (Greenwood, 1974). Sentiments of this kind resonate through the self-congratulatory speech of Viscount Haldane (1922), arguably the most provincial-rights-minded of all the British judges who presided over the Privy Council as Canada's constitutional arbiter.

In interpreting the federal provisions of the Canadian constitution the Judicial Committee made little use of American Supreme Court decisions. By way of contrast the judges of the Supreme Court of Canada soon after it was established in 1875 looked to American jurisprudence for guidance. In 1878 in *Severn v. The Queen*, for example, they justified an extremely broad interpretation of the federal commerce power on the basis of the U.S. Supreme Court's liberal interpretation of the more limited commerce power in the American Constitution (Russell et al., 1989: 31). But the Canadian Supreme Court at this time and until 1949 was supreme only in name. Its approach to judicial review soon succumbed to the higher authority of the Judicial Committee of the House of Lords in London.

If the Judicial Committee's treatment of the Canadian constitution had an American root it was not the decisions of the U.S. Supreme Court but the British judges' theoretical conception of the American Constitution. The understanding of federalism that the Law Lords brought to bear on the Canadian constitution may well have been influenced by English texts on American constitutionalism. Dicey's *An Introduction to the Study of the Law of the Constitution* had its first edition in 1885 and must have been widely read by British lawyers and judges. It was Dicey (1961: 144) who, on the basis of his understanding of the American Constitution, insisted that the three essential characteristics of a "completely developed federalism" were "the supremacy of the constitution—the distribution among bodies with limited and coordinate authority of the different powers of government—the authority of courts to act as interpreters of the constitution. These propositions provided the intellectual rationale for the Judicial Committee's approach to Canadian judicial review.

Whatever the causes and influences, the result was clear: by the end of the nineteenth century the practice of judicial review was firmly established in Canada. British judges applying their understanding of American federalism had made constitutional federalism a first principle of the Canadian system of government. In the twentieth century the federal executive's power of veto over provincial legislation fell into disuse as it conflicted with the ideal of classical federalism and the view that the enforcement of constitutional limitations on government was exclusively the responsibility of the courts. Although crafted by a foreign court, judicially enforced classical federalism at this stage in Canadian history fit reasonably well the fragmented nature of the Canadian polity.

It is important to note that the approach to judicial review of legislation forged by the Privy Council was based narrowly on federalism and not on a broader conception of constitutionalism. British and Canadian judges carried over into constitutional interpretation techniques they used for ordinary statutory interpretation and, employing the categories of administrative law, simply determined whether challenged legislation was *intra vires* or *ultra vires*—within or beyond—the powers bestowed on the legislature by the BNA Act. So keen were they to underline the limited scope of judicial review that they frequently asserted that the federal division of powers was the only constitutional limitation on legislative power in Canada, ignoring provisions of the constitution such as the language rights in Section 133 and provisions guaranteeing the independence of the judiciary that appear to restrict both levels of government (Scott, 1959). Insistence on this so-called exhaustion theory—the theory that the BNA Act divides all possible powers of government between the federal and provincial legislatures—minimized the political significance of judicial review: in ascertaining the constitutionality of legislation the judiciary was deciding not whether legislation ought to be passed at all but simply which level of legislature may enact it.

THE ADVENT OF THE CHARTER OF RIGHTS AND FREEDOMS

With the adoption in 1982 of a constitutional Charter of Rights and Freedoms and a clause declaring the "the Constitution of Canada is the supreme law of

Canada,'' the basis of judicial review has broadened to encompass a full sense of constitutionalism. The mutation from imperialism to federalism to constitutionalism as the underlying rationale of judicial review in Canada is complete.

International influences have had their effect in propelling Canada through this latest transformation of its constitutional culture. The founding of the United Nations in 1945 and the 1948 UN Universal Declaration of Human Rights provided the first impetus toward developing a Bill of Rights in Canada (Tarnopolsky, 1975). Subsequently, the European Convention of Human Rights and the International Convention of Civil and Political Rights (which came into force for Canada in 1976) became models for Canadian Bill of Rights enthusiasts. While not discounting these broad international forces that stimulated worldwide interest in the constitutional codification of fundamental rights, in the Canadian case there was in addition an especially potent American influence. The relatively greater strength of this American influence is the most likely explanation of the fact that the general idea of protecting individuals and minorities through judicially enforced constitutional rights gained much more currency in Canada than in the sister Commonwealth countries, Australia and New Zealand.

It is of no small consequence that the liberal civil rights decisions of the Warren Court in the United States coincided with the dawning of the age of television. Most of what Canadians watch on their television screens comes from the United States (Babe, 1988). And on their screens in the 1950s, 1960s and 1970s they were exposed to the attractive image of liberal judges upholding the rights of the downtrodden. This impact of the American mass media helps account for the general popularity of the Charter of Rights project in Canada. Polls registering that popularity fueled the federal government's determination to press ahead with the Charter against the opposition of most provincial governments. A 1987 social science survey conducted by three colleagues and I shows overwhelming support for the new Charter of Rights among both English and French Canadians (Sniderman et al., 1989).

The Liberal Party led by Pierre Trudeau made the Charter of Rights its top priority in constitutional politics primarily for its symbolic value. By expressing the common values of Canadians, the Charter was looked upon as an instrument for promoting national unity and for reversing the centrifugal tendencies in Canada's constitutional politics (Russell, 1983). The Charter's political sponsors showed little concern for the judicial review implications of the Charter. Those who pushed for the Charter tended to play down or ignore the role of the judiciary in interpreting and applying its terms. The Supreme Court of Canada, since 1949 Canada's highest court, had been markedly restrained in its treatment of the statutory Canadian Bill of Rights. It did not give politicians any cause to fear excessive judicial activism on the part of a court enforcing constitutional guarantees.

The only serious resistance to the Charter project was at the elite level (Milne, 1982; Romanow et al., 1984). Some provincial political leaders were wary of the way a constitutional charter might shift power from legislatures to courts and of the centralizing implications of the Supreme Court in Ottawa applying national standards to provincial legislatures. The legal sector of the intelligentsia was predominantly pro-Charter, many of its members having taken postgraduate studies at American law schools where they were dazzled by the Warren Court's activism. However, a few academics on the Left and a number of political scientists raised concerns about the tendency of a Charter of Rights to "legalize" politics and to move Canada's political culture away from its traditional collectivism toward a more American accented Lockean liberalism.

Although this resistance did not stop the movement to entrench rights and freedoms, it did leave its mark on Canada's constitutional Charter of Rights and Freedoms and on the scope and nature of judicial review flowing from it. In order to maintain the broadest possible political support for the Charter, the Trudeau Liberals, at the insistence of the NDP (Canada's democratic socialist party), kept property rights out of the Charter. The communitarian strand in Canada's political culture is reflected in clauses recognizing the rights of minority language communities, multiculturalism, and aboriginal peoples (Monahan, 1987). Positive freedom is given precedence over negative freedom in the equality section of the Charter, which recognizes affirmative action to ameliorate the conditions of disadvantaged individuals or groups as legitimate grounds for modifying the right to equal benefit of the law. There is a further balancing of collectivism against individualism in Section 1, the Charter's general limits clause, which invites the courts to balance individual claims against the general interest of the community.[1] And finally the Charter's override clause, which permits legislatures for five years at a time to immunize their legislation from judicial review based on the Charter's most important universal rights, represents a quintessential Canadian compromise between American and British constitutionalism (Weiler, 1984).

In the few years in which the Charter has been in force it has become a major factor in Canadian public life (Morton, 1987; Mandel, 1989; Russell, 1988). The media and academic journals are stuffed with Charter chatter. Most of the litigation has been generated by lawyers representing accused persons in the criminal justice system. But the courts' activism has also encouraged political interest groups to pursue their policy objectives through Charter claims. While the Canadian judiciary, led by the Supreme Court of Canada, has been much more activist in its treatment of the Charter than was generally expected, this new dimension of judicial review is not untouched by some characteristic Canadian moderation. In applying the reasonable limits section, judges have frequently shown deference to the legislature's judgment.[2] The Supreme Court has shown that it is opposed to reading economic rights into the Charter.[3] While the Court struck down Canada's national abortion law, it did so primarily on procedural grounds and in a manner that left ample room for a legislative resolution of the substantive issue (Russell et al., 1989: 515).

There is also some resistance to the Americanization of Canada's constitutional law. In interpreting rights in the Charter that have counterparts in the American

Bill of Rights, Canadian judges have been reluctant to adopt American juris-prudence uncritically. Justice LaForest gave vent to this sense of judicial na-tionalism when he stated in one of the Supreme Court's early Charter decisions that "Canadian legal thought has at many points in the past deferred to that of the British; the Charter will be no sign of our national maturity if it simply becomes an excuse for adopting another intellectual mentor. American juris-prudence, like the British, must be viewed as a tool, not as a master" (Russell et al., 1989: 21).

JUDICIAL REVIEW UNDER THE CHARTER

In the first six years of Charter application, courts of appeal in Canada struck down 65 statutes on Charter grounds (Morton et al., 1989). This degree of activism has not aroused a great deal of controversy. The Court's decision striking down the law restricting abortions did provoke a writer for one of the country's leading magazines to ask "Who's Running the Country Anyway?" (Frum, 1988). But such reactions have not been widespread. At the level of public opinion, judicial review has not encountered a legitimacy crisis. The survey of opinion on the Charter conducted in 1987 indicates that a clear majority of Canadians prefer judges over legislatures as the final decision makers on questions pertaining to rights and freedoms.[4]

The override clause in the Charter has been used only once to reverse a Supreme Court decision. This was a dramatic event that may be a watershed in Canada's constitutional evolution. In December 1988 the Supreme Court in a unanimous "opinion of The Court" ruled that Quebec legislation prohibiting commercial advertising in any language other than French violated the Charter's guarantee of "freedom of expression" (Russell et al., 1989: 557). Within a few days of this decision Quebec's Liberal government, under pressure from francophone opinion in the province, brought in legislation restoring the French-only rule for all outdoor advertising. The override clause was employed to protect this leg-islation from judicial review. This provoked a tremendously hostile reaction throughout English Canada—a reaction that appears to be the final nail in the coffin of the so-called Meech Lake Constitutional Accord, the amendments designed to win Quebec's support for the 1982 constitutional settlement (Hogg, 1988).

The legislative override in the Charter is now in very bad odor in all parts of the country except Quebec. Prime Minister Mulroney and several provincial premiers have pledged their determination to remove it from the Charter. They sense the extent to which the public has come to believe the Charter's rhetoric of fundamental rights and accept the judiciary's legitimacy as the final arbiter of those rights. In English-speaking Canada the override may quickly experience the fate of the federal disallowance power and become politically unusable. But this is not likely to occur in Quebec. There, in the minds of the French majority, Charter rights have not preempted provincial rights nor the right of the Quebecois to ensure their cultural survival. In the future, the Charter, far from being an instrument of national unity, may accentuate the cleavage between Quebec and the rest of Canada.

CONCLUSION

For now judicial review appears to be well-established in Canada, playing a major role in its governance and politics. In a recent contribution to the *International Political Science Review*, Fred Riggs (1988: 276) argues that constitutional review is primarily a requirement of presidentialist regimes. He acknowledges that judicial review has come to play a more important role in "a Commonwealth country, like Canada, where there is now a written constitution" but doubts "that it equals that of the USA in importance." Riggs, like many contemporary Americans, does not appreciate the importance of judicial review in maintaining federalism. He overlooks the fact that whereas the contemporary U.S. Supreme Court has virtually withdrawn from the role of federal umpire,[5] the Supreme Court of Canada continues to play a vital role in adjudicating disputes over the division of powers. With the addition of Charter review to federalism review and with a reasonably activist judiciary sustained by a public, still relatively naive and unrealistic about judicial power, arguably Riggs is wrong, and the importance of judicial review in Canada at the present time equals if it does not exceed its importance in the United States.

An interesting question for the future is whether the Canadian variant of judicial review with its peculiar combination of British and American influences will now diffuse outward and precisely because of its mongrel quality become a model at least for older members of the Commonwealth. For a Canadian accustomed to living at the margin of empire, this is an untypically chauvinistic sentiment to harbor.

NOTES

1. Section 1 states that "the *Canadian Charter of Rights and Freedoms* guarantees the rights and freedoms set out in it subject only to such reasonable limits prescribed by law as can be reasonably justified in a free and democratic society."

2. This is particularly evident in decisions upholding limits on the right to counsel in order to permit random roadside breathalizer tests. See *R. v. Hufsky* (1986) 1 S.C.R. 621 and *R. v. Thomsen* (1986) 1 S.C.R. 640.

3. This view is explicitly expressed in a recent decision of the Court (*Irwin Toys* [1989] 1 S.C.R. 927) rejecting a challenge to a Quebec law prohibiting advertising aimed at children.

4. This is the survey whose results on language rights issues are reported in Sniderman et al., 1989). The question asked was as follows: "When the legislature passes a law but the courts say it is unconstitutional on the grounds that it conflicts with the Charter of Rights, who should have the final say, the leg-

islature or the courts?'' While 60 percent of the 2,000 respondents in the sample of citizens preferred courts, a majority of legislators in the elite sample preferred legislatures.

 5. This is the clear implication of the U.S. Supreme Court's decision in *Garcia v. San Antonio Metropolitan Transit Authority* 105 S Ct. 1005 (1985).

REFERENCES

Babe, R. E. (1988). Emergence and development of Canadian communication: Dispelling the myths. In R. Lorimer and D. Wilson (eds.), *Communication Canada*, 3rd ed. Toronto: Kagan & Woo.

de Smith, S. A. (1973). *Judicial review of administrative action*, 3rd ed. London: Stevens.

Dicey, A. V. (1961). *An introduction to the study of the law of the constitution*, 10th ed. London: Macmillan.

Frum, D. (1988). Who's running the country anyway? *Saturday Night*, 103: 10–14.

Galligan, B. (1987). *Politics of the high court: A study of the judicial branch of government in Australia*. St. Lucia: University of Queensland Press.

Greenwood, M. F. (1974). Lord Watson, institutional self-interest and the decentralization of Canadian federalism in the 1890's. *University of British Columbia Law Review* 9: 224–279.

Haldane, R. (Viscount). (1922). The work for the empire of the Judicial Committee of the Privy Council. *Cambridge Law Journal* 1: 2.

Hogg, P. W. (1988). *Meech Lake constitutional accord annotated*. Toronto: Carswell.

Jennings, I. W. (1937). Constitutional interpretation: The experience of Canada. *Harvard Law Review* 51: 1–39.

MacDonald, V. C. (1951). The Privy Council and the Canadian constitution. *Canadian Bar Review* 29: 1021–1037.

Mandel, M. (1989). *The Charter of Rights and the legalization of politics in Canada*. Toronto: Wall & Thompson.

McGovney, D. O. (1944). The British origin of judicial review of legislation. *University of Pennsylvania Law Review* 93: 1–49.

Milne, D. (1982). *The new Canadian constitution*. Toronto: James Lorimer.

Monahan, P. (1987). *Politics and the constitution: The charter, federalism and the Supreme Court of Canada*. Toronto: Carswell/Methuen.

Morton, T. (1987). The political impact of the Canadian Charter of Rights and Freedoms. *Canadian Journal of Political Science* 20: 1–49.

———, Solomon, G., McNish, I., and Poulton, D. (1989). Judicial nullification of statutes under the charter 1982–1988. Paper presented to joint session of Annual Meetings of the Canadian Political Science Association and the Canadian Law & Society Association, Quebec City, June 3.

Riggs, F. W. (1988). The survival of presidentialism in America: Para-constitutional practices. *International Political Science Review* 9: 247–278.

Romanow, R., Whyte, J., and Leeson, H. (1984). *Canada notwithstanding: The making of the constitution 1976–1982*. Toronto: Carswell.

Russell, P. H. (1983). The political purposes of the Canadian Charter of Rights and Freedoms. *Canadian Bar Review* 61: 30–54.

———. (1988). The Canadian charter: A political report. *Public Law* (Autumn).

————, Knopff, R., and Morton, T. (1989). *Federalism and the charter: Leading constitutional decisions, a new edition.* Ottawa: Carleton University Press.

Scott, F. R. (1959). *Civil liberties and Canadian federalism.* Toronto: University of Toronto Press.

Smith, J. (1983). The origins of judicial review in Canada. *Canadian Journal of Political Science* 16: 115–134.

Sniderman, P., Fletcher, J., Russell, P. H., and Tetlock, P. (1989). The problem of double standards: Mass and elite attitudes toward language rights in the Canadian Charter of Rights. *Canadian Journal of Political Science* 22: 259–284.

Strayer, B. (1983). *The Canadian constitution and the courts: The function and scope of judicial review.* Toronto: Butterworths.

Tarnopolsky, W. (1975). *The Canadian Bill of Rights.* Toronto: Carswell.

Vipond, R. C. (1985). Constitutional politics and the legacy of the provincial rights movement in Canada. *Canadian Journal of Political Science* 18: 267–294.

Weiler, P. (1984). Rights and judges in a democracy: A new Canadian version. *University of Michigan Journal of Law Reform* 18: 51–92.

4

Abstract Constitutional Review and Policy Making in Western Europe

Alec Stone

Constitutional review has exploded into prominence in Western Europe. In the 1970s, Greece, Portugal, Spain, and Sweden joined Austria, the European Community, France, West Germany, and Italy as polities with effective review mechanisms. Yet before 1950, the power of European courts to control the constitutionality of legislation was nearly unknown. Comparative political scientists have all but ignored this development and constitutional courts generally (Sigelman and Gadbois, 1983). The French case, where *no major book or article on the Constitutional Council has yet been produced by native social scientists*, is a telling, if extraordinary, example. But in all European countries, academic discourse on law and courts is the privileged domain of law professors, the vast majority of whom are exercised exclusively by traditional, jurisprudential concerns. In this discourse, there is a fierce resistance to the notion that constitutional courts are political actors at all; a radical dissociation between legal and policy-making processes is propagated; and the impact of courts on macro politics is obscured or altogether ignored.

This chapter is an overview and assessment of the establishment and subsequent development of abstract review in Europe, focusing on the interaction between constitutional courts, governments, and parliaments in the making of public policy. First, I examine the creation of constitutional jurisdictions set apart from the ordinary and administrative court systems in Austria, Germany, France, and Spain. This creation had the particular advantage of allowing for the *constitutional review* of legislation by special judges while preserving the main tenets of European separation of powers doctrines, tenets that had long enshrined an uncompromising hostility to *judicial review*. In the second section I describe aspects of the structure, mandate, and activity of European courts that exercise abstract review—in Austria, France, West Germany, and Spain. Abstract review differs from American judicial review in that it is not dependent on, or incidental to, concrete litigation or controversy involving a statute. The abstract review process results in a decision on the *prima facie* constitutionality of a legislative text; a concrete tort is not a requisite condition; the process is a purely exegetical exercise. In the third section I examine the impact of abstract review on legislative processes, focusing on the cases we know the most about—France and Germany. In both of these countries, policy making has been transformed, and in remarkably similar ways.

ORIGINS

The development of judicial review in Europe constitutes an extraordinary departure from an established constitutional orthodoxy long thought to be utterly resistant to fundamental change. In civil law systems, statutes traditionally are conceived and treated as concrete expressions of the general will, or of state sovereignty, sovereignty to which the work of the judiciary and of legal science is to be an obedient, if at times, creative, servant. In this orthodoxy, the constitutional document is not necessarily considered superior to statute. Historically, basic laws not only failed to provide judges with the power to review the constitutionality of legislation, they placed no limits on the substantive content of legislation (including the areas of public liberties and fundamental rights). Even more important, constitutions could be amended or even abrogated by ordinary legislative processes.

Partly as a consequence, the role and function of the judiciary in the classic European politicolegal system were rigidly circumscribed. The judge's role was a subservient and bureaucratic one: he was required to verify the existence and applicability of statutory norms to a case at hand, but he could investigate the work of the legislature no further. To recognize a judge-made law in this system was to diagnose pathology: lawmakers had promulgated either an unclear law or one in conflict with established legal regimes, precipitating judicial interpretation; or the judge had simply, and illegitimately, overstepped constitutional bounds. Judicial review was all but unthinkable. From 1780 in Germanic states and from 1791 in France, judicial interpretation of statutes was explicitly prohibited by constitutions, and penalties were prescribed in the penal codes for any transgression.

It is worth noting that during the latter half of the nineteenth century, public law came to be taught as a separate branch of the law in continental countries, and doctrine began to evolve independently. From this time onward, legal scholarship proved increasingly hostile to the prohibition of judicial review, and by the 1920s an important international doctrinal movement made the achievement of judicial review *the* central concern of the public law field (Duguit, 1923; Friedrich, 1963: 262–263; Hauriou, 1929; Neumann, 1964: Ch. 2). This movement largely failed, and for two reasons. First, political authorities in control of the state consistently and overwhelmingly reiterated their opposition to a grant of interpretive powers to judges, an opposition that became all the more resolute when they were told that judicial review in the United States had led to a "government of judges" (Lambert, 1922). Second, judges were constrained by the internalization of their bureaucratic role, and by their lack of independence from political authorities.

Constitutional courts replete with at least potential review authority had existed at various times in the federal systems of Germanic states, Switzerland, and Austria between 1848 and 1945 (Deener, 1952). But the most innovative pre-World War II experiment in constitutional review occurred in Austria, during its short-lived first republic (1920–34) at the instigation of Hans Kelsen, an extraordinarily influential law professor and legal theorist who had been asked to draft what became the Constitution of 1920 (Eisenmann, 1986 [orig. 1928]). Kelsen (1928), like many of his French and German peers, argued that if a constitution were to mean anything at all, it had to be considered superior to statute, and this hierarchy had to be defended if the rule of law (or *rechtsstaat*) was to be assured. But Kelsen also understood that *judicial* review would not likely be acceptable, and he searched instead for another means by which the constitution could be defended. The result was the creation of the Austrian constitutional court, the first example in history of a special jurisdiction whose exclusive purpose was to decide constitutional controversies. The court possessed wide-ranging powers of abstract and concrete review. Cursed by the turbulent times into which it was born, the institution was subject to periodic, virulent attacks by right-wing political parties and their press organs, and its review powers were finally all but rescinded by government decree in 1933 (Gulick, 1948: 785–86, 877–878, 1075–1077). The republic was engulfed shortly thereafter by Nazism.

The Austrian precedent is considered, in Cappelletti's terms (1986), "seminal for Western Europe," and the Kelsenian court is today recognized as the prototype of the "European" model of "constitutional" (because it is not formally "judicial") review, in contrast to the American model (Favoreu, 1986). But the political environments in which post-World War II courts find themselves differ fundamentally from those of their predecessors. Most important is the central place accorded to constitutions—and by extension to constitutional courts—as institutional bulwarks against a recurrence of authoritarianism. The drafting of the Federal Republic's Basic Law and the decision in 1945 to revive and modernize the Austrian constitution of 1920–29 were above all reactions to the Nazi experience. Much the same can be said of the drafting of the Spanish Constitution of 1978. In all three cases, the founders explicitly gave to constitutional courts the burden of protecting citizens from abuses by public authorities. In Germany, an extensive bill of rights comprises the first 18 articles of the Basic Law, repudiating traditional theories that the state necessarily presupposes and is responsible for the existence of individual rights. In Spain, "by far the longest section of the Constitution deals with fundamental rights and the obligation of the state to uphold and guarantee these rights" (Donaghy and Newton, 1987: 13). In Austria, the situation is more complicated since there is no charter of rights in the constitution proper, but the constitution does require the court to protect rights and freedoms, and the court has made use of a number of texts that it has elevated to constitutional status to achieve that end (Ohlinger, 1982: 347–351). Furthermore, the desire to decentralize German and Austrian state power permanently led to the adoption of federal structures, which in turn virtually required the existence of a constitutional court (Dicey, 1961: Ch. 3). The dominant issue confronting the Spanish framers was that of regional autonomy, and they also relied heavily on the constitutional court as an instrument of supervision over what is a quasifederal system.

The French case is exceptional. The 1958 constitution does not contain a bill of rights, and the Constitutional Council was not created in order to protect fundamental rights and liberties. Moreover, federalism is absent. The fact that the French Council is actively involved in constitutional review is due to judicial activism, and to the politicization of its offices by politicians. Created by Gaullists to ensure that parliament would not overstep its constitutionally prescribed limitations, the Council's early years were uneventful and it was wholly subservient to the executive. In 1971, however, the Council annulled its first piece of governmental legislation and in the process incorporated an expansive bill of rights into the constitution, which includes the 1789 Declaration of the Rights of Man, the preamble to the 1946 constitution, and the unnamed "fundamental principles recognized by the laws of the republic." The Council's current role, then, has virtually no relation to the framers' intentions (Keeler and Stone, 1987).

Two general statements should be made now. First, the proliferation of constitutional courts in Europe on the Austrian model—as a general phenomenon—is due not least to the fact that such institutions preserve the traditional legal order and judicial function, while at the same time enabling effective review. Second, the review activity of these courts is tolerated by politicians largely because it works to protect individual rights, and it has been embraced by legal scholars because it provides a stable and creative source for the building of constitutional law. The support of the scholarly community accorded to constitutional courts has proved enormously important in their struggle to appropriate power or—what amounts to the same thing—to gain legitimacy. Whether European- or American-style, however, the power to judge the constitutionality of legislation, and to set it aside or annul it, is also the power to participate in the making of public policy.

STRUCTURE AND ACTIVITY

There is significant variation in the constitutional mandate and activity of the European courts that exercise abstract review authority. As Table 4.1 shows, a constitutional court may possess abstract review powers alone, or in combination with powers of concrete review. Further, there exist two modes of abstract review:

Table 4.1
Structure and Mandate of European Courts that Exercise Abstract Review*

	France(1958)	W. Germany(1951)	Austria(1920/1945)	Spain(1980)
Composition and Recruitment:				
Number of Members	9	16	14	12
Appointing Authorities	President(3) Pres. Nat. Ass.(3) Pres. Senate(3)	Bundestag (8) Bundesrat (8)	Federal Govt. (8) Nationalrat (3) Bundesrat (3)	Congress (4) Senate (4) Govt. (2) Judiciary (2)
Length of Term	9 years	12 years	until 70 years of age	9 years
Age Limit	None	40 year minimum 68 year maximum	70 year maximum	None
Requisite Qualifications	None	6/16 must be federal judges: others must be qualified to be German judges	8/14 must be judges functionaries, or law professors; others must be lawyers or political scientists	All must be judges, lawyers or law professors with at least 15 years experience
Constitutional review authority:				
Attached to court systems	No	Yes	Yes	Yes
Abstract Review				
-- a priori	Yes	No	No	Abolished(1985)
-- a posteriori	No	Yes	Yes	Yes
Concrete Review	No	Yes	Yes	Yes
Power to refer constitutional controversies to the court possessed by:				
Politicians (abstract review)	President Pres. Nat. Ass. Pres. Senate 60 deputies 60 senators	Fed. Govt. Lander Govts. 1/3 of Bundestag	Fed. Govt. Lander Govts. 1/3 Nationalrat 1/3 lower houses of Lander	Prime minister Pres. Parliament 50 deputies 50 senators Executives autonomous regions
Ombudsman (abstract and concrete review)	-	-	-	Yes
Judiciary (concrete review)	No	Yes	Yes	Yes
Individuals (concrete review)	No	Yes	Yes	Yes

* A complete list would include Portugal, whose constitutional court was established in 1983.

a posteriori (Austria, Portugal, Spain, West Germany), and *a priori* (France, Spain until 1985, Portugal). In the former, laws are referred to the constitutional court after promulgation; in the latter, laws are referred after final adoption by parliament, but *before* promulgation. In all cases, abstract review is initiated by politicians, who refer legislation directly to the court. Courts cannot refuse to rule, and governments and legislative majorities cannot avoid having their legislation examined. *Abstract review therefore functions to extend what would otherwise be a concluded legislative process*—referrals in effect require the court to undertake a final ''reading'' of a disputed bill or law.

The highly partisan nature of this process places constitutional courts in delicate situations, and the possibility of explosive judicial-political confrontation might appear to be virtually permanent. However, *for every European court excepting the French, abstract review processes do not constitute a major source of caseload or of public perceptions about their role in the political system.* Whatever impact abstract review might have on debates and controversies about a court's institutional legitimacy is counterbalanced by routine lower profile tasks. That is, in countries other than France, what constitutional courts do most of the time is not salient to partisan politics: political parties are not involved directly in these processes, and they do not actively question and debate the legitimacy of the work being performed.

Statistics show the extent to which abstract review constitutes only a small fraction of total activity outside of France. The German court, for example, receives 99 percent of all of its cases via direct appeal by individuals—who, as in Austria and Spain where similar mechanisms exist, must demonstrate that their rights have *already* been violated. Since 1951, individuals alone have filed on average over 1,500 complaints per year (more than 3,300 were filed in 1987) seeking concrete review, while referrals of legislation by politicians seeking abstract review average less than three per year.

In Austria, concrete review of cases originating in the administrative court system comprises well over 90 percent of the Vienna court's caseload. The court has dealt with over 1,000 such cases per year during the 1980s, and its docket is chronically backlogged (there are some 2,000 cases pending at present). The court, which also receives approximately 25 individual referrals each year, is motivated above all else by its desire or responsibility to harmonize the legal order, and not by politically initiated reviews. *Abstract review is exceedingly rare in Austria, and, indeed, is politically insignificant.* In 1975, the right of referral was granted to one-third of the deputies in the federal and state lower houses—that is, to the minority party. Whether due to the consensual nature of Austrian politics, to a belief that referrals are not altogether legitimate, or to both, the court has received only five referrals to date, resulting in only one ruling of unconstitutionality. In consequence, the legislative process has *not* been significantly altered by the existence of such review.

The work of the Spanish court, like that of its German counterpart, is dominated by individual referrals (90 percent of all cases that reach the court). These referrals (*amparos*) may not attack a law directly, but instead are requests that the court defend against alleged administrative infringement those fundamental rights enumerated in Articles 14 and 30 of the constitution. From 1981, when the court began its work, through 1985, it has handed down 422 decisions on nearly 4,000 individual referrals. Moreover, the court has clearly signaled that it considers the protection of individual rights to be its top priority. *As in Germany, this is largely due to the court's wish to contribute to the stability of a democratic regime created in the wake of fascist rule.* And, as in Germany, it would be politically dangerous for any major party in Spain to attack the court on issues concerning individual rights. Abstract review referrals for *a posteriori* control have averaged 8 per year, while the court received a total of 13 petitions for *a priori* control until 1985. In 1985, the *a priori* power was rescinded because it was considered to be an illegitimate affront to parliamentary sovereignty.

The French Constitutional Council exercises *a priori* abstract review exclusively, and solely upon referral by political authorities. Once promulgated, laws are immune from scrutiny by the Council or by any other jurisdiction. Further, not only is the Council detached from the greater judicial system (any influence it may exercise upon ordinary or administrative courts is neither systematic nor formal), it is also cut off from direct popular contact with the citizenry. Political scientists (including myself), comparativists, and non-French legal specialists have consistently conceptualized the Council as something other than a court, and as an institution that fulfills more a legislative than a judicial function. Unable to claim that it performs a function of harmonizing legal decisions or administrative activity with the exigencies of the constitution, and bereft of a stable constituency, the Council may be said to possess relatively fewer resources with which to counter criticisms of its activities. These occur with greater frequency and are much more public and vitriolic than those directed at other European courts. At the same time, the Council's role has vastly expanded: from 1974, when the power of referral was granted to any 60 deputies or senators, through 1987 the Council received 191 referrals—in the 1958–73 period, it received a total of 9.

The French Council has also been heavily criticized for its "political" composition. As Table 4.1 shows, whereas in the German, Austrian, and Spanish cases minimum levels of judicial expertise are requisite conditions for appointment, there are no such standards in France. Of the 41 members who have served on the Council from 1958 to 1988, 59 percent were selected from the ranks of parliamentarians and/or ministers. While in Germany, the tendency has been toward greater "juridicization" of the selection process (that is, the number of members of the court with previous careers on the bench or tenure on law faculties has increased over time), such has not been the case in France. In 1968, the nine-member Council contained six (67 percent) former professional politicians, increasing to seven (78 percent) in 1983, and to eight (89 percent), in 1986. Nevertheless, it is important to note that the Council's jurisprudence has become more dense, sophisticated, and attendant to French judicial norms during the past two decades.

The "juridicization" of constitutional courts does not imply that the recruitment process is apolitical. On the contrary, in both Germany and Austria, formalized negotiations among the major political parties determine which party will fill vacancies on the court (allocations are roughly proportionate to parliamentary strength); in Spain as well, although it is too early to draw firm conclusions, the appointment process is largely a process of bargaining among political parties.

THE "JURIDICIZATION" OF POLICY MAKING

The development of abstract constitutional review in France and Germany has transformed the customs and conduct of politicians and policymakers. Indeed, policy making can be described as "juridicized" to the extent that a constitutional court's decisions, the pedagogical authority of its past jurisprudence, and the threat of future censure alter legislative outcomes. When a constitutional court rules on the constitutionality of legislative provisions, this influence is direct but not always negative. The court may have an indirect influence to the extent that governments and their parliamentary majorities sacrifice policy preferences in order to avoid constitutional censure. This indirect impact also might be said to constitute a court's legislative behavior.

The jurisdicization of policy-making processes in France and Germany can be explained by four interrelated structural and behavioral factors: (1) the modes of constitutional review exercised by the respective constitutional courts over legislation; (2) the use by politicians of the courts' offices for political ends; (3) judicial activism and the attendant development by courts of creative techniques of controlling legislation; and (4) the strict application of decisions by legislators. The study of "juridicization" thus focuses empirical attention on the interaction between courts and legislative institutions in the making of public policy. Space limitations preclude close analysis of particular legislative processes and decisions. I have therefore sought to generalize from my own research (Stone, 1989a and b, 1992) and that of Christine Landfried (1985, 1988), work based on in-depth case studies of the impact of constitutional courts on policy output.

Mode of Control

In his pathbreaking, now classic essay on conceptualizing the U.S. Supreme Court as a "national policymaker," R. Dahl (1957) argued that "what is critical is the extent to which a court can or does make policy decisions by going outside established 'legal' criteria found in precedent, statute, and constitution." Creative judicial interpretation will have policy impact in any political system. But Dahl's focus is too limited for our purposes, reflecting strictly the realities of the American judicial review mechanism and a specifically American separation-of-powers tradition. Abstract control is typically justified as providing for a more complete, potentially systematic, and therefore efficacious defense of the supremacy of the constitution within a hierarchy of judicial norms (Weber, 1987: 50–57). *Abstract review is of interest to policy studies because it requires or enables constitutional courts to intervene in and alter legislative processes and outcomes.* This intervention is virtually immediate: in France, bills must be referred to the Council within 15 days after their adoption in Parliament, and may not be promulgated until a decision has been reached by the Council; in Germany, politicians have one month from the date of promulgation to refer legislation. Thus, it should not be surprising that the subsequent decision is viewed by politicians as the true final stage of the legislative process.

Juridicizing Legislative Politics

The remarkable development of abstract constitutional control in France and Germany is a result of, and a response to, the exploitation of the courts by politicians for partisan political ends. In France, successive oppositions in the 1980s correctly viewed petitions to the Council, or the mere threat of petition, to be their most effective means to obstruct or enforce changes in legislation proposed by the government and its parliamentary majority. Because governments can not prevent such petitions, they are obliged either to work on the assumption that the opposition will refer important projects to constitutional judges or to risk court censure, embarrassment, and lost time. Since 1981, such major reforms as the laws on decentralization (1982), press pluralism (1984), audiovisual communications (1986), and the Chirac government's penal code reforms (1986) were subject to massive autolimitation processes, as majorities sacrificed important policy objectives due to threats of referral and fear of censure. In West Germany, governments and their supporters are apparently even more willing to compromise with the opposition, so risk-averse have they become in constitutional matters, and in consequence policy making is "overloaded with legal arguments and considerations" (Landfried, 1988) as the "opposition in the Bundestag [works] to attain its political goals by judicial means" (Landfried, 1985: 541). The laws on codetermination (1976) and on military service for conscientious objectors (1978) are just two important reforms that were substantially altered by the juridicized process. Constitutional debate is therefore not limited to official judicial intervention, but may occur during all stages of the legislative process.

That said, juridicization is not a permanent state within ministries and parliament. The most important aspects of a great number of bills either raise no fundamental constitutional objections or are treated as though they do not by politicians. The opposition does not waste time and resources in threatening court intervention if compelling objections as to the constitutionality of legislation in question do not exist or can not be found. Moreover, even debates that can be empirically characterized as juridicized are not juridicized evenly or in the same way. Any given policy area has its own dynamic of constitutional possibility or constraint, conforming to jurisprudential development. Legislative debate is more or less juridicized as a function of this variation—that is, oppositions have a greater chance of juridicizing processes to the extent that constitutional courts have already laid the ground rules for legislating in that policy sector. The French Council's annulments of the Socialist's bills on nationalization (1982), press pluralism (1984), and electoral reform in New Caledonia (1985) thus structured the policy processes and debates on the Chirac government's privatization program (1986), press and audiovisual reform (1986), and the reform of the electoral system in metropolitan France (1986). In a similar manner, no West German government engaged in reforming party finance law (a pressing issue these days) can afford to ignore the court's rulings of 1966, 1967, and 1983.

In juridicized debates, the constitutional text is a site of partisan conflict. For the opposition, threats of referrals are useful weapons in the pursuance of its policy positions—but they will be credible threats only if jurisprudence is taken seriously. Accordingly, oppositions in both countries have come to employ outside constitutional specialists and court watchers to develop constitutional arguments for juridicized debate and to write petitions. For the government and its majority, the increased tendency for parliamentary debates to be juridicized poses even greater technical, practical, and political problems. They are forced to address a multitude of often contradictory claims of constitutional obligation or enjoinment emanating from opposition bancs, their own ranks, and from special experts. The opposition can proliferate constitutional arguments with impunity, but only the government can be punished for misunderstanding constitutional principles. As a result, the role of the Council of State, the French government's official legal advisor, has been enhanced, as ministers seek to insulate bills from future censure. In Germany, long Bundestag hearings have been organized during which selected legal experts, jurists, and former constitutional judges are asked to engage in what Landfried (1988) calls "Karlsruhe-astrology"—attempts to predict the future position which the court will adopt. In any event, the task of insulating a bill from constitutional censure is not a simple one, since official advisers, politicians, and private constitutional consultants may have radically differing conceptions of the legislator's legal obligations and predict different rulings. More problematic, governments usually set limits on how far they are willing to compromise, and these are largely determined by partisan and not judicial considerations.

Judicial Activism

Constitutional courts are intervening in legislative processes at an increasing rate, as statistics show. In France, in the 1958–80 period, the Council examined 45 laws referred to it by politicians; in the 1981–87 period, the number more than doubled—to 91. In the 1974–80 period, an average of 6.1 percent of the bills adopted by Parliament were referred; since 1981, the percentage is 13.8 percent, with a high of 24 percent in 1986. In the 1980s, therefore, nearly one in seven laws adopted by the French Parliament was subjected to constitutional review, a remarkably large fraction since a majority of laws are only of the narrowest technical interest and take up practically none of the time and resources of the average parliamentarian. Indeed, Council intervention in the legislative process can be said to be systematic: *All budgets since 1974 have been scrutinized by the Council as has virtually every major piece of legislation since 1981.*

In West Germany, the intervention is relatively limited: 71 laws were referred to the Constitutional Court between 1951 and 1981; in the 1981–87 period, 23 laws were referred. Several points should be made about the German statistics. First, in terms of the legislative process in the Bundestag, partisan battles over legislation occur—if they are to occur—at the committee stage, accounting for the fact that nearly nine of every ten laws are adopted by unanimity. The approximate three laws per year that are referred are those on which the parties were not able to achieve prior consensus. The impact of the court can therefore not be assessed or measured by examining referrals and decisions alone. The researcher must be willing to wade through committee debates in searches for autolimitation. Second, the power of the Lander governments to refer federal legislation has been used without reference to problems of federalism. Parties in opposition at the federal level but making up the governments of Lander have used the referral in service of the national party, in what are essentially national conflicts. Thus, the Social Democratic Party (SDP) used its control of state governments to refer federal legislation on rearmament (1950s) and social welfare policy (1961), and the Christian Democratic Union-Christian Social Union Lander governments did the same, after 1969, to refer to the Court the SDP legislation on abortion (1974), and the Ostpolitik treaties with East Germany (1973). Moreover, as in France since the first *alternance* in 1981, the number of referrals is highest after national elections yielding an alternation in power—that is, during a new government's so-called honeymoon period and when reform spirits are highest (Von Beyme, 1983: 186). Thus, in 1970–71, 1976–77, 1983–84, and 1987 the number of referrals jump significantly—1 to 5 or more per year.

These figures measure only the volition of politicians to use constitutional courts as a means of obtaining their political goals, and not "judicial activism." However, there is a structured complicity between politicians in opposition and constitutional courts. Referrals to courts act as a kind of jurisprudential transmission belt: the more petitions the court receives, the more opportunity they have to elaborate jurisprudential techniques of control; this elaboration, in turn, provides oppositions with a steady supply of issues, expanding the grounds of judicial debate in parliament and in future petitions. In addition, constitutional principles are most effectively enshrined when legislative choices are invalidated (or rewritten by the court)—a more acceptable raw measure of activism. Since 1981, substantially more than 50 percent of the laws referred to the French Council were judged to be unconstitutional, in whole or in part, as adopted, up from 24 percent in the 1958–74 period. In West Germany, where concrete control also exists, judicial invalidation rose dramatically in the 1980s: in the 1951–80 period, 85 federal laws were judged to be in whole or in part unconstitutional; since 1981, the number is 94.

As important, constitutional courts have developed a host of techniques of controlling the legislator other than through declarations of unconstitutionality. The most important of these are the declaration of "strict reserves of interpretation"—that is, a declaration "that one particular interpretation of the law is the only constitutional one" (Landfried, 1985: 531–532)—and the acceptance of the *principle* of a reform but not of the *means* chosen by the legislator. These "weapons of limited warfare against constitutionality" (Cappelletti and Cohen, 1979: 94) were initially developed as means of judicial self-restraint. In both countries, the practical result has been to give positive law-making authority to constitutional judges because lawmakers have responded simply by copying the terms of the courts' decisions directly into subsequent laws on the same legislative subject.

Last, constitutional judges in both countries have aroused controversy in both political and academic milieux by "going outside of established 'legal' criteria found in precedent, statute, and constitution." In France, as noted above, the Council has willfully expanded its field of reference by incorporating into the constitution an ever-expanding bill of rights. In 1986, a number of government ministers and high parliamentary officials called the Council a "deviation," and "a new kind of legislator" exercising "discretionary power over parliament," and called for a codification of constitutional obligations to eliminate "arbitrary" rulings. The German court, for its part, has been accused of "drawing conclusions from the basic law which one can hardly relate to the text of the constitution" (Landfried, 1988: 162). That judges are creatively building constitutional law is undeniable, if a natural response to the fact that many of the problems they are asked to solve are highly complex socially and politically, and do not fall into neat constitutionally fixed categories.

"Overdone Scrupulousness" and Corrective Revisions

The application of negative court decisions by legislators is best illustrated by in-depth case study, but some comments should be made here. Theoretically, legislators would have a range of options available to them in response to constitutional censure or control: they could, on one extreme, copy word-for-word relevant jurisprudence directly into new legislation, could seek creative ways to circumvent a court's dictates on the other, or strike balances between the two. What Landfried concludes with respect to West German legislators could also describe their French counterparts: "The problem is not so much the absence, but rather the excess of obedience . . . towards the court"—there is an "overdone scrupulousness" (Landfried, 1988: 157–158). The practical effect of many of the most important decisions of unconstitutionality is to force a second legislative process, which I call a "corrective revision" process—the reelaboration of a censured text in conformity with judicial prescriptions in order to avoid a second censure. This conformity can be characterized as strict, and no legislative project has ever been censured twice, despite multiple referrals.

In cases such as these, legislators simply allow constitutional courts to dictate, often word-for-word, the terms of new legislation. Policy outcome may have no relation to initial policy preferences as expressed by the respective parliaments. Indeed, revised laws reflect the policy preferences of constitutional judges unambiguously overriding those of elected officials. A few examples will suffice. In 1982 the French Council struck down a nationalization bill on the grounds that its provision for compensation to expropriated stockholders violated property rights. It then went on to state how the government could save the bill, by employing different formulas for arriving at the valuation of the companies concerned. The government was obliged to write the formulas into the law; the bill survived a second referral, but the revision raised the cost of nationalizations by a full 25 percent. In 1986 the Chirac government was forced to revise both its press and audiovisual bills after they had been struck down because, the Council asserted, they did not adequately protect media "pluralism"—a concept that is not mentioned in any constitutional text (including in those incorporated by the Council). In both cases, the government simply copied word-for-word, comma-for-comma, long sections of the Council's decision directly into the law. In 1967, the German parliament all but unanimously passed an electoral finance law elaborated, or so it was thought, in accordance with a 1966 decision on the same topic. The court, however, struck down the law as unconstitutional because it provided for reimbursements of campaign expenses only for those parties that had received at least 2.5 percent of the vote. The Court ruled that the floor should be placed at .5 percent, though of course it could point to no constitutional text in support of such a judgment. The subsequent corrective revision process enshrined the court's solution. Again, this result is the rule not the exception; indeed, Kommers (1976: 275) reports that strict compliance is more prevalent in cases of abstract review than for any other forms.

The macropolitical effect of the evolving "juridicization of policy-making processes" has been to close off reform routes that would otherwise be open to reform-minded governments. Said differently, because these courts have never reversed themselves, because politicians perceive the effects of judicial review as binding upon them forever, and because lawmakers choose to incorporate constitutional court jurisprudence directly into legal regimes, more and more political issues are no longer open to legislative activity, and the web of con-stitutional obligation and enjoinment becomes more and more "close-meshed." The situation has led some, including Landfried, to argue that the "juridicization of parliament [is] dangerous for democracy," and that abstract control mecha-nisms "should be abolished" (Landfried, 1988: 165; Landfried, 1985: 541). It is perhaps inevitable that normative debate attends any discussion of juridici-zation, for it is there that a complex set of political, academic, and ideological commitments intersect in the concrete world of policy making.

At times, abstract review itself is put on trial, as in France from 1981 to 1987 when a succession of ministers and parliamentarians from both the Left and the Right decried what they viewed as a dangerous development toward a "gov-ernment of judges" and publicly threatened the Council with curtailing its pow-ers. The case of Spain, where review has at times paralyzed the government since the Left came to power in 1983, provides another dramatic example (Bon and Moderne, 1985). Until 1985, the Spanish court possessed *a priori* review authority over organic laws and those laws governing the status of the autonomous regions. Upon coming to power, the Socialist Workers embarked on a number of wide-ranging reforms of both legislative and constitutional regimes, and these required extensive organic legislation. In the 3-year period 1983–85, the opposition referred 6 laws (of a total of 27 that could have been referred) to the court according to the rules governing *a priori* review, 3 of which were judged to be in whole or in part unconstitutional. Unfortunately, these referrals delayed the reforms for ludicrous periods of time. In France, the Council is required to rule within one month, and in Germany referrals do not suspend the law's effect unless a negative decision has been rendered. The Spanish referrals suspended promulgation, but worse for the government, in five of these six cases the court took over one year to render a judgment. Two main arguments—both of which have been heard in France and West Germany—were most widely made for this suppression. First, *a priori* control was considered—by the governing party, the major press, and significantly by the scholarly community—as manifestly "political," because its effect was to implicate the court directly in day-to-day politics. Second, it was judged that the use of the *a priori* procedure was being used primarily as a means of parliamentary obstruction, as parliamentary politics by other methods.

CONCLUSION

From the perspective developed here, the constitutional politics of abstract review are legislative politics by another name. As a description of function, constitutional courts exercising politically initiated abstract review can be conceptualized profitably as third legislative chambers whose behavior is nothing more or less than the impact—direct and indirect—of constitutional review on legislative outcomes. This is not to imply that courts exercise legislative powers identical to those of governments and parliaments, or that judges behave as card-carrying members of political parties. It is to assert that abstract review requires these courts to participate in policy-making processes, and to the extent that *legislative* outcomes are substantively altered by such review, its function is easily and profitably assimilated into a legislative one. Some may protest that this confuses behavior with the effects of constitutional jurisprudence on policy output. If this is a confusion, it is willful and, I believe, necessary. Study of juridicization has the advantage of focusing empirical attention on how abstract review actually functions in political systems, and on how these courts are shaped by and in turn shape their political environments. It is thus a profitable approach for political scientists, especially those whose primary interests lie *beyond* the study of public law, courts, and judicial processes more narrowly conceived. Nevertheless, courts, unlike legislators, produce jurisprudence, and that aspect of their activity, judged to be central by academic lawyers, is admittedly deemphasized here, with certain negative effects.

Still, it is crucial to note that when constitutional judges are engaged in abstract review, their decision-making processes are closer to legislative decision-making processes than when they are applying a code, or even the constitution, to decide disputes arising from concrete litigation. That is, in abstract review processes, the lawmaking function of these courts is far more important than is dispute-resolution. Moreover, the "dispute" at hand is primarily partisan-political, rather than judicial. Blair (1978: 354) reports that the German court readily understands this and is thus "far more cautious" when engaging in abstract review than for other activities. The French Council, on the other hand, can never engage in anything but abstract interpretation, and thus it is in a much more vulnerable institutional position than are other European constitutional courts. The implicit assumption here—borne out, I believe, in empirical studies—is that politically initiated, abstract review is inherently more destabilizing than is concrete review, precisely because it poses the "countermajoritarian difficulty" unambiguously, from the moment it is initiated.

The eminent German jurist Carl Schmitt (1958) long opposed the establishment of an organ replete with the power of constitutional review on the grounds that it would lead either to the "judicialization of politics" or to a "politicization of justice." Of course, from a policy-making perspective, it led to both. In all cases, whether in Spain, France, Germany, or Austria, abstract review exists only to the extent that politicians seek to alter legislative outcomes, by having their policy choices ratified or the government's and parliamentary majority's choices watered down or vetoed. If politicians ceased to use referrals as political weapons, abstract review would disappear, and the countermajoritarian difficulty would no longer be posed.

REFERENCES

Blair, P. (1978). Law and politics in West Germany. *Political Studies* 26: 348–362.
Bon, P., and Moderne, F. (1985). Chronique (Chronicle). In *Annuaire international de justice constitutionnelle: 1985* (International annual of constitutional justice: 1985). Paris/Aix-en-Provence: Economica/PUAM, 339–367.
Cappelletti, M. (1986). Rapport general (General Report). In L. Favoreu and J. A. Jolowicz, (eds.), *Le controle juridictionnel des lois* (Judicial review). Paris/Aix-en-Provence: Economica/PUAM, 301–314.
———, and Cohen W. (eds.) (1979). *The modern systems of judicial review: Comparative constitutional law*. New York: Bobbs-Merrill.
Dahl, R. (1957). Decision-making in a democracy: The supreme court as a national policy-maker. *Journal of Public Law* 6 (2): 279–295.
Deener, D. (1952). Judicial review in modern constitutional systems. *American Political Science Review* 46 (4): 1079–1099.
Dicey, A. V. (1961). *An Introduction to the study of the law and the constitution*, 10th ed. London: Macmillan.
Donaghy, P. J., and Newton, M. T. (1987). *Spain: A guide to political and economic institutions*. Cambridge: Cambridge University Press.
Duguit, L. (1923). *Traite du droit constituionne* (Treatise on constitutional law). Paris: Sirey.
Eisenmann, C. (1986) (orig. 1928). *La justice constitutionnelle et la haute cour consti-*

tutionnelle d'Autriche (Constitutional justice and the high constitutional court of Austria). Paris/Aix-en-Provence: Economica/PUAM.

Favoreu, L. (1986). *Les Cours constitutionnelles* (Constitutional courts). Paris: Presses Universitaires de France.

Friedrich, C. J. (1963). *The philosophy of law in historical perspective*, 2nd ed. Chicago: University of Chicago Press.

Gulick, C. (1948). *Austria between Hapsburg and Hitler*. Berkeley: University of California Press.

Hauriou, M. (1929). *Precis du droit constitutionnel* (Presis of constitutional law). Paris: Sirey.

Keeler, J.T.S., and Stone, A. (1987). Judicial-political confrontation in Mitterrand's France. In S. Hoffmann, G. Ross, and S. Malzacher (eds.), *The Mitterrand experiment*. New York: Oxford, 161–181.

Kelsen, H. (1928). La garantie Jurisdictionnelle de la constitution (Constitutional justice). *Revue du droit public* 15: 197–257.

Kommers, D. P. (1976). *Judicial politics in West Germany*. Beverly Hills, CA: Sage Publications.

Lambert, E. (1922). *Le gouvernement des juges et la lutte contre la legislation sociale aux Etats-unis* (The government of judges and the struggle against social legislation in the United States). Paris: Giard.

Landfried, C. (1985). The impact of the German constitutional court on politics and policy-outputs. *Government and Opposition* 20 (4): 522–541.

———. (1988). Legislation and judicial review in the Federal Republic of Germany. In C. Landfried (ed.), *Constitutional review and legislation: An international comparison*. Baden-Baden: Nomos Verlag.

Neumann, F. (1964). *The democratic and the authoritarian state*. New York: Free Press.

Ohlinger, T. (1982). Objet et portee de la protection des droits fondamentaux en Autriche (Object and scope of the protection of fundamental rights in Austria). In L. Favoreu (ed.), *Cours constitutionnelles europeennes et droits fondamentaux* (European constitutional courts and fundamental rights). Paris/Aix-en-Provence: Economica/ PUAM, 335–381.

Schmitt, C. (1958). Das reichsgericht als huter der verfassung (The federal court as a guardian of the constitution). In *Verfassungsrechtliche aufsatze* (Essays on constitutional law). Berlin: Duncker and Humboldt, 63–100.

Sigelman, L., and Gadbois, G. (1983). Contemporary comparative politics: An inventory and assessment. *Comparative Political Studies* 16 (3): 293–295.

Stone, A. (1989a). In the shadow of the constitutional council: The 'juridicization' of the legislative process in France. *West European Politics* 12 (2): 12–34.

———. (1989b). Legal constraints on policy-making: The Constitutional Council and the Council of State. In P. Godt, (ed.), *Policy-making in France: From De Gaulle to Mitterrand*. London: Pinter, 28–41.

———. (1992). *The birth of judicial politics in France: The Constitutional Council in comparative perspective*. New York: Oxford University Press.

Travaux preparatoires de la Constitution due 4 octobre 1958, Avis et debats due Comité consultatif constitutionnel (1960). (Preparatory work for the Constitution of October 4, 1958: Opinions and debates of the Constitutional Consultative Committee). Paris: Documentation francaise.

Von Beyme, K. (1983). *The political system of the Federal Republic of Germany.* Aldershot, UK: Gower.

Weber, A. (1987). Le Controle juridictionnel de la constitutionnalite des lois dans les pays d'Europe occidentale (Judicial Review in Western Europe). In *Annuaire international de justice constitutionnelle* (International annual of constitutional justice). Paris/Aix-en-Provence: Economica/PUAM, 39–79.

5

Establishing and Exercising Judicial Review in the Soviet Union: The Beginnings

William Kitchin

As of early 1991, judicial review was part of the Soviet legal system. Until December 1989, judicial review had never existed in Soviet law (Kerimov, 1989: 3).[1] However, the Soviet Union then created the Committee on Constitutional Oversight, which had the power of judicial review (*Izvestiia*, 1989: 1).[2] In the context of intense, increasingly desperate focusing in the Soviet Union on democratization and the creation of a law-governed state (Stepovoy, 1990a: 1), judicial review was adopted primarily for two purposes: to protect human rights and to resolve conflicts involving the distribution of power between the central government and the republics (Feofanov, 1990: 2).[3]

First, this chapter uses a political concept of judicial review to place the now defunct Soviet system into a comparative context. Next, the structure and processes of the Soviet mode of judicial review are described, and finally, the early decisions of the short-lived Soviet Committee on Constitutional Oversight are described.

A POLITICAL CONCEPT OF JUDICIAL REVIEW

Judicial review is the power of a court to declare acts of other political entities to be in conflict with a fundamental set of norms (usually a constitution). This is clearly the power to allocate values authoritatively, but its appearance in the judicial garb creates the impression of something quite different from what a legislature or an executive does. The political reality is that judicial review is binding policy making. Thus, it is easy to understand that before judicial review could be adopted in the Soviet Union, the Communist Party's constitutional lock on political power had to be abolished. By the middle of 1989, with the abolition of Article 6 of the Soviet constitution,[4] the democratization of Soviet political

Table 5.1
Typology of Judicial Review

STATUS OF JUDICIAL INDEPENDENCE +	EFFECT OF RULING AT JUDICIAL REVIEW =	TYPE OF JUDICIAL REVIEW	EXAMPLES
Independent	Coercive	Independent - Coercive	Austria, Italy, USA
Independent	Advisory	Independent - Advisory	Japan, Poland (1989), USSR - 2
Independent	Restricted	Independent - Restrictive	Finland, France
Dependent	Coercive	Dependent - Coercive	Iran, Yugoslavia
Dependent	Advisory	Dependent - Advisory	Hungary (1989)
Dependent	Restricted	Dependent - Restricted	USSR - 1

Definitions:

Coercive: Ruling at judicial review is binding on other political entities.

Advisory: Other political entities may ignore or override ruling at judicial review.

Restricted: Judges are prohibited from issuing rulings at judicial review.

Independent: Judges are relatively free of control by other political entities.

Entries:

USSR - 1:   The Soviet Union until January, 1990.

USSR - 2:   The Soviet Union from January, 1990 to approximately the creation of the "Commonwealth of Independent States."

institutions, the creation of the elected Congress of People's Deputies, the empowerment of its elected Supreme Soviet, democratic local elections, and increasing political flexing by the republics, not only the possibility but the necessity of judicial review became apparent.

To understand the range of options for a nation in the process of adopting a form of judicial review, we should consider both (1) the structural independence the judges have and also (2) whether a court's rulings at judicial review are binding upon other political entities or are only advisory.[5] Table 5.1 summarizes and gives examples of six modes of judicial review that these two dimensions suggest.[6]

In 1989 when Soviet legal reformers were fully involved in drawing up a law on judicial review, there were, as Table 5.1 shows, several Communist states that had already put into place some form of judicial review (Ludwikowski, 1988). The Soviet and, to a lesser extent, the Polish model had features relevant to Soviet plans. In the early stages of Soviet deliberations—that is, when the idea of judicial review was being considered at the Institute of State and Law prior to its introduction into the Supreme Soviet—the Yugoslavian system was considered unacceptable and incompatible with the constitutional monopoly of political power possessed by the Communist Party.

In 1989 the perplexing and exacting task for Soviet legal reform was, consequently, to accommodate the pressures of glasnost and democratization but not to reform at such a pace as to create a political vacuum or to encourage a dissolution of one legal system before the other was in place. Once Article 6 of the Soviet constitution was abandoned, thus ending the political monopoly of the Communist Party and enabling the establishment of a multiparty political system, the major conceptual barrier to judicial review was removed and the dissolution of the old legal system took on new speed and energy. The political landscape of the Soviet Union by mid-1989 had fundamentally changed to the point that the issue of judicial review became not whether the Communist Party would resist judicial review but whether the legislature would allow it.

Besides the abolition of Article 6, two other developments cleared the path for the arrival of judicial review to the Soviet Union. First, legal reform by 1989 had become so energized toward the goal of establishing a law-governed state that its own demiurgical force eliminated any possibility that judicial review in some form would *not* be established. Second, as political forces associated with a centrist position created an "iron hand" (authoritarian) presidency, judicial review looked more and more promising as a means of controlling legal excesses from the republics (Kitchin, 1990). Thus, President Gorbachev and more conservative political forces supported the establishment of judicial review, presumably as a means of holding the union together.

The result was the establishment of the Committee on Constitutional Oversight. In Table 5.1, the committee is classified as an "independent-advisory" system since its members were guaranteed legal and political independence and its rulings could have been overturned by the Congress of People's Deputies, the Soviet Union's constitutional legislature.[7]

THE COMMITTEE ON CONSTITUTIONAL OVERSIGHT

The Congress of People's Deputies in its historic first session (1989) appointed a commission to study the establishment of a Committee on Constitutional Oversight. Because the Baltic republics feared that such a committee would use its power primarily at the behest of the center to force deviant republics into line by finding their laws unconstitutional, Baltic deputies opposed the entire idea.[8] A vote in the Congress on actually creating such a committee was not taken.

At the time of that session of the Congress, there did exist a legislative committee charged with supervising the development of the constitution, but that committee did not have the power to make decisions about republic laws, nor could it review all-union laws. Valery Savitsky of the Institute of State and Law of the Soviet Academy of Sciences believed that the power of a constitutional committee to "mediate between the federation and its constituent parts" was the key issue in expanding the committee's powers (*Moscow News*, 1989: 4).

The initial thrust of reform discussions was to revise the powers and functions of that committee in order to transform it into a constitutional court whose members would be drawn from the legislature. However, that initial direction did not prevail, and a completely new institution was created.

In December 1989 the second session of the Congress of People's Deputies established the USSR Committee on Constitutional Oversight. This entailed the passage of the Law on Constitutional Oversight and the amendment of Article 125 of the Soviet constitution.[9] The new law revealed the compromises produced by the year's debates and also reflected the decisive political strains produced by the multinational nature of Soviet federalism.

Composition of the Committee on Constitutional Oversight

The law provided for a committee of 27 members, 15 from the republics and 12 others. Members were elected for 10-year terms by the Congress of People's Deputies. Elections for half the members were to be held every five years. Members were not explicitly required to renounce their party affiliation, but they could not be members of other state or all-union political institutions, such as the Supreme Soviet or the Congress of People's Deputies. Thus, members were guaranteed independence insofar as a statute could make such a guarantee.

According to D. A. Kerimov (1989: 3), members were not conceptualized as "representatives" of their republics. They were to be elected based merely on their residency in the republics. The obvious implication was that the perspective of the committee's members should remain national, that the committee was not a representative institution.

Powers of the Constitutional Oversight Committee over National Laws

The committee could consider the compliance with the USSR constitution of (1) laws passed by either the Congress or the Supreme Soviet, and (2) drafts of laws not yet passed but under consideration by either of those bodies.

Until a long-term resolution of republic-union relationships was achieved, the committee's power was not to extend to issues of whether provisions of the constitutions or laws of the republics complied with the USSR constitution.[10] This was a major concession to the Baltic republics that opposed the establishment of the committee because they feared it would become a means of denying their sovereignty. However, this moratorium on republican application of the committee's power did not apply if the issue was whether a provision of a republic constitution or law violated a "citizens' basic rights and liberties" (Stepovoy, 1990: 3). This linkage of the Committee's power to issue rulings concerning republic constitutions or laws to the revision of the Union Treaty was passed by the Congress of People's Deputies at the same session in which the Law on Constitutional Oversight itself was passed.

This not only indicated a realistic political compromise within the Congress, but it also suggested the priority of human rights issues over issues of institutional power. These two missions—protecting human rights and resolving conflicts of political power—guided the committee's work to the extent that presumably the committee could not deal with an issue that did not directly concern one of those missions.

Thus, the committee apparently would have considered the compliance of a republic law with a Soviet constitutional provision concerning one's exercise of his or her freedom of speech, but not if the same law allegedly only conflicted with an all-union law or a provision of the Soviet constitution dealing not with the exercise of the freedom of speech, but with which body—the all-union body or the republic body—had the legal power to regulate that freedom. The operating assumption was that issues of power distribution would be more susceptible to solution once a governing body of principles had been adopted through the Union Treaty, but that the principles governing human rights issues are constant and do not depend upon the renegotiation of the treaty.

Extensive Oversight Power over State Authorities

Whereas laws and draft laws were to be considered as to their consistency with the constitution, other legally binding instruments could be considered *both* as to their consistency with the constitution and with the laws of the USSR. Thus, presidential decrees, laws of the republics (assuming the Union Treaty delay described above), orders and decrees issued by the Council of Ministers, plenum instructions issued by the Supreme Court of the USSR, international treaties submitted for ratification, and directives and advisories issued by the procuracy were required to be consistent with the laws passed by the central government as well as with the constitution of the USSR. Finally, the committee's oversight power reached any normative legislative instruments of any other state organs. In effect, with exceptions described below, the oversight power could reach every governmental institution of the national government.

Oversight Power over Public Organizations

Significantly, the committee could also consider any normative act (such as a directive, advisory, or decree) of a *public* organization. The apparent intent here was to extend the committee's power to embrace any organization that has the power to initiate legislation (Kerimov, 1989: 2). This included party organizations. Thus, the committee could review the compliance to the Soviet constitution and to USSR laws of legally binding instruments issued by the Communist Party and presumably other parties.

This provision reflected the extraordinary breadth of the committee's oversight jurisdiction. To the extent that an organization can issue a legally binding instrument, a construction in *pari materia*[11] of the committee's power supported

extension of that power to functionally public but technically private organizations. Whether or not the committee's jurisdiction would have proved this elastic,
the statutory, organizational jurisdiction of the Soviet committee appeared far
broader than comparable jurisdiction of constitutional courts found in other
countries.

Limitations on the Oversight Power

The committee's oversight power did not extend to rulings of courts of law
(Kerimov, 1989: 3). Thus, the committee was not an appellate court and was
not even organizationally part of the Soviet judicial system. If the committee
were a part of the appellate hierarchy, its powers would necessarily have been
exercised within the framework of specific cases. The committee's exercise of
powers was structured as an abstract power of review in which the committee
was to examine specific legal instruments, such as laws, drafts of laws, decrees,
and so on, rather than specific cases of litigants (Feofanov, 1990: 2).

Moreover, placement of the committee within the judicial system would have
entailed a decrease in the powers of the Supreme Court. The framers of this
legislation did not want to use this law as a vehicle for judicial reform beyond
judicial review itself, nor did they want to introduce the notion of precedent into
the Soviet legal system. The committee's power was by definition precedential
and if exercised by a court of law would have constituted too massive an expansion of the nonprecedential nature of the Soviet civil law tradition.

Though the committee could not reach court rulings in specific cases, it could
reach plenum instructions from the USSR Supreme Court. Plenum instructions
were conceptual clarifications of the law and are binding upon lower courts.
Thus, they were precedential but did not concern and did not arise out of a
particular case. They were judicial analogues to laws passed by the legislature
and were similarly subject to the committee's oversight jurisdiction.

A second jurisdictional limitation on the power of the committee was that the
committee could not handle those matters that were already within the purview
of the procuracy.[12] The Soviet procuracy was the uniquely Soviet amalgam of
prosecutor-ombudsman-public monitor. Its power to prosecute cases as well as
its power of general supervision—that is, its power to monitor the legality of
the actions of ministries, government officials, economic enterprises, many state
organs, individual government officials, and individual citizens (Oda, 1987:
1339) made the procuracy one of the eyes of the state. Whereas the procuracy's
power included the power to protest (the power to go to court against an offending
party in order to correct an illegal practice) (Osakwe, 1983: 461), the procuracy
could not invalidate a law. In contrast, the power of the Oversight Committee
included the power to invalidate a law or decree (Osakwe, 1983: 461), but the
committee had no power of protest whereby it could bring a court action against
an offending party.[13]

Finally, the committee did not have oversight jurisdiction over state arbitration matters. Disputes arising out of economic contracts between state enterprises and associations were usually handled through the arbitration procedures known as *arbitrazh* (Kiralfy, 1988). Thus, unfulfilled contractual obligations to supply certain quantities or qualities of products to some domestic enterprises as part of the central plan led to state arbitration.[14] The Committee on Constitutional Oversight could not review specific *decisions* made at arbitrazh. However, the committee probably could have reviewed the *procedures* employed at arbitrazh since those procedures would be promulgated through advisories, directives, and substatutes that were subject to the committee's jurisdiction.

Two aspects created the possibility that decisions at arbitrazh would be different from decisions what might be rendered by a law court. First, the procedures and substantive principles as arbitrazh though similar to the Soviet law of obligations that a law court would apply to contractual disputes were substantively and procedurally not identical. More importantly, arbitrazh could consider political variables and the public interest in making decisions (Kiralfy, 1988: 95). Its orientation was toward policy and results. In contrast, courts, and specifically the Committee on Constitutional Oversight, were prohibited from considering political variables since they were by definition institutions of law. Consequently, arbitrazh could render decisions at arbitration that were not strictly in accord with the law or the constitution. Such decisions could by definition be unconstitutional. However, the 1989 Law on Constitutional Oversight placed these arbitration decisions outside the committee's jurisdiction.

The independence of arbitrazh might have proved especially important in the attempts of the Soviet Union to transform its planned economy into a market economy. Arbitrazh was simply more flexible than judicial resolution, especially judicial resolution in an era when the rule of law was being established. Politically motivated and public-interest-based decisions were conceptually counter to the idea of rule of law,[15] and the attempts to create a law-governed state would only be discredited if the courts were perceived of as arbitrarily and unpredictably departing from the law in economic, contractual matters.

The Initiation of the Oversight Power

The Law on Constitutional Oversight provided that a matter could be brought to the Oversight Committee by a one-fifths vote of the Supreme Soviet, the Presidium of the Supreme Soviet, the chairman of the Supreme Soviet, the highest body of state power of a republic, and, for certain matters, committees of the Supreme Soviet, the Council of Ministers, the Soviet People's Control Committee, the USSR Supreme Court, the Procurator-General, the head of arbitrazh, the Academy of Sciences, and public organizations.

The exhaustive list of those who could initiate actions before the committee is actually a list of those who under Article 133 of the Soviet Constitution could initiate legislation in the Supreme Soviet. As was true with the designation of the committee's jurisdiction, the political prominence of public organizations, and again the rapidly evolving nature of Soviet distinctions between public and private organizations, inevitably had major impact on the application of this provision of the Law on Constitutional Oversight.

The committee, by a majority vote of its members, could initiate certain actions itself. This highlights the idea that the committee was not a constitutional *court* but an institution of constitutional *oversight*.[16] The intent, according to the then chairman of the Oversight Committee (Sergey Alekseyev), was that it be an active force in the establishment of a law-governed state (*Krasnaya Zvezda*, 1990: 1). The Committee's power to initiate actions was limited to its review of laws or drafts before the Congress of People's Deputies, the Supreme Soviet, or bodies created by them.[17]

This included the presidency, since President Gorbachev was elected by the Congress of People's Deputies and the office was created by that body. (This enabled the committee to review a presidential decree as its first major action. This is discussed later.) Had the Soviet presidency come to be elected by the public rather than the Congress, the intriguing question would have been whether presidential acts could be reviewed at the committee's initiative or whether they could only be reviewed on the request of some other body. Since the governing structure of the USSR lacked a theoretical basis for separation of powers, one cannot automatically assume that the initiative power was restricted to legislative targets.

The only limitations on the agenda of the committee were those set by the Law on Constitutional Oversight itself. The significant limitation was that the committee could not of its own initiative review the compliance of a republic's normative instruments (its constitution or laws) to the USSR constitution. This preserved the juridical autonomy of the republics and mitigated against the committee's being an instrument of unlimited, centralized control over the laws and constitutions of the republics. Otherwise, the power of the committee was fully exercisable of its own initiative.

A Committee Ruling on a National Law or Draft Law

A ruling that a national law or draft law violates the USSR constitution did not immediately rescind or even suspend that law. Instead, the committee referred the offending law to the Congress of People's Deputies, and a three-month clock began to run. By the end of the three months, the provision in conflict with the constitution must have been corrected, or else the committee would communicate to the Congress the effective revocation of the law in question. The Congress, by a vote of two-thirds of its members, could during the three months override the committee.

Though the Law on Constitutional Oversight was not completely clear on the path of referrals, a law passed by the Supreme Soviet would apparently have been referred to the Supreme Soviet before being referred to the Congress. If the Supreme Soviet did not satisfactorily modify the law, then the committee presumably would have informed the Congress of the impending invalidation, and the Congress was required to reject the committee's finding by a two-thirds vote or the law automatically would be void.

A Committee Ruling on a Republic Law or Republic Constitution

A similar procedure was to be followed once the Union Treaty was revised when the committee invalidated a republic law or a provision of a republic constitution for violating an all-union law or the USSR constitution. The provision would have stayed in force, at least for three months. The law seemed to require that the provision at issue be submitted to either the Congress or to the Supreme Soviet for correction as well as to the issuing body in the republic concerned. Such channeling of a republic law into the national legislature was clearly a means by which the central government could, if it chose, exercise control over republic laws and constitutional provisions. This was the basis of the continuing Baltic suspicion of the centralizing potential of the committee's power.

If after three months the law had not been corrected, the committee informed the Congress, the Supreme Soviet, or the USSR Council of Ministers of the impending revocation of the law in question. If the Supreme Soviet or the Council of Ministers rejected the committee's finding,[18] it was mandatory that the Congress examine the issue. By a two-thirds vote of its members, the Congress could reject the committee's finding, and the law or constitutional provision would have survived. Otherwise it would become void.

The requirement of an extraordinary majority (two-thirds of the membership) of the Congress to overrule the committee strongly reinforced the power of the committee as a *political* body. It also constructed a far stronger basis on which to build a rule of law than would have been the case if a normal majority vote could have overruled the committee and in this sense solidified the position of the committee as a *legal* body.

Committee Findings That Result in Immediate Suspension

In two instances, committee rulings would have resulted in the immediate suspension of the legal provision in question. First was the significant human rights priority. A legally binding instrument, including all-union and republic laws, found to violate a basic human right was considered to be immediately invalid. The source of the basic rights to which laws must conform were the Soviet constitution as well as international treaties agreed to by the Soviet government. The three-month clock ran, and the provision in question remained invalid unless the cause of the invalidity was remedied or unless the Congress by a two-thirds vote overrode the committee.

A second instance resulting in immediate suspension was if the committee found a lack of constitutional compliance of any type of provision other than an all-union law, all-union draft law, republic law, or provision of a republic constitution. Automatic suspension thus applied to any other normative instrument promulgated by any juridical person or any public organization. The organization involved had three months to remedy the deficiency of the law. If the law was not remedied by the expiration of the three months, it would become void unless the Congress by a two-thirds vote overrode the committee and reinstated the law.

Statutory Independence of Members of the Committee

The Law on Constitutional Oversight provided that committee members may not simultaneously belong to any body whose instruments are subject to committee oversight. This meant that committee members could not be deputies, members of the Council of Ministers, or presumably even members of juridical bodies. Though membership in a political party was not explicitly forbidden, since instruments of the Communist Party were subject to committee oversight, the effect of the law seemed to prohibit Communist Party membership during one's committee tenure.

Though committee members were prohibited from being members of the Congress of People's Deputies, they could attend meetings of the Congress, the Supreme Soviet, or the Presidium of the Supreme Soviet. In addition, the committee itself had the power of legislative initiative. Thus, it was contemplated that the committee would submit to the Congress or the Supreme Soviet the recommendations for legislation needed to obtain compliance with various provisions of the Soviet constitution.

Members of the committee had absolute criminal immunity and also immunity to administrative punishment. However, a majority of the committee could waive the immunity for any of its members. The law explicitly provided that no member of the committee could be arraigned for any opinion expressed or vote cast as a member of the committee.

EARLY ACTIONS BY THE COMMITTEE ON CONSTITUTIONAL OVERSIGHT

Committee Invalidation of a Presidential Decree

The committee held its first official meeting on May 16, 1990, and on September 14, 1990, issued its first finding of unconstitutionality (Stepovoy, 1990a: 2). In April, 1990 President Gorbachev issued a decree that banned demonstrations within the Moscow Ringroad and took the power to regulate such demonstrations from the Moscow City Council and gave it to the Council of Ministers, a body that Gorbachev controlled. The Committee on Constitutional Oversight accordingly held that the decree invaded the powers of the Moscow City Council and the Russian republic and struck down the decree pending correction of its "unconstitutional" feature. The three-month period did toll and the committee's ruling became permanent in December 1990.

This first major test of the power of the committee was unique in several ways. Most obviously, it involved President Gorbachev himself. It is noteworthy that the striking down of a presidential decree was unimaginable as recently as 1989. The committee was, of course, fully appreciative of the symbolic significance of its first use of the power of judicial review. The striking down of a presidential decree dramatically communicated to all that the committee will boldly use its powers.

Second, the committee struck down a decree that Tass described as having "extensive support" ("Constitutional Compliance Committee Begins Work," 1990: 30). Thus, the committee demonstrated a willingness to tackle issues that were politically controversial and had noticeable public backing.

Third, the committee took this action at its own initiative. Though such *sua sponte* actions by the committee were supposed to be the exception (Feofanov, 1990: 2), this again indicated that the committee was quite capable of being a daring, active institution.

Fourth, this action concerned the distribution of power between the central government and the governments of the republics. Although committee rulings on such power conflicts then awaited the completion of the new Union Treaty, this particular presidential decree also concerned human rights and, thus, was subject to immediate committee consideration (Khatuntsev, 1990: 1).

Perhaps most significantly, the committee decision was apparently being complied with by the other political entities and was largely accepted by the public. At that very early stage in the creation of a law-governed state, this compliance was a very positive signal.

Committee Consideration of Residency Permit Regulations

In September 1990 the committee's very *consideration* of the residency permit rules of the USSR caused the USSR Council of Ministers to repeal many of the rules *before* the committee even had a chance to make a finding concerning constitutionality (Nikitinsky, 1990: 1). The mere threat of committee action apparently was all that was needed to achieve this result. One must also remember that this particular threat of committee action closely followed the committee's earlier invalidation of Gorbachev's decree. The committee had indicated the skill and will to use its power and resources. Apparently, the anticipation of committee action led the Council of Ministers to eliminate rules that had given the police the arbitrary power to forcibly haul from a city or town peace demonstrators, black marketeers, those convicted of previous crimes, and others "behaving in an unbecoming manner" (Nikitinsky, 1990: 1). In addition, other previously secret rules were declassified, and many were repealed. The very fact that the committee was contemplating the constitutionality of the residency permit regulations had the desired effect of leading to their abolition.

The basic requirement of having a residency permit was then still in effect. Consequently, one still had to acquire a residency permit before one could live in a certain area. The residency permit was also a prerequisite to getting health care, housing, and other services. Persons without residency permits were not permitted to work in the larger (and more desirable) cities. The issue then was simply whether a requirement that one must get administrative permission before one could live in a certain area or city violated the Soviet constitution.

Other Issues before the Committee

Finally, as this chapter was in preparation, the committee was considering several other constitutional issues, including the constitutionality of a law that prevented the courts from using certain procedures in handling individual labor disputes, the constitutionality of certain provisions of the Civil Code concerning the sale of substandard goods, certain criminal laws, and certain rules of criminal procedure. Indications then were that the permit requirement would be struck down by the committee.

CONCLUSION

The Soviet Union was clearly involved in profound reform of its substantive laws and the institutions that administer those laws. The creation of judicial review was a testament to the basic nature of current legal reform in the Soviet Union. The very creation of a constitutional compliance entity of any type was remarkable. The creation of an Oversight Committee that was at the same time independent and had extraordinarily wide jurisdiction—in a nation that had not known the rule of law for 70 years—was perhaps even more remarkable.

But herein lies perhaps the greatest cause for concern. The political and legal culture of the Soviet Union was one replete with arrogant disregard for a rule of law, and its history was an embarrassing collage of the flaunting of law and the simultaneous manipulation of legal symbols to legitimize totalitarianism. Can such a 70-year history and its consequent political and legal culture be deliberately and systematically transformed into its opposite—a law-governed state? Can this be accomplished at all? Can it be accomplished before the Soviet Union, or its successor, under the pressure of a collapsed economy and a disintegrated federal system, reverts to its more familiar pattern of arbitrary rule incompatible with the rule of law?

My initial impression after conducting interviews in Moscow and examining the oversight processes but before the disintegration of the Soviet Union was positive for a number of reasons. The committee was functioning. It was addressing issues of enormous importance on the Soviet constitutional scene. It had wisely been restrained from considering the political questions related to republic sovereignty and the distribution of power between the central and republic governments other than as those questions involve basic human rights. Human rights issues were given statutory priority over issues of the distribution of governmental power. The first two items on the committee's agenda—the voiding of Gorbachev's decree concerning demonstrations in Moscow and the government's voluntary repealing of many of the residency permit rules—were resolved in a way compatible with the establishment of a law-governed state. The committee proceeded in the name of human rights in its consideration of both issues. The public and the other agencies of government accepted the committee's power and therefore implicitly ratified the institution of judicial review.

Although this chapter considers only judicial review, the context of this particular reform is, of course, much broader and much deeper than can be seen from this examination of one subject. Other legal reforms that faced the then Soviet Union included the revision of the Fundamental Principles of Criminal Law and the implicit reformulation of the whole concept of socialist legality. The Code of Criminal Procedure was being completely revised. This entailed an overhaul of the system by which objective truth has in the past been sought, all too often at the expense of individual rights. The prerogatives of the system of administrative law and the prerequisites for the legal applicability of substatutes were then being reformed. Trade unions' rights were in a state of revision. Property law was in an advanced state of reform, and new concepts of property had already invaded Soviet law. Family law and the law of domestic relations were being revised.

Not only were the areas of legal reform numerous but also the nature of the reforms was conceptually significant. Indeed, the building of the law-governed state represented something even more fundamental than legal reform. We are quite possibly witnessing the deliberate creation (rather than the gradual evolution) of a new type of legal system. This new system is already intermerging principles of Soviet law, the European civil tradition, even some principles of the Anglo-American common law system, and other *sui generis* principles born of the moment.

Judicial review is an essential prerequisite to the rule of law. Barring some type of political reversion, or the breakup of the Soviet Union, one could have expected the Soviet Committee on Constitutional Oversight or its successor to play a prominent role in the establishment of the Soviet law-governed state and perhaps serve as midwife to the birth of a fundamentally new type of legal system.

We can only hope that such a prospect will survive under the Commonwealth of Independent States, or under the several fully independent states that may follow the disintegration of the Soviet Union.

NOTES

1. I am indebted to Dean David Roswell of Loyola College for his continuing and significant support of my research into Soviet law.

2. Definitions of judicial review vary, but I am using a rather inclusive definition: It is the power of a court to find an action of a political branch of government or another political entity null and void. This definition includes the invalidation of laws passed by a legislature, actions of the executive, orders of the bureaucracy (i.e., administrative law), and such. It also includes the issuance of judicial findings that are merely advisory as well as those that are binding on other institutions of government.

3. In August 1989 I conducted interviews in Moscow with legal scholars who were responsible for drafting the proposal that the Soviet Union establish a power of judicial review in a newly structured constitutional committee. The conclusions in this paragraph and other material in this chapter concerning the purposes of the law and the motivations of some of the framers rely on those interviews.

4. The abandoned Article 6 reads as follows:

> The Communist Party of the Soviet Union [CPSU] is the leading and guiding force of Soviet society and the nucleus of its political system and of state and social institutions. The CPSU exists for the people and serves the people.
>
> Armed with Marxist-Leninist doctrine, the Communist Party determines the general perspective of the development of society and the course of domestic and foreign policy of the USSR, directs the great creative activity of the Soviet people, and imparts a planned and scientifically sound character to their struggle for the victory of communism.
>
> All party organizations function within the framework of the Constitution of the USSR.

5. This way of classifying forms of judicial review is discussed more fully in Kitchin (1991).

6. For another approach, see Mauro Cappelletti (1989), *The Judicial Process in Comparative Perspective*. He discusses centralized and decentralized forms of judicial review and whether courts handle questions of constitutionality in the context of regular cases ("incidenter" review) or as abstract questions in a specially adopted format ("principaliter" review). Such a taxonomy is instructive in terms of the legal framework in which judicial review occurs but ignores the fact that regardless of judicial dress, the emperor is still political.

7. Overriding a decision of the Soviet Union's new Committee on Constitutional Oversight required a two-thirds vote of the Congress of People's Deputies. The result was that the committee's power, though technically advisory, was as a practical matter coercive.

8. Indeed a major reason that even some conservatives supported the committee idea was that it provided a means by which questions of republican sovereignty could be handled under the rubric of law. Judicial review could be used to strike down laws of the republics incompatible with the Soviet constitution.

9. Article 125 before it was amended simply gave the Supreme Soviet the power to appoint commissions to monitor the work of government agencies.

10. The Union Treaty is the "agreement" between the 15 republics to constitute the Union of Soviet Socialist Republics. Perestroika and democratization unleashed the forces of nationalism in the republics such that the existing treaty was clearly rendered obsolete. The renegotiation of the treaty was intended to handle the seemingly intractable issues of conflicting republican and union power over the economy, property, resources, the

making of foreign policy, the nature of republican sovereignty—in short, all of the issues that eventually tore apart the Soviet Union.

11. That is, upon the same matter or subject.

12. The committee's oversight power likewise did not include oversight of the investigations of the police, the KGB, or other agencies involved in the criminal preliminary investigation.

13. The procuracy's power of general supervision did not extend to the highest organs of government, such as the Council of Ministers, the Supreme Soviet, the Congress of People's Deputies, the presidency, and so on.

Sergey Alekseyev, the first Chairman of the Constitutional Oversight Committee, was careful to distinguish between the procuracy's oversight power and the committee's power, primarily by describing the committee as a "legal court" (Feofanov, 1990: 2).

14. Joint-venture contracts—that is, contracts between a Soviet partner and a foreign partner—were not directly subject to arbitrazh but were subject to the law of the forum (Soviet law) or the law specified in the contract. Nevertheless, if a Soviet partner could not meet its obligations to the joint venture because of a contractual violation of a Soviet subcontractor, that dispute between the Soviet partners would be handled at arbitrazh. Thus, the foreign partner was indirectly subject to the procedures and principles of arbitrazh.

15. Of course, the power of judicial review was a *political* power, but it was cloaked as a legal power. Thus, Alekseyev referred to the Committee as a "legal court" (Feofanov, 1990: 2).

16. Sergey Alekseyev emphasized the *judicial* nature of the committee and believed the term "oversight" is a misnomer. Rather, he argued that the committee should be designated as a "constitutional court" or a "constitutional council" (Alekseyev, 1990: 3).

17. It, of course, remained to be seen whether a procedural norm would develop whereby the Congress or Supreme Soviet would defer to the republic body or whether the national body would exercise control over the republic provision. In any event, the law was so structured that if the committee's finding of unconstitutionality was rejected by another (issuing) body, the Congress would have to exercise the final say.

18. The law did not specify that rejection at this stage required a two-thirds vote; therefore, one assumes that a majority vote would suffice. It does not matter, however, since rejection by either the Supreme Soviet or the Council of Ministers triggered the mandatory action by Congress. This meant that the Congress approved the committee's finding *unless* it rejected it by the two-thirds vote.

REFERENCES

Alekseyev, S. (1990). Konstitutsionnii nadzor: Pervii shagi i problemi (Constitutional oversight: First steps and problems). *Izvestiia*, August 28, p. 3.

Cappelletti, M. (1989). *The judicial process in comparative perspective*. Oxford: Oxford University Press.

"Constitutional Compliance Committee Begins Work" (1990). Foreign Broadcast Information Service Daily Report. Soviet Union, May 17.

Feofanov, Y. (1990). Uredecheskii sovetnik, eelee polnopravnii strazh zakonnosti (Legal advisors, or competent guardians of legality). *Izvestiia*, June 12, p. 2.

Izvestiia, (1989). O konstitutsionnom nadzore v CCCR (Concerning constitutional law of the USSR). December 26, pp. 1–3.

Kerimov, D. A. (1989). Opora pravovogo gosudarstva: Navstrechu vtoromu sbezdy narodnix deputatov CCCR. (Buttresses of the rule of state: Preparing for the Second Congress of the USSR People's Deputies). *Pravda*, December 8, p. 3.

Khatuntsev, V. (1990). S pozistii prava i umanizma (From the standpoint of law and humanism). *Pravda*, May 17, p. 1.

Kiralfy, A. (1988). A comparison of civil procedure and state arbitration procedure in the USSR. In D. D. Barry (ed.), *Law and the Gorbachev era*. Dordrecht: Martinus Nijhoff, 91–103.

Kitchin, W. (1990). The mechanics of independence: Soviet judges in the grip of the iron hand. Paper delivered at the Interim Meeting of the Research Committee on Comparative Judicial Studies of the International Political Science Association, London.

———. (1991). The implications for judicial review of the current legal reforms in the Soviet Union. *Policy Studies Journal* 19: 96–105.

Krasnaya Zvezda. (1990). Sworn In. April 28, p. 1.

Ludwikowski, R. (1988). Judicial review in the socialist legal system: current developments. *Traditional and Comparative Law Quarterly* 37: 89–108.

Moscow News (1989). Expertise. June 25–July 2, p. 4.

Nikitinsky, L. (1990). Pravdii (Home truths). *Komsomolskaya Pravda*, September 14, p. 1.

Oda, H. (1987). The procuracy and the regular courts as enforcers of the constitutional rule of law: The experience of East Asian states. *Tulane Law Review* 61: 1339–1363.

Osakwe, C. (1983). Modern soviet criminal procedure: A critical analysis. *Tulane Law Review* 57: 439–601.

Pravda (1989). O proekte zakona konstitutsionnom nadzore v CCCP (Concerning the draft law on constitutional oversight in the USSR). December 22, p. 2.

Stepovoy, A. (1990). Kimitet nachinaet deistvovat (Committee gets down to work). *Izvestiia*, May 18, p. 2.

Part III

Judicial Review and Its Policy Impacts

6

Social Action Litigation in India: The Operation and Limits of the World's Most Active Judiciary

Carl Baar

The expanded use of judicial review in the past generation to place constitutional limitations on government has been greeted warily by many scholars. Entrenched rights and increased judicial activism have been seen by critics on both the Left and Right as a threat to rather than a realization of the democratic order (Mandel, 1989; Glasbeek and Mandel, 1984).

Whatever the merits of this argument, it cannot be assessed without additional evidence drawn from the experience of countries in which entrenched rights and judicial activism are a part of the political fabric. The absence of such evidence has, for example, dramatically misled scholars in Canada who have criticized both the 1982 entrenchment of a Canadian Charter of Rights and Freedoms and the subsequent increase in the judiciary's visible role in major areas of public policy. Consider this broadside in a 1984 symposium in *Socialist Studies*:

[J]udicial activism is a peculiarly American phenomenon. It is an expression of the place which the courts, and especially the Supreme Court of the United States, occupy in that country's political and ideological systems. I doubt whether the courts in any other state occupy a similar place. This must raise questions about the possibility of judicial activism anywhere other than in the U.S. (Martin, 1984: 78).

The author's reaction is understandable, since Canada is a country with a constitution explicitly "similar in principle to that of the United Kingdom"—a system based on the supremacy of Parliament, not on American-style separation of powers. Reinforcing this difference is the long experience that common law parliamentary systems such as England, Canada, and Australia have had with a more conservative judiciary whose restraint in tolerating governmental intrusions into civil liberties is matched by an historic suspicion of labor and social welfare legislation (Griffiths, 1985).

In such comparative analysis, an examination of contemporary judicial review in India is particularly relevant. India has a legal system built on English practices, a federal parliamentary system with a strong executive (not unlike Canada), and a set of entrenched constitutional rights interpreted by a judiciary prepared to intervene in the most sensitive national political issues (not unlike the United States). What has emerged from this mix is an extraordinarily high degree of judicial activism—one that would even surprise Americans, both in terms of the procedures that have been developed and the principles of law enunciated.

Judicial review is not only used more extensively in Indian than American courts, but also quite differently. The Indian judiciary has adapted the wide discretion characteristic of English practice, principally via interim orders, to support its interventionist approach. Its distinctive techniques, partly a response to massive arrears and delay, have allowed the delays themselves to reinforce judicial activism and fundamental rights. At the same time, the real impact of judicial activism remains problematic, since it occurs in an activist state capable of marginalizing even the most courageous and controversial interventions by the courts.

JUDICIAL ACTIVISM IN INDIA

Western political scientists who have studied Indian politics still focus on the judiciary's efforts to undermine socialist programs in the name of property rights. It was these efforts that led Prime Minister Indira Gandhi to make changes in the courts that became part of the background of the 1975–77 Emergency. In the decade since then, however, judges have become outspoken supporters of the political, social, and economic rights of oppressed peoples. The vehicle for this new form of judicial activism is usually termed public interest litigation (PIL) or social action litigation (SAL), the term preferred by some of its leading advocates.

Public interest litigation had its origins not in a popular or even a professional movement. It began in the Supreme Court of India itself, initially in two-judge panels of reform-minded judges who sought new ways to bring issues affecting unrepresented Indian people before the courts. By mid-1980s, public interest litigation "would comprehend any legal wrong or injury or illegal burden, caused or threatened" (Agrawala, 1985: 9). It would extend beyond individual rights to collective or social rights that "require active intervention by the State and other public authorities for their realization, including freedom from indigency, ignorance and discrimination as well as the right to a healthy environment, to social security and to protection for massive financial, commercial and corporate oppression" (Bhagwati, 1987: 21). "[A] determinate class of persons . . . threatened . . . by reason of poverty, helplessness or disability or socially or economically disadvantaged position" would be covered even when that class was "unable to approach the court for relief."[1] The scope of public interest litigation would go beyond its American namesake's efforts "to secure greater fidelity to the parlous notions of legal liberalism''; ''while labels can be borrowed,'' wrote scholar-activist Upendra Baxi (1987: 33), ''history cannot.''

ELEMENTS OF SOCIAL ACTION LITIGATION

Judicial activism is built into the very procedures of social action litigation, in some cases extending the activism of Indian courts well beyond that of its American counterparts. SAL's key procedural elements (summarized in Bhagwati, 1987) include:

1. *Epistolary jurisdiction.* The Supreme Court of India, as well as the High Courts in the various states, can convert a letter from a member of the public into a writ petition. Thus access to judicial redress may be obtained without a lawyer or even the filing of formal papers. The earliest epistles were addressed to individual members of the Supreme Court, and reports abound of individual judges soliciting petitions (see Baxi, 1987: 41; Agrawala, 1985: 16–17). The number of letters has remained high enough to justify the creation and continuation of a ''PIL cell'' within the Supreme Court to process the paperwork— and perhaps to place administrative controls on individual judges (Cassels, 1989). No similar procedure exists in the United States or Canada; prisoners can gain access in some circumstances by letter, but not members of the public.

2. *Broadened roles of standing (locus standi).* ''[A]ny member of the public or social action group acting bona fide'' can apply on behalf of an individual or class unable to do so on its own (Bhagwati, 1987: 24). Social activists filed ''a preponderant number'' of some 75 SAL writs in 1980–82; among the petitioners have been law professors, a third-year law student, a social worker, and journalist (Baxi, 1987: 38–39). This is a dramatic change from strict English-style rules of standing; even a critic of PIL found ''virtual unanimity'' for liberalization (Agrawala, 1985: 14).

3. *Sociolegal commissions of inquiry.* Once a litigant group was given standing and its petition accepted, a lack of resources would likely make the development of a case extremely difficult. A ''passive approach'' by the Court would mean ''fundamental rights would remain merely an illusion,'' wrote Justice P. N. Bhagwati (1987: 26–27), requiring a ''departure from the adversarial procedure without in any way sacrificing the principle of fair play.'' The result was the creation of sociolegal commissions of inquiry:

The Supreme Court started appointing social activists, teachers, researchers, journalists, government officers and judicial officers as Court Commissioners to visit particular locations for fact-finding. The Commissioners were required to submit a quick and detailed report setting out their findings and also their suggestions and recommendations.

While there is precedent for commissioners of inquiry in British administrative regulation dating back to the Public Health Act of 1848 (see E. Baar, 1987: VIII–22), no American court of last resort uses this approach to fact-finding, and American trial courts would do so in a much more modified and limited form.

4. *New remedies and monitoring.* Finally, social action litigation has resulted in a wide variety of remedial court orders. Many would have a familiar ring to American public interest litigators (see, for example, Weisbrod, Handler, and Komesar, 1978; Cooper, 1988), but they represent radical departures from British legal practice all within a short time period. A particularly important element is the establishment of a monitoring agency, by which social activists or judicial officers check on compliance. In practice, District Court Judges are frequently designated inquiry commissioners or monitors, although they are state-appointed judges of limited jurisdiction.

A review of the major cases and substantive principles enunciated through social action litigation will not be attempted here. It is sufficient to note that cases have involved not only the prison conditions (for example, *Dr. Upendra Baxi v. State of Uttar Pradesh*, 1981) and pretrial detention rights (for example, *Hussainara Khatoon v. State of Bihar*, 1979) familiar in American litigation, but have extended to bonded laborers (*Bandhua Mukti Morcha*, 1984), pavement dwellers (*Olga Tellis v. State of Maharastra*, 1979), rickshaw pullers (*Azad Rickshaw Pullers v. Punjab*, 1981), construction workers (*People's Union for Democratic Rights v. Union of India*, 1982), and thousands of *adivasis* and *dalits*[2] (*Times of India*, 1988: 3; for other examples, see Baxi, 1987; and Gupta, 1987: 219). In this process, Indian judges have rendered interpretations of constitutional language that are much broader than comparable American interpretations: antislavery provisions of the constitution have been extended to a setting in which workers were paid below the minimum wage; the state has been given a positive obligation to protect the environment; and a commuter was able to sue the state railway for failing in its constitutional obligation to guarantee freedom of movement (Agrawala, 1985: 12).

JUDICIAL ACTIVISM IN CROWDED COURTS

Overcrowded dockets in Indian Courts have been a subject of scholarly concern within the country (Dhavan, 1978, 1986) and amazement outside. But what is important to our current analysis is how arrears and delay, by reinforcing an English-style approach to judicial discretion, have promoted judicial activism by facilitating selective judicial intervention.

The Supreme Court of India's caseload is staggering by any calculation. The Court's own monthly statement for January 1988 showed a total of 39,454 "regular hearing matters" pending, plus 137,622 "admission and miscellaneous matters"—a combined total of 177,076. In January alone, over 4,000 matters had been disposed of, but over 5,000 matters had come in. While the bulk of the pending cases are not constitutional, the Court shows a total of 7,611 constitutional matters pending on February 1, 1988, including 104 civil writ petitions from 1978 that are listed as ready for hearing.

These gigantic numbers suggest that the very concept of litigation and readiness for hearing must be treated differently in India than in other common-law countries. Thus an advocate who had recently completed a Supreme Court appeal in a nonconstitutional matter that had commenced 52 years earlier brushed aside my concerned questions, referring to the case as "luxury litigation." If a matter is important, it will come on for hearing; what the Court considers a priority is handled expeditiously.

And so it is. When a controversial television miniseries on partition led to protests and riots, the Bombay High Court "stayed further screening of the serial on the basis of a writ petition filed by a Bombay businessman" (Tripathi, 1988: 75). Two days later (January 23, 1988), a two-judge panel had viewed the six-part film and lifted the interim order. The petitioner appealed to the Supreme Court, but the Court dismissed the petition on February 1 (*Indian Express*, 1988: 1). The entire matter was resolved within the short life of the series and without an episode being missed. To do otherwise would have prevented the judiciary from bringing its own distinctive approach and concerns to bear at a time of major national debate. While the American or Canadian Supreme Courts would have waited for an opportunity for sober second thought and for the quieting of public debate, the Supreme Court of India heard arguments and delivered a 23-page judgment within two weeks after the first action in a lower court.

What is happening is quite simple: the Indian courts are operating on interim orders. In contrast, the U.S. Supreme Court uses doctrines of ripeness and exhaustion of remedies to ensure that lower court action is complete. This is done not just because of that court's delicate constitutional position, but because American courts have generally rejected the use of interlocutory appeals (appeals from the decisions of trial judges on preliminary motions). In contrast, British courts (and their Canadian and Australian counterparts) make extensive use of interlocutory appeals, usually through a single superior court judge hearing an appeal from the ruling of an inferior trial judge. The Indian courts, following British practice, also make extensive use of interim orders—so that even when there is no time to complete a case, steps can be taken to control state action.

The use of interim orders is a key to the success of social action litigation. Even by the early 1980s, Baxi (1987: 42) noted that "not a single leading SAL matter has yet resulted in a final verdict. . . . In the meantime, the Court rules through interim directions and orders. Bit by bit, it seeks improvement in the administration, making it more responsive than before to the constitutional ethic and law." When a letter came to the Supreme Court on behalf of adivasis and dalits claiming harassment by forest and revenue authorities, a two-judge bench not only accepted the letter as a writ petition, but issued a restraining order against the authorities—shifting the burden of court delays from the petitioners to the state (*Times of India*, 1988: 3).

The use of interim orders allows the Indian judiciary to cope with delay. At the same time, extensive delays can be used and not merely coped with. Delays legitimate the need to reset priorities for hearing, giving the judiciary wide discretion to pick and choose from among those demanding a hearing. Jumping the queue is no longer deemed unfair when the queue is ten years long. Thus a court committed to an agenda of social justice could advance matters on its docket whose resolution would promote that goal, and avoid cases that are either marginal or detrimental to the goal. By analogy, the Indian courts operate more like North American graduate schools than North American law schools. A smaller proportion of students flunk out of graduate school than out of law school, yet at the same time a smaller proportion actually graduate. Similarly, constitutional petitioners may not lose in great numbers, but neither is a high proportion successful. Numerous cases simply fall by the wayside, never reached by the courts. In this process, however, the Indian judiciary does hear a wide range of matters that provide opportunities to teach symbolic lessons to the state and the society. And those lessons are given at the very moment when the attention of that audience is most intense.

CONSTITUTIONAL CONDITIONS FOR SOCIAL ACTION LITIGATION

Social action litigation did not develop out of a history of judicial restraint and institutional weakness. It has flourished because of the judiciary's original constitutional position and subsequent constitutional role. Consider four constitutional factors that have facilitated the development of social action litigation:

1. There is the tradition of judicial activism going back to the beginning of the constitution in 1950, culminating in the two great cases of *Golak Nath* in 1967 and *Kesavananda Bharati* in 1973. In the former, the Supreme Court effectively declared a constitutional amendment unconstitutional, by holding that Parliament could not amend the constitution in a manner that would abridge the Fundamental Rights in Part III. An 11-judge bench heard the case for two months; its four separate opinions took 173 pages. In *Kesavananda*, the Court modified its earlier holding, allowing Parliament to amend the constitution, including Part III, but only as long as the "basic structure" of the constitution was preserved. That decision followed a six-month hearing before a 13-judge bench, and resulted in 11 opinions running a total of 701 pages.

The Court in both cases was reviewing land reform legislation in the name of property rights, thus arraying itself as a conservative institution challenging the authority of a redistributive regime in a highly visible political event. If *Kesavananda* could be India's *Marbury v. Madison* (because, as argued by the Rudolphs [1987:110], it "establish[ed] an acceptable ground for judicial review"), it could also be Indian's *Schechter Poultry* case (the most newsworthy of the U.S. Supreme Court's decisions invalidating New Deal legislation in the 1930s). For just as President Franklin Roosevelt responded to *Schechter* by appointing a number of Supreme Court judges more sympathetic to his social and economic reforms, and saw those judges go on to become judicial activists when individual rights were violated by government action, so it was that the

Indira Gandhi government, in the years following *Golak Nath*, appointed a number of more left-wing judges, including Bhagwati, V. R. Krisna Iyer, and O. Chinnappa Reddy, who accepted an active state role in socioeconomic policy, but supported judicial activism in cases of government infringement of civil liberties.

2. There is a constitution that includes not only fundamental rights but also "Directive Principles of State Policy." Sections 12–35 of the Indian constitution entrench a full range of fundamental rights, enforceable in the Supreme Court (s.32). Sections 36–51 go in a different direction, enunciating a set of directive principles that are not judicially enforceable (s.37). Derived from the Irish constitution, these positive obligations extend to a variety of areas of economic and social policy, providing a context for the application of fundamental rights. For example, the Canadian fear that a doctrine of substantive due process would be read into Section 7 of its Charter to promote a conservative economic agenda, in the style of the *Lochner*-era U.S. Supreme Court, would be mitigated by the understanding that fundamental rights gain meaning from their relationship to directive principles. Thus, for example, the Supreme Court of India saw the two as "complementary to each other," with directive principles "prescrib[ing] the goal" and fundamental rights "lay[ing] down the means" (*Minerva Mills*, 1980).

3. There is an administratively independent judiciary. Section 50 of the Indian Constitution provides that "the State shall take steps to separate the judiciary from the executive in the public services of the State." While this language is part of the nonenforceable "Directive Principles of State Policy," the goal it enunciates has been achieved in India to an extent greater than in any other common law parliamentary system. Thus Indian courts are administered under the direction of the judiciary, as in the United States, and not by the executive, as in Canada, Australia, and the United Kingdom. The registrars (chief administrators) of the Supreme Court and the state High Courts are appointed by the judges of those courts; the current Supreme Court registrar was formerly a District Court judge in the neighboring state of Rajasthan. As in the United States (see C. Baar, 1975), the Indian courts are still subject to external budget constraints; however, the Indian judiciary has control over internal allocation of resources— an authority that would be condemned as contrary to principles of parliamentary government in Canada, Australia, or the United Kingdom.

Differences in the constitutional and political setting of court systems generate different administrative strategies for meeting the maintenance and enhancement needs of those institutions. It was argued a decade ago that the independent administrative base of American courts has led to an organizational growth and empowerment strategy, while the administratively dependent status of the Canadian courts has led to an encapsulation and professional alliance strategy (C. Baar, 1977). The Indian judiciary has, following its British counterpart, traditionally relied on its linkages to the senior bar to reinforce its independence, but control over its own administrative apparatus has allowed the judiciary to shift to an empowerment strategy. As a result, the administrative infrastructure needed to support social action litigation (the Supreme Court's PIL cell, the sociolegal commissions of inquiry) is within the judiciary's control; a chief justice, for example, need not go to an executive official to request that a unit be created to handle a new wave of court-encouraged letters and writ petitions.

4. There is a Supreme Court with broad jurisdiction. The Supreme Court of India has a wide range of both original and appellate jurisdiction entrenched in the constitution itself. Section 32 gives access to the Supreme Court to anyone who claims their fundamental rights are violated. While the Court has urged public interest litigants to start in their state High Courts, original petitions continue to be filed, and continue to be admitted for hearing. The Supreme Court, consistent with its surrounding political culture, has emphasized the need to maintain access rather than move to the kind of tight docket control that has been used in the courts of last resort in the United States and Canada. One of the trade-offs has been the growth of the Court (18 members by the mid–1980s, and more recently up to 25) and the use of the "double bench"—two-judge panels that hear the overwhelming majority of constitutional arguments in PIL cases. Participants are aware of the cost of these steps in potentially reducing doctrinal coherence, but there has been no move to reduce Supreme Court jurisdiction.

The Supreme Court's original jurisdiction reinforces its activist character in comparison with other national courts of last resort. One of the reasons why India's Supreme Court is so much more active than the U.S. Supreme Court is that a large number of the matters before the Indian Court would be handled in the United States by federal district courts. It is these federal trial courts that have been in the forefront of institutional reform litigation, which bears the closest resemblance to Indian social action litigation in its use of interim orders and designation of officials to monitor enforcement of court orders. Thus the contrast between the Indian and American judiciaries may not be as great as the contrast between the two countries' highest courts.

THE LIMITATIONS OF JUDICIAL ACTIVISM

The Indian judiciary, I have argued, is at least as active as its American counterpart, and by some key indicators is even more so. As well, its activism is built on a different set of legal traditions, manifested through a different set of techniques, developed under more extreme caseload pressures, and in service to a different ideology (see Baxi, 1985: 15–18). Yet at the end of the day, it appears that even a judiciary whose energy and activism would amaze outsiders is no match for the energy and activism of the Indian state and its political leaders. The social action litigation that has captured the imagination of North American legal scholars (for example, Cassels, 1989; Cunningham, 1987) was dealt with in two paragraphs of the latest major book by the leading American political science scholars on India (Rudolph and Rudolph, 1987: 122–123. Why is it that an activist judiciary has relatively less impact in India than if it arose in other democratic polities?

Part of the judiciary's limited impact may be a product of the absence of other checks on government power in general and national political power in particular. For example, the states are relatively weak units in the Indian federal system. Constitutional amendments, even changes to provisions for fundamental rights, require only approval in the union parliament. It is no wonder that the Supreme Court developed the "basic structure" doctrine; no other institution outside the government in power at the center could check so fundamental an exercise of authority.

Nor is there an independent upper house to challenge judicial appointments in the style of the U.S. Senate. In practice, it is the Supreme Court again that has provided a check. No justice has been appointed to the Supreme Court of India since independence without the consent of the chief justice, and the veto has gained strength as its conventional use has continued. The chief justice's pivotal role has made his appointment all the more sensitive. The chief justiceship normally goes by seniority, and attempts by government to move past the most senior justices have given rise to supercession controversies (see Dhavan and Jacob, 1978). It is also rare for a Supreme Court appointee not to have had extensive experience on a state High Court, further constraining the central government appointing authorities.

Balanced against these constraints, however, is the provision for compulsory retirement of Supreme Court justices at age 65 (High Court justices retire at 62). The retirement age, reflecting the shorter life spans at the time the constitution was written 40 years ago, produces an enormous turnover, with the resulting opportunity for a new government to remake the Court in short order. For example, 14 of the 18 Supreme Court justices sitting on May 1, 1985, had retired by the end of 1988.[3] The longest period of service among those 18 was a term of 13 years, 5 months.

The impact of social action litigation is mitigated by the absence of a bar with sufficient independent resources to support litigation challenging the legitimacy of government action. In the United States, public interest law grew through the public and private financial support of a network of law firms with the resources and expertise to vindicate new and expanded rights for their clientele. In India, no similar structure exists for perfecting challenges to state authority through the courts. Once again, the initiative fell to the Supreme Court; the PIL procedures that originated within the judiciary were in this sense a matter of necessity.

In summary, judicial activism in India is in a very real sense a constitutional imperative. The underdevelopment of other checks on a powerful central government has widened the scope and use of accountability mechanisms in the hands of the judiciary. India has neither the strong provincial governments that operate in Canada, the separation of powers that operates in the United States, nor the referenda used in Australia. As a result, the judiciary has become both a first and a last resort. It has responded to its role with a vigor and creativity that are breathtaking to outside observers. Yet, whether additional checks can develop to relieve some of the pressures on the Indian polity remains to be seen.

NOTES

Research for this chapter was conducted primarily during a stay in New Delhi and Bombay, India, February–March 1988. I would like to thank the numerous lawyers, judges, court officials, and scholars who shared their views and knowledge with me, and especially Dr. L. M. Singhvi of the Supreme Court Bar and Professor Upendra Baxi of the Indian Law Institute for their help and encouragement. Earlier versions of this chapter were presented to the Constitutional Law Group of Osgoode Hall Law School, York University, April 1988, and India Group, York University, March 1989.

1. See *S. P. Gupta v. Union of India*, A.I.R. 1982 S.C. 149 at 189, reasons by Bhagwati J., as quoted in Agrawala, 1985: 9.

2. *Adivasis* are aboriginals (literally, "original inhabitants"), usually members of scheduled tribes designated for protection under Part XVI of the Constitution, sections 330ff. *Dalits* refer broadly to the depressed or downtrodden, members of "backward classes."

3. Derived from biographical material in *Judges of the Supreme Court and the High Courts As on 1st May, 1985* (New Delhi: Government of India, Ministry of Law and Justice, Department of Justice, 1986).

REFERENCES

Agrawala, S. K. (1985). *Public interest litigation in India: A critique*. Bombay: Tripathi.

Baar, C. (1975). *Separate but subservient: Court budgeting in the American states*. Lexington, MA: D. C. Heath.

———. (1977). Patterns and strategies of court administration in Canada and the United States. *Canadian Public Administration* 20, 242–74, reprinted in *Law Society of Upper Canada Gazette* 11, 79–110.

Baar, E. (1987). *Positive compliance programs: Their potential as instruments for regulatory reform*. Ottawa: Department of Justice of Canada.

Baxi, U. (1985). *Courage, craft and contention: The Indian Supreme Court in the eighties*. Bombay: Tripathi.

———. (1987). Taking suffering seriously: Social action litigation in the Supreme Court of India. In N. Tiruchelvam and R. Coomaraswamy (eds.), *The role of the judiciary in plural societies*. New York: St. Martin's Press, 32–60.

Bhagwati, P. N. (1987). Social action litigation: The Indian experience. In N. Tiruchelvam and R. Coomaraswamy (eds.), *The role of the judiciary in plural societies*. New York: St. Martin's Press, 20–31.

Cassels, J. (1989). Judicial activism and public interest litigation in India: Attempting the impossible? *American Journal of Comparative Law* 37: 495–519.

Cooper, P. J. (1988). *Hard judicial choices*. New York: Oxford.

Cunningham, C. D. (1987). Public interest litigation in Indian Supreme Court: A study in the light of American experience. *Journal of the Indian Law Institute* 29: 494–523.

Dhavan, R. (1978). *The supreme court under strain: The challenge of arrears*. Bombay: Tripathi.

————. (1986). *Litigation explosion in India*. Bombay: Tripathi.

————, and Jacob, A. (1978). *Selection and appointment of supreme court justices: a case study*. Bombay: Tripathi.

Glasbeek, H. J., and Mandel, M. (1984). The legalization of politics in advanced capitalism: The Canadian Charter of Rights and Freedoms. *Socialist Studies* 2: 84–124.

Griffiths, J.A.G. (1985). *The politics of the judiciary*, 3rd ed. London: Fontana Press.

Gupta, V. K. (1987). Concept and organization of the Supreme Court of India—a study in retrospect. *Indian Bar Review* 14: 201–228.

Indian Express (1988). Tamas will prevent communal riots: SC. February 17, p. 1.

Mandel, M. (1989). *The charter of rights and the legalization of politics in Canada*. Toronto: Wall and Thompson.

Martin, R. (1984). The judges and the charter. *Socialist Studies* 2: 66–83.

Rudolph, L. I., and Rudolph, S. H. (1987). *In pursuit of lakshmi*. Chicago: University of Chicago Press.

Times of India. (1988). SC allows Adivasis, Dalits to till land. February 16, p. 3.

Tripathi, S. (1988). Tamas: fresh target. *India Today*, February 15, p. 75.

Weisbrod, B. A., Handler, J. F., and Komesar, N. K. (1978). *Public interest law: An economic and institutional analysis*. Berkeley: University of California Press.

CASES CITED

Azad Rickshaw Pullers v. Punjab (1981) 1 SCC 366.

Bandhua Mukti Morcha v. Union of India & Others (Faridabad stone quarries), AIR 1984 SC 802.

Dr. Upendra Baxi v. State of Uttar Pradesh, 1981 (3) SCALE 1136.

Golak Nath v. Punjab, AIR 1967 SC 1943.

Hussainara Khatoon v. State of Bihar (Bihar undertrials case), AIR 1979 SC 1360; AIR 1979 SC 1369; AIR 1979 SC 1377; AIR 1979 SC 1819.

Kesavananda Bharati v. Kerala, 1973. 4 SCC 225.

Marbury v. Madison, 5 U.S. (1 Cranch) 137 (1803).

Minerva Mills v. Union of India, 1980. 3 SCC 625.

Olga Tellis v. State of Maharastra, AIR 1979 SC 1825.

People's Union for Democratic Rights v. Union of India, AIR 1982 SC 1473.

Schechter Poultry Corp. v. U.S., 295 U.S. 495 (1935).

S. P. Gupta v. Union of India, A.I.R. 1982 S.C. 149.

7

Judicial Review and Public Policy in Italy: American Roots and the Italian Hybrid

Mary L. Volcansek

Judicial review, broadly defined, is the power of a court "to hold unconstitutional and hence unenforceable any law, any official action based on a law, or any action by a public official . . . [deemed] to be in conflict with the basic law" (Abraham, 1986: 292). Such a conception of judicial power was, in a sense, novel when the framers of the U.S. Constitution met in Philadelphia in 1787, but it is one that is widely imitated throughout the world.[1] The process of transplanting a legal rule such as judicial review from one culture to another does not, however, insure that the rule will be observed or used in an expected fashion in its new cultural setting, for law and culture are often mirrors of one another and law parallels a country's social fabric (Liebesney, 1981: 1).

The Italian Republic, created at the end of World War II, consciously imitated the American practice of judicial review, but the process has assumed the character of the Italian legal culture. Grafting a legal institution from one culture onto another may or may not be successful, and even where the imported practice takes root, it may be altered to fit the attitudes and beliefs that have evolved historically in the new legal culture. Italy and other European nations who copied the U.S. system of judicial review instituted some calculated changes, like limiting the power to a single constitutional court in lieu of the "decentralized" American tradition of according such power to all courts. In practice, moreover, European courts have also been noticeably more aggressive in asserting their authority of judicial review than have their brethren in the United States. The first difference was necessary because of the character of civil law: for example, the absence of rigid adherence to precedent, the large number of jurists on most courts, and a preference for fidelity to the notion of separation of powers. The other shift was most likely caused by the continental approach to judicial decision making, one that is not based on pure interpretation (Cappelletti and Golay, 1981: 24–27).

This chapter compares the origins, acceptance, and practice of judicial review in the United States and its adaptation to the Republic of Italy. U.S. practices, because of their familiarity and two centuries of evolution, need not be recounted in the same detail as the Italian development of judicial review and its mere four decades of maturation. The U.S. experience, rather, reveals the growth of an original prototype that has been altered, modified, and perhaps even improved in its transplanted setting in southern Europe.

JUDICIAL REVIEW IN THE UNITED STATES

Judicial review is not explicitly mentioned in the U.S. Constitution, a fact that has fueled a lively debate for the century and three-quarters since Chief Justice John Marshall proclaimed the power for the U.S. Supreme Court.[2] The concept was, however, not without basis in British common law and in the practice of the colonies. Edward Coke had, in 1610, asserted that acts of Parliament must be declared void by British judges if they offended "fundamental," "higher law," or "common rights and reason" (Corwin, 1978: 221), and colonial legislatures had more than once seen their actions nullified by the English Privy Council (Grosman and Wells, 1988: 104). Courts in Rhode Island and South Carolina exercised judicial review in 1786 and 1787 to abrogate legislative actions, though their assertions of this authority were not favorably received by their respective legislatures (Volcansek and Lafon, 1987: 24–25). The debates at the Constitutional Convention in 1787 suggest that most of the delegates assumed some sort of judicial power to annul legislative acts contrary to the Constitution. These assumptions were illustrated in their discussion of a proposed Council of Revision, an institution that was ultimately rejected by the Convention.[3] At the Convention, however, there were also those who registered their reservations about the wisdom of granting such power to judges.[4] These fragments of debate or discussion by the framers seem to validate the conclusion of Robert McCloskey (1960: 9) that "neither the words of the Constitution nor the probable intent of those who framed and ratified it justified in 1790 any certitude about the scope or finality of the Court's power to superintend either the States or Congress." The most commonly cited justification for the exercise of judicial review by the Supreme Court can be found in Alexander Hamilton's *Federalist* No. 78:

If, then, the courts of justice are to be considered as the bulwarks of a limited Constitution against legislative encroachments, this consideration will afford a strong argument for the permanent tenure of judicial offices . . . which must be essential to the faithful performance of so arduous a duty (Hamilton et al., 1969: 508).

The reality of judicial review was first manifested in the tour de force opinion of Chief Justice John Marshall in the case of *Marbury v. Madison*.[5] Marshall

and attacks by the parties.'' Opponents, primarily from the leftist parties (PSI and PCI), argued that a Constitutional Court with the power of judicial review threatened popular sovereignty, by removing ultimate power from Parliament and creating a ''democracy of the judges.'' That position, assumed by PCI leader Palmiro Togliatti, was reinforced by Socialist leader Pietro Nenni, who cited the experience of Franklin Roosevelt, whose New Deal initiatives had been blocked because the judges deemed them to be unconstitutional. The leftists supported a rigid constitution and a mechanism to check laws that violated it, but, to preserve popular sovereignty, felt that power should be vested in the representatives of the people sitting in Parliament (Rodota, 1986: 14–15). Empowering a court to serve as the ultimate arbiter of constitutional principles was seen as a guarantee, by the leftists, that Italy would be liberal and catholic; moreover, the judges under fascism had not demonstrated any penchant for preserving democratic principles nor for asserting independence from the regime in power. The reservations expressed caused the twin issues of the Constitutional Court and judicial review to be returned to the Commission of 75 for reconsideration; the questions were not resolved until near the end of the deliberations of the Constituent Assembly some ten months later (Laurenzano, 1983: 15–17).

The compromises that resulted in the final Constitution are not surprising since the Constituent Assembly was composed of representatives of ''the political forces of Catholicism, Marxism and liberalism'' that made the process one of ''reciprocal concessions'' (Martines, 1986: 27).[8] When the Constitutional Court was debated again in December 1947, interest was low and passage was uncomplicated. In the final constitution, Article 134 defines the powers of the Court as extending to determination of the constitutionality of laws and of acts having the force of law, conflicts among the three branches of government, controversies between the national government and the regions, and impeachments of the president of the republic and any ministers. The method for appointing members of the Court is defined in the next article.[9] Article 136 clarifies that a law declared unconstitutional ceases to be effective the day following the publication of the Court's decision, and Article 137 provides for parliamentary action to make all ''other provisions necessary for the constitution and functioning of the Court'' and clarifies that there are no appeals from decisions of the Constitutional Court. Article 138, however, presents a new wrinkle in the notion of judicial review and was added to satisfy those in the Constituent Assembly who feared that the Constitutional Court might thwart popular sovereignty. The constitution may be amended—that is, decisions of the Constitutional Court may be overruled—by absolute majority votes in each house of Parliament. A referendum may be called upon demand of one-fifth of the members of either house of Parliament, of 500,000 voters, or of five regional councils, but *no* referendum is possible if both houses of Parliament pass the amendment by a two-thirds majority on the second vote. The next and final article of the constitution makes a single exception: ''the Republican form of Government is not subject to constitutional amendment.''

Though the constitution became effective in 1948, a series of events, both within and without Italy, conspired to prevent implementation either of the Constitutional Court or of control of the constitutionality of laws. The "Red Threat" emerged in 1947 and affected the elections in 1948 for Italy's first Parliament,[10] as the joint vote for the PCI and PSI dropped to only 31 percent, while the Christian Democrats won an absolute majority of parliamentary seats (although only 48.4 percent of the popular vote), enabling the DCs to form a coalition government that did not include the leftists. The Christian Democrats, then, planted Italy firmly in the Western alliance by joining NATO and decided not to allow any diminution of their domestic power that might result from implementation of the Constitutional Court or of the constitutionality mandated regional governments. This turn of events left Italy with "a Liberal Constitution, a Catholic government and Fascist laws" (Clark, 1984: 31).

The Communists and Socialists were, after 1948, excluded from power in Rome and, as the opposition, became champions of decentralized government, specifically of judicial independence, the Constitutional Court, and devolution to the regions (Kogan, 1983: 105–106). The dominant Christian Democrats, on the other hand, were bent on consolidating their power and even attempted to pass an electoral law, the so-called Legge Truffa or Fraud Law, that would have enabled them to obtain an even more disproportionate number of seats in Parliament than the popular vote would dictate.[11] However, the 1953 elections ended the DC majority in Parliament.[12]

In advance of the 1953 elections Parliament finally engaged in debates on the implementation of the Constitutional Court. Two laws passed that year were of primary importance for the future of the Constitutional Court. The first, Constitutional Law No. 1, 1953, added one power to the Constitutional Court that was not mentioned in Article 134 of the constitution: that of controlling popular referenda to abrogate laws passed by Parliament, as stipulated in Article 75 of the constitution. This law further prescribed that decisions of the Court were to be by a two-thirds majority and judges were protected from prosecution for any vote or expression of opinion in the performance of their duties.

Form and shape for the Constitutional Court were given in Law No. 87 (March 11, 1953). That law defined the jurisdiction of the Court and the procedures for naming jurists to do it. The Court was, by the law defining its jurisdiction, prohibited from making any evaluation of a political nature or any censure of the discretionary power of Parliament. The merit of a parliamentary decision was not, therefore, available for judicial scrutiny, only its constitutionality was at issue in a strict sense.[13] Procedures were provided for disputes to reach the Court, either by direct or indirect access. Direct access is from Parliament, the prime minister (presidente del consiglio dei ministri), or regional governments when there is an alleged conflict among the powers of the state or between the regional governments and the national government, or from Parliament when the president of the republic or a minister is accused of abuse of power or a crime. Indirect access is from the ordinary and administrative courts when a party to a case contends that a law or an official act involved in the case is contrary to the Constitution. The Court, in cases reaching it indirectly, responds only to the constitutional question posed and returns the case to the referring court for disposition consistent with its interpretation.

A major issue in the debates on implementing the Court was the method for Parliament to name its five judges. The constitution had specified only that the judges were to be named in a joint session of the two houses. The 1953 law allowed that a majority of three-fifths was necessary in two separate votes for a judge to be named, a provision motivated by fears of the centrist coalition parties that an absolute majority might facilitate the selection of leftist judges.[14] Between the passage of the law designating the procedures for naming judges to the Court and the actual nomination of the first ones, the composition of Parliament was altered by the 1953 election results. The battle to name the five parliamentary judges began in October 1953 and did not conclude until 25 months later, after a major compromise among the parties of the majority and the major parties of the opposition. The final two selections were Nicola Jaeger (a "leftist," but not a member of the PCI), and Giovanni Cassandro (PLI) (Rodota, 1986: 22). Subsequently the parties have negotiated various formulas to distribute the positions on the Court; currently, the Christian Democrats name two and the PCI, PSI, and lay parties each choose one.

The remaining problem for staffing the Court was the naming of judges by the president of the republic. Since the president is largely a ceremonial figure, the constitution provides in Article 89 that his actions are invalid unless countersigned by the Council of Ministers, who submit proposals and assume responsibility for them. President Einaudi, of the PLI, claimed that the responsibility for naming judges was his alone, citing Article 135 on Court personnel as an exception to the general rule of Article 89. The Council of Ministers, controlled by the DCs, asserted that he was only able to ratify the candidates that were submitted to him by the Council. Einaudi eventually won, naming people more for their legal abilities than for partisan advantage.[15]

The Court held its first session in April 1956 and promptly asserted its power to act independently and to uphold the values of the republican Constitution. The first case heard by the Constitutional Court involved a conflict between Article 21 of the constitution (freedom of expression and press) and a public security law of fascist vintage.[16] The state argued that the Court lacked the competence to invalidate any law that preceded the Court's implementation in April 1956, a position that would have maintained the entire corpus of fascist law, unless altered by Parliament, and any other laws passed prior to 1956. The Court emphatically declared the security law to be constitutionally illegitimate and asserted its authority to review laws from any era that were in conflict with the constitution (Judgment No. 1, May 5, 1956).

A complete review of the jurisprudence of the Constitutional Court is not possible, and firm statistics of the precise number of laws declared invalid are not available and would be misleading if they were. Much of the positive reputation of the Court for aggressive protection of the Italian constitution results more from its rulings on laws persisting from the fascist era and less for its confrontations with Parliament, the Council of Ministers, and the ordinary judiciary. The court has, indeed, been reticent to interfere in the affairs of the three branches of government because of its rather stringent interpretation of the separation of powers. Both the Chamber of Deputies and the Senate have established procedures to examine and, if necessary, redraft legislation that has been invalidated by the Court.[17] The Court, however, has repeatedly asserted its authority to review replacement or remedial legislation that results as a consequence of its earlier invalidation of a law.[18] The Court has, at the same time, made a policy of rigorous self-restraint by recognizing the discretionary powers of Parliament whenever assertions are made that the legislative branch has exceeded its constitutional powers.[19] Some of the Court's most controversial decisions have been those made in *support* of the power of Parliament, rather than in opposition to it.[20]

The Court has been more active in dismantling laws and traditions inherited from the fascist era and clarifying the influence of extra-state powers, in particular the authority of the Catholic Church, to achieve consistency with the constitution. The penal code, of fascist vintage, provided that a married woman and her "accomplice" could be sentenced to one year in prison for the crime of adultery; a married man, on the other hand, was criminally liable only if he lived with another woman "consistently and notoriously." The distinctions were initially sustained by the Court (Judgment No. 64 of 1961), because of the harm to the family if the wife is unfaithful. However, the Court recanted seven years later (Judgment No. 126 of 1968), by recognizing equality of treatment for husbands and wives.[21]

Divorce and abortion, both strictly prohibited by Catholic doctrine and by Italian law, were issues in which the Constitutional Court assumed an active role. The Fortuna-Baslini law legalizing divorce was passed by Parliament in 1970 and upheld by the Constitutional Court against the charge that it violated Article 7 of the constitution that had incorporated the Lateran Pacts.[22] The Constitutional Court upheld the legitimacy of the divorce law, relying also on Article 7 of the constitution and emphasizing that the provision granted independence and sovereignty to both the Church and the State, each in their appropriate sphere (Judgment No. 169 of 1971).[23] The Court dealt another blow to Catholic dominance of marital relations when it upheld the 1975 reform of family law that forbids marriage contracts among minors, against the challenge that Catholic law (Lateran Pacts in Article 7) permitted marriages at ages 16 for males and 14 for females (Judgment No. 16 of 1982).

The next question involving church-state relations was that of abortion. The Constitutional Court had, in 1971, invalidated the fascist-era law that prohibited the use of contraception, and, in a decision that foreshadowed the abortion question, nullified that portion of the penal code that made a woman's consent to an abortion, even when there existed a threat to her health, a criminal act

(Judgment No. 127 of 1975). Parliament in 1978 legalized abortion for adult women, during the first trimester of pregnancy.[24]

The Court was empowered by the constitution not only to review the legitimacy of legislative acts, but also to arbitrate among the powers of government. The Court has narrowly construed that power to exclude minor organs of government or actions of a single minister, because the executive is a single not a diffuse power (Judgment No. 150 of 1981). It has further asserted that the Court should not intervene to decide contests about "the appearance of power," but only when as a consequence of the exercise of power by one organ another is disabled (Judgments No. 13 of 1975, No. 231 of 1975, No. 65 of 1978, and No. 129 of 1981). This self-imposed limitation has kept the Court out of the potentially prickly circumstance of umpiring among the president of the republic, the Council of Ministers, Parliament, and the Superior Council of the Magistrates.

The Court was also enabled by the constitution to act on usurpations of power between the central government and the regions,[25] an authority that has placed the Court in the position of delineating divisions of power. Before the regions were even functional entities, the Constitutional Court declared that they were limited in their competence because they lacked sovereignty, which resided in the national government (Judgment No. 6 of 1964). The line of decisions thereafter regarding regional devolution appeared to favor the national government at the expense of the regional government. In 1983, however, the Court invalidated a number of decree laws that were preludes to the local finance laws, because they violated the fundamental relationship between the national government and the regions, economic emergencies notwithstanding (Judgment No. 12, 1983). The Court similarly defended the constitutional jurisdiction of the regions against the national government in the areas of health service, agriculture, and forestry.

The Court has had to face a number of obstacles in cementing its place in the power-sharing scheme of Italian politics. The executive branch initially was disinclined to enforce decisions of the Court, and was so blatantly persistent in its refusal that the first president of the Constitutional Court, Enrico De Nicola, resigned in protest. His complaints were echoed by his successor (Kogan, 1983: 107). Senior judges in the ordinary courts were also hostile to the Court at first, and, since indirect access is through the other courts, they refused to refer cases to the Constitutional Court when appropriate (Spotts and Wieser, 1986: 152). The Court's early performance was characterized as "cautious rather than daring" (Kogan, 1983: 107), but over the mere three decades of its existence, the Italian Constitutional Court has managed to win a rather favored place in the Italian political scheme, admired at least for its "solid prestige" (Spotts and Wieser, 1986: 152).

JUDICIAL REVIEW: HEIR OR MUTATION?

The Italian experience with judicial review at first blush seems to be at considerable odds with the practice of the United States. When the U.S. Constitution was written in 1787, the notion of judicial review was not unknown, but there was no experience with its practice. By the time the Constituent Assembly met in Italy in 1947, there were a number of models of judicial review available, with track records of success and disappointments. Those who wrote the 1948 Italian Constitution sought to extract the best feature of judicial review as it was known in other nations. The decentralized system of the United States, whereby *all* judges might invalidate acts of legislative and executive branches, was rejected in favor of reposing the power in a single judicial body, separate from all three organs of government. This strict adherence to separation of powers owed more to the French example than to the American. It also was particularly well-suited to Italy, where holdover fascist judges remained on the benches of the other courts until eventually removed by retirement or death. The control of constitutionality would have been under a shadow had jurists with questionable loyalties and political persuasions been entrusted with the authority.

Judges on the U.S. Supreme Court are nominated and confirmed in a political fashion; likewise the jurists on the Italian Constitutional Court, at least those named by Parliament, owe their selection to partisan ties. The extent to which ideological and partisan predispositions influence decisions is repeatedly commented upon, but the conclusion that the Italian Constitutional Court "is no more politicized than is the Supreme Court of the United States" (LaPalombara, 1987: 226) seems warranted.

The dilemmas of Franklin Roosevelt and the "Nine Old Men" prompted the Constituent Assembly to limit the terms of judges on the Constitutional Court to 12 years, though that was later reduced to 9. Fresh views and new personnel were certain to be present on the Court as the judges rotated off in staggered years, assuring that, unlike the Roosevelt and Carter administration's experiences, each president of the republic, each Parliament, and each new sitting of senior judges would be assured of naming people to the Constitutional Court.

The U.S. Supreme Court has been assailed as the undemocratic organ of the American system (Dahl, 1967: 150), partially because its unaccountable justices wield the power to veto effectively actions of the democratically elected branches of government. A similar concern was voiced by Togliatti (PCI) and Nenni (PSI) in the Constituent Assembly, prompting the provision in Article 138 of the Constitution for an amending process whereby Parliament could counter a decision of the Constitution Court. Though the procedure to amend the U.S. Constitution is far more cumbersome, three amendments have been passed to overturn decisions of the Supreme Court,[26] and multiple other attempts have been made to curb the court (Nagel, 1973: 9). The Italian Parliament, rather than attacking the Constitutional Court, has established procedures to handle every decision that invalidates a law and has successfully amended the constitution by the requisite two-thirds majority in both chambers, without resort to public referenda.[27]

Writing a constitution that describes or implies judicial review is hardly the measure of the concept; how the practice of judicial review evolves is more telling. The U.S. Supreme Court has wielded its pen against laws enacted by Congress rather sparingly, incurring public or political rancor only in certain historical eras. The habit of the Italian Constitutional Court has been different, for it invalidated numerous legislative enactments, particularly those that predated the republic. The Court acted when Parliament had neither the will nor the ability to act. It risked the ire of an extralegal, but nonetheless substantial, power in the nation, that of the Catholic Church, to force conformity with mandates and guarantees in the constitution. The U.S. Supreme Court has used its power of judicial review far more liberally to nullify state laws that conflicted with the Constitution, and the Italian Constitutional Court has emulated that example in its treatment of the regional governments. The actions of both appear to give particular validity to the comment of Oliver Wendell Holmes (1920: 295) that the nation could survive without the power to invalidate congressional acts, but not without the power to nullify offending state statutes.

The highest tribunal in the United States has been wary of direct clashes with the president or even of sustained disagreements with Congress. A mere handful of cases have been decided that declared the illegitimacy of presidential actions, particularly when directed at a sitting president. The wisdom of this approach to arbitrating among the powers of government is imitated by the Italian Constitutional Court, which has enshrined a series of rules to guide it when considering policy questions decided by Parliament or when asked to define the lines of power among the organs of government. Both courts have chosen, probably wisely, to walk softly around issues that could evoke the wrath of more powerful branches of government. The American president and Congress are well-armed with weapons to retaliate against an overly aggressive court; the Italian constitution even permits abolition of the Constitutional Court through an amendment requiring only a two-thirds vote of each chamber of Parliament.

The parallels between the practice of judicial review in the United States and Italy are striking, but the circumstances in which they have occurred are in stark contrast. Those who drafted the U.S. Constitution inherited a tradition of representative government and were largely homogenous in their political, social, and economic outlooks. The Italian Constituent Assembly that was elected in 1946 represented the opposite. Italy was unified as a nation only in the late nineteenth century, and that unification was the result of diplomatic agreements and military conquests. Its resulting governing structure could not meet even the minimal requirements of a democracy and it was easily converted into a totalitarian state, with the acquiescence of the monarch and Parliament, under the leadership of Mussolini. Italy had no democratic tradition, nor did those who wrote the new constitution share the same assumptions about or visions of government and governing. Marxists, Leninists, liberals, conservatives, Catholics, and neofascists gathered to find a compromise scheme of government. Each had its own agenda and its own strategy to eventually achieve power. That agreement could be found for 139 articles that comprise the constitution is remarkable. What was founded was a guarantee, a compromise that least divides (DiPalma, 1987: 1).

Judicial review has evolved and developed in these two nations against wholly different backdrops. The United States has enjoyed a rather stable political life, interrupted only by the Civil War. Two parties have dominated the political scene and have peacefully alternated in power. The Italian Republic is governed by a perpetual coalition of political parties, always dominated in the postwar era by the Christian Democrats, the party of the relative majority. In a mere four decades, Italy has had more governments than the United States has had presidents.[28] The institution of judicial review, however, has persisted and has resisted encroachments upon the guarantees of the constitutions in both Italy and the United States.

Henry Abraham (1986: 291–292) proposes that a stable tradition of judicial review is most likely to exist in nations with regime stability, a competitive party system, horizontal power distribution, a strong tradition of judicial independence, and a high degree of political freedom. At the conclusion of the fascist era, when a republican constitution was written for Italy, virtually none of these attributes was present. The new constitution was designed to create and foster such ideals. Italy still is not generally regarded as having horizontal power distribution and, although the republican regime persists, governmental turnover is frequent. Judicial review, even with a beginning retarded by eight years of political posturing, has nevertheless achieved stability on the Italian peninsula. The Constitutional Court and the practice of controlling for constitutionality have survived, and even flourished. The Constitutional Court, like its counterpart in North America, has the potential to profoundly influence the nation's life. It has invited controversy from some quarters, but its influence has tended to be subtle; its very presence causes the other players on the political stage to pause and to measure the legitimacy of their intended actions against the constitution and the interpretations of the Constitutional Court. The Court has, in a brief period of only three decades, achieved legitimacy, "the power to command acceptance and support from the community so as to render force unnecessary" (Cox, 1976: 103), the most important quality that law can have.

Montesquieu proposed that laws, because they must harmonize with the general conditions of a nation, could not function outside the country for which they were intended. Henry Ehrmann (1976: 5) has concluded to the contrary that legal institutions have frequently migrated from one country to another, and the success of these grafts has been determined by the necessity of reform and the absence of any existing mechanism to handle a new situation. The successful transplantation of judicial review onto the Italian political culture was prompted by the perceived need for a constitution that could not be molded to the desires of one person, and there were no other existing institutions that could preserve the integrity of constitutional guarantees. The institution and the practice of judicial review in Italy are not a mirror image of those in the United States, but benefiting from experiences from the other shore of the Atlantic, the Italians may have improved upon the concept.

NOTES

1. Henry Ehrmann claims that "almost one-half of the nations of the world have by now officially adopted some form of judicial review" (Ehrmann, 1976: 139), while Henry Abraham suggests a more modest figure of "about sixty-five countries" (Abraham, 1986: 291).

2. For a sample of the debate, see Wechsler (1959: 1) and his references to the positions of others on the question. For a more current version of the controversy, see the special edition of *Judicature* 71 (August–September 1987), "Judicial Power and the Constitution."

3. On June 4, 1787, in the discussions of a Council of Revision, Mr. Gerry questioned whether the judiciary ought to form part of the proposed council, since "they will have a sufficient check ag[ain]st encroachments on their own department by their exposition of the laws, which involved a power of deciding on their constitutionality" (Farrand, 1966: I, 97). Mr. King, on that same day, opposed inclusion of the judiciary on the Council because "the Judges will have the expounding of those Laws when they come before them: and they will no doubt stop the operation of such as shall appear repugnant to the Constitution" (Farrand, 1966: I, 109).

Arguments supporting representatives of the judiciary on the Council of Revision also presumed a power of judicial review. For example, Mr. Wilson explained on July 21: "Laws may be unjust, may be unwise, may be dangerous, may be destructive; yet not be so unconstitutional as to justify the Judges in refusing to give them effect" (Farrand, 1966: II, 73). Similar reservations were echoed by Mr. Martin (Farrand, 1966: II, 76) and Col. Mason (Farrand, 1966: II, 78).

4. Mr. Mercer, on August 15, stated his disapproval for the doctrine that judges could nullify laws, for "laws ought to be well and cautiously made, and then to be uncontrollable." Mr. Dickenson concurred, saying that "no such power ought to exist . . . for the Justiciary of Aragon . . . became by degrees the lawgiver" (Farrand, 1966: II, 298–299).

5. Between 1789 and the writing of *Marbury*, courts in ten states exercised judicial review by declaring laws unconstitutional (Abraham, 1986: 322); three cases before the Supreme Court in advance of the 1803 decision in *Marbury* had also involved questions of the constitutionality of legislative enactments (Grossman and Wells, 1988: 105).

6. When the Constituent Assembly met for the first time on June 25, 1946, it delegated to a commission of 75 members the responsibility of writing a draft constitution. The 75 were to be named by the provisional head of state, but in proportion to the relative strength of the political parties. The Commission presented its draft to the Assembly at the end of January 1947 and discussions, lasting until mid-December, began. Many provisions passed, while others were repeatedly tabled and discussed at later times. The assembly approved the entire constitution on December 22, 1947, by a vote of 453 to 62; it was promulgated on December 27 and became effective on January 1, 1948.

7. The prior constitution (Statuto albertino) that had been granted to Piedmont in 1848, in advance of the unification of Italy, was flexible and allowed Italy to become fascist. A degree of rigidity had been introduced by Law 2693 of 1928, whereby the

Grand Fascist Council was given the authority to resolve all questions of a constitutional character (Martines, 1986: 225). This translation and all others from sources in Italian are mine.

8. Perhaps the best example of "reciprocal concessions" was the decision to include the Lateran Pacts, originally negotiated between the Catholic Church and Mussolini, in the constitution in Article 7. The Lateran Pacts provided for Catholicism as the national religion, for state stipends to be paid to the Holy See, and for religious (catholic) education in the public schools. The Communist Party supported inclusion of that provision.

9. The Constitutional Court is composed of 15 judges, one-third named by the president of the republic, one-third by Parliament in a joint sitting, and one-third by judges on the highest ordinary and administrative courts. Only judges sitting on or retired from the highest ordinary and administrative courts and full professors of law or lawyers who have practiced for a minimum of 20 years are eligible for positions on the Court. The constitution originally provided for 12-year, nonrenewable terms, but the limitation was changed to 9 years by Parliament *without* a referendum by Law No. 2, November 22, 1967.

10. The fear of Communism in Italy was fueled by the Communist coup in Czechoslovakia in February 1948 and the Berlin Blockade that autumn. In June 1948 PCI leader Togliatti failed to dissociate himself or the Italian Communist Party from Stalin's condemnation of the renegade Communist Premier Josip Broz Tito in Yugoslavia.

11. The Legge Truffa, so named by opponents, would have assigned to the party or parties that managed to win 50 percent of the vote to take 390 seats in the Chamber of Deputies, leaving only 200 seats to be divided among the parties of the minority. The scheme was offered by the ruling coalition of Christian Democrats, Social Democrats (PSDI), Liberals (PLI), and Republicans (PRI) in 1952–53. In the 1953 elections, however, the four partner parties won only 49.8 percent of the national vote; the law was defeated (Pallotta, 1985: 271–274).

12. No political party has won a majority of the popular vote in postwar Italy, and none since the first Parliament (1948–53) has managed an absolute majority of seats in either house of Parliament.

13. The jurisprudence of the Constitutional Court has indicated three criteria that it uses to determine if Parliament has exceeded its power: (1) if the motives of the law are absolutely illogical, incoherent, or arbitrary or if there are evident contradictions in the assumptions behind the law; (2) if the law is irrational in terms of the concrete results expected; and (3) if there is no congruity between the means prescribed and the ends intended (Martines, 1986: 546–547).

14. Luigi Sturzo was the foremost proponent of the two-thirds requirement because of his fear of naming one or more Communists, "with the troublesome eyes of Moscow," to the Court (Rodota, 1986: 20).

15. Einaudi's selections were Enrico de Nicola, the provisional Head of State until 1946; Tomaso Perassi, professor of international law and a member of the Constituent Assembly; Gaetano Azzariti, ex-president of the highest ordinary court; Giuseppe Capograssi, professor of philosophy of law; and Giuseppe Avolio, ex-president of the highest administrative court (Rodota, 1986: 22).

16. The law in question had already been challenged as contradictory to Article 21 by 18 *pretori*, 8 *tribunali*, and 3 courts of appeal (Rodota, 1986: 25).

17. The Rules of the Chamber of Deputies, in Article 108, and the Senate, in Article 139, each establish methods for reviewing decisions of the Constitutional Court. These

procedures were first used in response to the Court's invalidating the agricultural pacts of 1947 and 1961 as a violation of constitution Article 44 regarding limitations on private land ownership (Judgment No. 107 of 1974).

18. See, in particular, Judgments No. 9 of 1959, No. 78 of 1984, and No. 154 of 1985.

19. See, for example, Judgment No. 187 of 1981.

20. The best illustration is the decision of the Court (Judgment No. 225 of 1975) in which the national monopoly of radio and television was upheld. That position was reaffirmed in Judgments No. 202 of 1976 and No. 148 of 1981.

21. These two decisions seem almost incomprehensible when viewed in hindsight by a non-Italian. The Court's difficulty is clarified by a reading of Article 29 of the Italian constitution, which the Court viewed as embodying two conflicting norms, at least when applied to the issue of adultery: "Marriage is based on the moral and legal equality of husband and wife within the limits laid down by law for ensuring family unity." Preservation of family unity prevailed in the first case, whereas moral and legal equality was accorded primacy in the second.

22. The Lateran Pacts, in Article 34, had provided for state recognition of the civil effects of the sacrament of marriage, a phrase that the Church contended gave it authority over marriage, annulment, and divorce.

23. That decision was challenged a second time two years later, but the Court remained firm (Judgment No. 175 of 1973). The church attempted to abrogate the law by calling for a referendum, the first since the 1946 plebescite on the form of government. In the referendum, held in May 1974, a "no" vote was to uphold the divorce law, a position that won 59.1 percent of the vote (Pallotta, 1985: 392).

24. The Catholic forces were again mobilized for a referendum to repeal the law; the Radical Party proposed another referendum, one that would further liberalize abortion laws. The two referenda were held in 1981 and both lost (Pallotta, 1985: 393).

25. Regional governments were prescribed and their powers enumerated in Articles 114–127 of the constitution. However, only the special regions located on the periphery of the Italian nation, where there were strong separatist movements, were implemented in a timely fashion. The other regions were not allowed to hold elections until 1970, and a full transfer of power from the central government occurred incrementally thereafter. The extent to which full constitutional devolution has yet occurred is not clear.

26. The Eleventh, Fourteenth, and Sixteenth Amendments each directly overturned a decision by the U.S. Supreme Court.

27. The two-thirds majority reflects a degree of consensus not regularly seen in the Italian Parliament, since no party has won a majority of the seats in either house since 1953 and between 9 and 17 parties are normally represented in each chamber.

28. Italy's 49th postwar prime minister was sworn into office in July 1989.

REFERENCES

Abraham, H. J. (1986). *The judicial process*. New York: Oxford University Press.

Adamany, D. (1973). Legitimacy, realigning elections and the Supreme Court. *Wisconsin Law Review* 3: 790–846.

Calasso, F. (1985). *L'unita giuridica dell'Europa* (Juridicial unity in Europe). Manelli: Rubbettino Editore.

Cappelletti, M. and Golay, D. (1981). Judicial review, transnational and federal: Its impact on integration. Florence: EUI Working Paper No. 4, European University Institute.

Clark, M. (1984). *Modern Italy, 1871–1982*. London: Longman.

Corwin, E. S. (1978). *The Constitution and what it means today*. Princeton, N.J.: Princeton University Press.

Cox, A. (1976). *The role of the Supreme Court in American government*. New York: Oxford University Press.

Cuocolo, F. (1988). *Istituzione di diritto publico* (Institutions of public law). Milan: Giuffre Editore.

Dahl, R. A. (1967). *Pluralist democracy in the U.S.* New York: Rand McNally.

DiPalma, G. (1987). Tout se tient: Constitution-making and constitutional culture in Italy. Paper presented at the American Political Science Association Meeting, Chicago.

Ehrmann, H. W. (1976). *Comparative legal cultures*. Englewood Cliffs, N.J.: Prentice-Hall.

Falzone, V., Palermo, F., and Cosentino, F. (1976). *La Costituzione della Repubblica Italiana* (The constitution of the Italian Republic). Milan: Arnoldo Mondadori Editore.

Farrand, M. J. (1966). *The records of the federal convention of 1787*. New Haven, Conn.: Yale University Press.

Grossman, J. B., and Wells, R. S. (1988). *Constitutional law and judicial policy making*. New York: Longman.

Hamilton, A., Jay, J., and Madison, J. (1969) (orig. pub. 1788). *The federalist or the new constitution*. New York: Modern Library.

Holmes, O. W. (1920). Law and the court. In *Collected legal papers*. New York: Harcourt Brace.

Kogan, N. (1983). *A political history of Italy*. New York: Praeger.

LaPalombara, J. (1987). *Democracy Italian style*. New Haven, Conn.: Yale University Press.

Laurenzano, E. (1983). *Corte costituzionale e parlamento* (Constitutional Court and Parliament). Rome: Bulzoni Editori.

Liebesney, H. J. (1981). *Foreign legal systems: A comparative analysis*. Washington, D.C.: George Washington University.

Martines, T. (1986). *Diritto costituzionale* (Constitutional law). Milan: Giuffre Editore.

McCloskey, R. G. (1960). *The American supreme court*. Chicago: University of Chicago Press.

Nagel, S. (1973). Court-curbing periods in American history. In T. Becker and Feeley, M. (eds.), *The impact of Supreme Court decisions*. New York: Oxford University Press, pp. 9–21.

Negri, G. (1984). *Il quadro costituzionale: Tempi e istituti della liberta* (The fourth constitution: Times and institutes of liberty). Milan: Giuffre Editore.

O'Brien, D. (1985). The imperial judiciary: Of paper tigers and socio-legal indicators. *Journal of Law and Politics* 2: 1–16.

———. (1986). *Storm center: The supreme court in American politics*. New York: W. W. Norton.

Pallotta, G. (1985). *Dizionario della politica Italiana* (Dictionary of Italian politics). Rome: Newton Compton Editore.

Rodota, C. (1986). *La Corte Costituzionale: Come e chi garantisce il pieno della nostra costituzione* (The Constitutional Court: How and why it fully guarantees our constitution). Bari: Riuniti Editore.

Sorace, A., Battaglina, A. A., and Ruffilli, R. (1983). *Diritto pubblico* (Public law). Florence: Le Monnier.

Spotts, F., and Wieser, T. (1986). *Italy: A difficult democracy.* Cambridge: Cambridge University Press.

Volcansek, M. L., and Lafon, J. L. (1987). *Judicial selection: The cross-evolution of French and American practices.* Westport, Conn.: Greenwood Press.

Wechsler, H. (1959). Toward neutral principles of constitutional law. *Harvard Law Review* 73: 1–35.

8

Temerity and Timidity in the Exercise of Judicial Review in the Philippine Supreme Court

C. Neal Tate

One of the most perceptive students of the Philippine political process once described the Supreme Court of the Philippines as "the most important legitimizing institution in the Philippines" (Grossholtz, 1964: 27).[1] Throughout its history prior to Ferdinand Marcos' declaration of martial law in 1972, observers noted the role of the Court as a legitimizer of the national political system. Thus in 1921 the Wood-Forbes report, which was critical of the lower Philippine judiciary and of much of the rest of the national government machinery, found that "the Supreme Court has the respect and confidence of the Philippine people" (quoted in Worcester, 1930: 748). Some 20 years later, political scientist and former Vice-Governor General J. Ralston Hayden (1942: 239) wrote that Philippine legal institutions, especially the Supreme Court, were "one of the cohesive elements of the national state that is being developed in the Philippines." In the 1950s, former colonial Philippine Supreme Court Justice George Malcolm (1957: 134) noted that "since the inauguration of the Republic of the Philippines in 1946, the Court has retained the confidence of the people even while the President and Congress lost prestige."

Similar sentiments were expressed by Philippine writers in the late 1960s. A popular journalist (Makabenta, 1968: 18) wrote in an assessment of the Court:

We are a nation that has grown callous to the promises of legislation and ambitious budgets for national progress, grown skeptical of anyone who occupies a public office, but there remains somehow that curious faith in the high Court and its glorious power as a source of remedy for the problems of society and the citizen.

And two Jesuit sociologists echoed Grossholtz in noting that the Supreme Court has "become a special repository of the Filipino's faith in legitimacy and legality" (Araneta and Carroll, 1968: 57).

This emphasis upon the function of the Philippine Supreme Court as system legitimizer might give the impression that the power of the Court was largely symbolic. The Court might have been seen as an elite of deference, using Lasswell's (1958: 13) terminology, which in fact exercised little control over the types of public policy that emerged from the governmental process. But, prior to President Marcos' imposition of martial law in 1972, the Philippine Supreme Court regularly shaped important matters of public policy through its exercise of judicial review. Many of the Court's closest students stressed the varieties of public policy in which it was intimately involved.[2]

The temerity of the Court's judicial review of public policy during the Philippines' colonial, commonwealth, and independent democratic existence changed, during the 14-year authoritarian reign of Ferdinand Marcos from 1972 to 1986, into a timidity that greatly reduced the Court's ability to serve, not just as an important shaper of public policy, but also as the system legitimizer it had previously been, and which the Philippine political system continued to need so badly.

JUDICIAL REVIEW IN THE PRE-MARTIAL LAW SUPREME COURT

The Pre-Independence Period

The present Philippine Supreme Court has been in continuous existence since the organization of a civil government of the Philippine Islands under American colonial control in 1901. It is the successor of two other supreme courts of the Philippines: the Audencia Territorial de Manila, which operated during the Spanish colonial regime, and a temporary Supreme Court established during the American military occupation of the islands at the time of the Philippine Revolution (1898–1901).

The permanent Supreme Court organized by the civil colonial administration in June 1901 consisted of seven—later nine, then eleven—justices, including a chief justice. The civil administration established a policy of maintaining an American majority on the Court, with the chief justiceship allotted to a Filipino. This policy was continued throughout the period of American sovereignty, long after all the other institutions of colonial government, except for the governor-generalship, were thoroughly Filipinized.

The reasons supporting the maintenance of an American majority on the Court apparently remained persuasive to a wide variety of American colonial officials. The requirements of judicial independence demanded that no colonial administrative authority have control over the decisions of the Philippine Supreme Court. But the Court exercised full judicial review over the actions of lower court judges, the legislature, and colonial administrative officials, and could be overruled only by the U.S. Supreme Court, an authority that might be remote from the goals of the colonial administration. If an American-oriented exercise of judicial review were to be possible within the Philippines, it was essential to maintain an American majority on the Court.[3]

The policy of reserving the chief justiceship for a Filipino was probably not consciously decided upon when the Court was established. Apparently, the two decades of service of the first chief, Cayetano Arellano, institutionalized the practice of reserving the chief justiceship for a Filipino. In addition, the colonial authority, by retaining a Filipino as the Court's chief justice, dampened, to some extent, nationalist criticism of its unwillingness to change the American majority policy.

There has not yet been the rigorous research necessary to analyzing the overall exercise of judicial review by the Philippine Supreme Court during the colonial period—or later, for that matter. Thus in discussing its exercise of judicial review, I rely upon general descriptions of its work, some empirical work, and a litany of example cases designed to give the reader an impression of the significance of the Court's decision making. I begin by offering evidence assessing whether the maintenance of an American majority appears to have sustained a pattern of exercise of judicial review that pleased the Philippines' American imperial masters.

Despite the intentions of the colonial authorities, there is strong empirical evidence that the American majority was not successful in maintaining control of the Supreme Court's exercise of judicial review, at least in controversial cases. Tate's (1971: 232–234) analysis of bloc voting in nonunanimous cases during the colonial period showed that the Filipino minority remained consistently more cohesive than the American majority, making it relatively easy to pick up the single American vote they needed to control case outcomes when unanamity was absent. Nevertheless, in what was perhaps the most controversial exercise of judicial review by the Supreme Court in the colonial period, the Board of Control cases, the position of the colonial administration prevailed when the American majority remained cohesive, while the Filipinos experienced a defection from their normally unified bloc.

Republican Governor-General Leonard Wood, appointed by President Harding in 1920, objected to the way Philippine affairs had been conducted under his predecessor, Democrat Francis Burton Harrison. Under Governor-General Harrison, Filipino nationalist leaders had been given a greatly increased role in making executive decisions. During Harrison's administration the government had established a number of public corporations. Voting control over the government's stock in these corporations was vested by legislative act in a Board of Control, composed of the governor-general, the Filipino speaker of the House of Representatives, and the Filipino president of the Senate.

Wood did not approve of the idea of public corporations, nor of the concessions that had been made to Filipino control during Harrison's administration. Although he did not at first move to reclaim the "lost powers" of the governor-general, in 1926 Wood issued an executive order abolishing the Board of Control as an unconstitutional device and asserted his sole right to vote the stock of government corporations. The Filipino leaders appealed to the Supreme Court, but the Court upheld the governor-general and was sustained by the U.S. Supreme Court.[4] The vote in the Philippine Supreme Court was sharply divided, with the American majority and one Filipino justice supporting Wood, and three Filipino justices supporting the Filipino leaders.

The issue in the Board of Control cases clearly involved—and was perceived by the justices as involving—whether the Court should exercise judicial review in favor of the prerogatives of the American governor-general, or in support of the growing nationalist aspirations of the Filipino political leaders. To the American colonial authorities, the Board of Control decisions affirmed the wisdom of maintaining an American majority in the Supreme Court. Their devotion to preserving that majority remained firm until very near the end of American colonial control of Philippine domestic affairs and the establishment of the Philippine Commonwealth in 1935 (see Tate, 1971: 45–36 for further discussion). The last Americans to hold constitutional office in the government of the Philippines—five Supreme Court justices—resigned only at the inauguration of the Commonwealth in November 1935.

The position of the Philippine Supreme Court during the colonial period was analogous to that of a state supreme court lacking an intermediate court of appeal: It was the first appellate court for the system of trial courts, was supreme in applying Philippine laws and regulations, but could have its decisions reviewed by the U.S. Supreme Court. Board of Control cases notwithstanding, it is not surprising that the Philippine Supreme Court's decision making typically involved it in a broad range of disputes, many of which did not require the exercise of judicial review on matters of earth-shaking public policy significance.[5] Despite this, the Court acted vigorously to establish the independence and policy prerogatives of the judiciary, ruling, for example, that the administration could not transfer judges from one district to another without their consent nor establish a judicial lottery for the periodic reassignment of judges.[6] It passed this legacy to the new Commonwealth Court.

The new constitution of the Philippines adopted in 1935 provided, familiarly, for "one Supreme Court and . . . such inferior courts as may be established by law" (*Constitution of the Philippines* 1935, Article VIII, Secs. 1, 4). Soon after the inauguration of the commonwealth, the Philippine Congress did provide for one inferior Court of Appeals intermediate between the courts of first instance and the Supreme Court. At the same time it provided, as it was constitutionally allowed to do, for a reduction in size of the Supreme Court from eleven to seven members.[7]

According to one authority, the reduction in the size of the Supreme Court was a result of the "onslaught" of a determined President Manuel Quezon (Wurfel, 1964: 738), who did not wish to see the Supreme Court become a burden on his vigorous exercise of presidential authority.[8] As the court began to deal with the constitutional issues that inevitably emerged from the Commonwealth's new governing document, it seemed to share Quezon's concern for the preservation and expansion of presidential powers. While asserting its right to continue to exercise judicial review over executive actions, it ruled that the separation of powers of the Philippine Constitution should be regarded as relative, establishing a system of interdependent authority that was not meant to hamstring a strong and activist executive (see *Vilena v. Secretary of Interior* 67 *Phil [Philippine Reports]* 451 [1939] and *Planas v. Gil* 67 *Phil* 62 [1939]).

The role of the Supreme Court changed dramatically with the Japanese occupation of the Philippines in December 1941. The Supreme Court was maintained as a separate political institution, though reduced in size to five justices and plagued by a rotating membership. It was not prominent during the occupation. It had little latitude for vigorous action. The Japanese favored, even more strongly than Manuel Quezon, a government with a powerful executive untrammeled by the other political institutions, and, in fact, formally deprived the Supreme Court of its power of judicial review in the constitution of the Japanese-sponsored Republic of the Philippines in 1943.

Despite its low profile during the war, the Supreme Court was able to maintain much of its reputation for independence and its legitimizing role. The postwar Supreme Court declared its general confidence in the Occupation Court by holding that its decisions were valid, so long as they did not partake of a "political character" (Tingson, 1955: 347). In addition, the prestige of the institution for the postwar period, though not of the Occupation Court itself, was greatly enhanced by the fact that its Chief Justice, José Abad Santos, appointed by Quezon before he fled the Philippines for exile, became a wartime martyr-hero when he was captured and executed by the Japanese for refusing to collaborate (see Aquino, 1967).

The Postwar Supreme Court, 1945–72

Acting under emergency powers granted the president in 1941, President Sergio Osmeña, who had succeeded Manuel Quezon on his death-in-exile, altered the structure of the judicial system at the end of the war. He abolished the Court of Appeals and expanded the size of the Supreme Court to eleven justices. Filling these eleven seats confronted Osmeña immediately with the controversy over collaboration with the Japanese that was to plague postwar Philippine politics. Osmeña named to the reorganized Court the three justices who had served on the Occupation Court, but had been first appointed by Quezon, and an uneasy mixture of anticollaborationists and his long-time political supporters.

Although Osmeña had the rare opportunity of naming all the sitting justices of the Supreme Court, he had little time to reap any possible benefits of the situation. In April 1946 he was defeated for president of the republic by Manuel Roxas, a powerful prewar politician, who had been associated with the occupation government but was personally cleared of any real collaboration by his friend

General Douglas MacArthur. Though Roxas won the election, the dispute over the issue of collaboration with the Japanese was not laid to rest. The Supreme Court was to play a major role in this controversy in the next year and a half, before Roxas finally ended it with a proclamation of amnesty in January 1948.

The Supreme Court exercised review over the decisions of an emergency People's Court, established in 1945 to handle treason trials arising out of collaboration activities. In reviewing the People's Court decision, the Supreme Court refused to accept the claims of the collaborators that what they had done was no crime. But, using very restrictive doctrines regarding admissability of evidence, it also did not sustain the conviction of any prominent collaborator before Roxas' amnesty made the whole question moot.

One possible interpretation of the Court's role in these treason trials is given by Steinberg (1967: 151): "Five of the eleven members of the Supreme Court ... had held some position during the war. The Supreme Court was a bastion of oligarchy, closely related literally and figuratively to the elite under indictment. To have expected these men to convict their *compadres* was to expect the impossible." Whether or not one accepts Steinberg's judgment, it is clear that the Court's review of the collaboration cases prior to Roxas' amnesty (for detail see Steinberg, pp. 151–163) sustained the rule of the country's incumbent sociopolitical elite, with significant effects for postwar Philippine politics.

The collaboration issue was only one of a series of issues that sharply divided the Supreme Court in the immediate postwar years. "Parity" was another. In the early postwar period, a bitter dispute raged among Philippine politicians as to whether the nation should approve the Parity Amendment to the Philippine constitution. The Parity Amendment provided that, notwithstanding other provisions of the constitution, citizens of the United States or businesses owned by them should have access to the exploitation and development of all public lands, natural resources, and public utilities under the same conditions as Philippine citizens (1935 *Constitution of the Philippines*, "Ordinance Appended to the Constitution"). The provisions to which the "notwithstanding" clause referred had specifically restricted these rights to Filipinos or corporations in which Filipinos owned at least 60 percent of the capital (1935 *Constitution*, Art. 13, Sec. 1). The United States pressed hard for approval, threatening to withhold vital economic aid and trade concessions if it were not forthcoming.

A number of antiparity senators and representatives were elected to the Philippine Congress in 1946, but they were excluded from sitting and voting on the amendment by the proparity legislators. The excluded congressmen appealed to the newly organized Supreme Court to affirm their right to sit and vote on the amendment. But the Court refused, by a vote of eight to three, to grant their petition (*Mabanang v. Lopez Vito* 78 *Phil* 1 [1947]). Five of the eight justices who voted with the majority held that the Court had no jurisdiction over such a "political question." But the real reason for the decision seems to be that the majority justices feared the economic consequences of letting parity be defeated. In any case, there can be little doubt that the *Mabanang* decision "helped facilitate [the Philippines] becoming economically dependent on the United States'' (Concepcion, 1955: 948), and provided structure to one of the most bitterly debated issues of postwar Philippine politics.

The collaboration and parity controversies did not give the Supreme Court the option of making a decision that would have avoided confronting all the important political forces involved in the disputes. But in both the Supreme Court had exercised judicial review in a manner that avoided a direct confrontation with the presumed wishes of the incumbent president. If this, combined with the colonial and commonwealth experience, indicates some timidity in exercising judicial review where the interests of the chief executive are affected, that timidity did not survive the Court's involvement in the next major postwar governmental policy disputes that followed on the death of President Roxas in 1948.

The first task to which Roxas' vice-president and successor, Elpidio Quirino, addressed himself was the serious agrarian problem posed by the Hukbalahap.[9] Declaring an all-out campaign to eradicate the rebels, Quirino attempted to rule, despite an uncooperative Congress, by using the emergency powers that had been granted to Quezon on the eve of the Japanese occupation. Quirino's action was challenged, and once again the Supreme Court was called upon to decide a thorny political dispute between groups of national governmental leaders. It responded by voiding Quirino's use of the executive powers (*E. Rodrigues, Sr., et al. v. Gella, et al.*, 92 *Phil* 603 [1953]).

The unpopular Quirino was defeated in 1953 by Ramon Magsaysay, whose massive victory established him as the most powerful Philippine politician since Quezon. Magsaysay's administration, too, soon became embroiled in a direct confrontation with the Supreme Court. This occurred when the Supreme Court reviewed the convictions obtained by the solicitor-general of leading Huks for the ''complex crime'' of rebellion with robbery, murder, arson, which would have been punishable by death. The Supreme Court ruled that there was no such complex crime; that if the multiple crimes were all committed in furtherance of the purpose of the rebellion, they were punishable only under the lenient provisions of the criminal code governing the latter. Though the Magsaysay administration vigorously attacked the Court's position, it was unable to change it and, instead, had to change its policies for combatting the rebellion.

Other of the Magsaysay administration's programs were more cordially treated by the Court. For example, the Court held constitutional a land reform law desired by the administration (*Primero v. Court of Agrarian Relations* 101 *Phil* No. L–10594 [1957]; see also Goco, 1968: 17), and a law providing for the Filipinization of the retail trade at all levels of the economy (*Inchong v. Hernandez*, 101 *Phil* 1155 [1957]; see also Agaplo, 1963). The Court also looked with reasonable favor upon the administration's attempt to create an atmosphere conducive to the growth of an active labor movement (Wurfel, 1964: 703).

In 1957, President Magsaysay was killed in a plane crash in the mountains in Cebu, and was succeeded by Vice-President Carlos Garcia. Relations between Garcia and the Supreme Court were relatively calm, but the same cannot be said for his successor, Diosdado Macapagal. Macapagal became embroiled in a full-fledged controversy over the Court's treatment of the actions of his "New Era" officials. From late 1962 through 1964, the Supreme Court rebuffed the Macapagal administration in some 12 key cases. Administration officials charged the Court with being hostile to progress. Secretary of Justice Juan Liwag dared to suggest the humanity of the justices (quoted in R. Locsin, 1964: 4; also see Liwag, 1963: 227–234):

But let us not look at the Supreme Court as if it were a paragon of perfection or that it is a body composed of supermen incapable of committing errors. Let us not worship the Supreme Court as gods with supernatural powers or better still as sacred cows who are beyond the reach of human touch and beyond reproach. Rather let us look at our Supreme Court as a body of men with feelings, affected by prejudices, possessed of caprices and susceptible to other frailties of human nature, whose imperfections are often reflected, wittingly or unwittingly, in their judicial pronouncements.

The president himself reacted strongly to a concurring opinion (*Garcia v. Executive Secretary*, 6 *SCRA* [*Supreme Court Reports Annotated*] 1 [1962]), which suggested that he had prejudged the culpability of a Garcia appointee whom Macapagal sought to remove on the grounds that he had illegally participated in "electioneering" on behalf of President Garcia in 1961.[10]

Macapagal openly interpreted his controversy with the Philippine Supreme Court as analogous to that of President Franklin Roosevelt with the U.S. Supreme Court. He urged the Supreme Court to keep above the "political and emotional stresses" accompanying the people's mandate for reform (Macapagal, 1968: 473). If the outlines of the controversy were indeed analogous to that between Roosevelt and his Supreme Court, so was the public reaction. Macapagal was almost universally denounced by the legal profession and the press for his attack on the Court, even though the president firmly announced his intention to "blindly respect the decisions of the Supreme Court" (*Philippines Free Press*, 1962: 8). The Supreme Court was defended as an "eloquent reminder of the rule of law in this country" (Macaraeg, 1963: 36), and its justices upheld as "men of the year 1963" by the influential *Philippines Free Press* (T. Locsin, 1964: 8).

The reaction of the Supreme Court to the controversy with Macapagal was quite different from that of the U.S. Supreme Court to Franklin Roosevelt's "court packing" plan, however. There could be no "switch in time that saved nine," for most of the decisions that had gone against the president were unanimous: even Macapagal's two initial appointees failed to support his position. The Court took no public notice of the controversy. Backed by overwhelming public and professional support, it went calmly about its business.

It seems likely that Macapagal's defeat by Ferdinand Marcos in 1965 was in part due to the controversy generated by his confrontation with the Supreme Court. Certainly it appeared at least during the first Marcos term that the Court's temerity in the exercise of judicial review had, if anything, enhanced its political power, popularity, and ability to legitimize the Philippine regime. The president was able to avoid the kind of direct confrontation with the Supreme Court that had characterized the regimes of most of his predecessors. Nevertheless, the Supreme Court continued to exercise judicial review of the actions of government agencies in impressive ways. One example of this exercise came when the Supreme Court moved to speed up the electoral process and startled the legal community by announcing that it would throw out electoral challenges that were contrary to "statistical probability" (*Lagumbay v. Commission on Elections*, 16 *SCRA* 175 [1966]) to avoid the time-consuming examination of individual ballots that often led to an office's term expiring before the courts could resolve the dispute over who should hold it. Another occurred when the Court refused, apparently contrary to the wishes of the Marcos administration, to allow the extension of the parity-guaranteed rights of American citizens to buy Philippine lands (*Philippines v. Quasha* 46 *SCRA* 160 [1972]; see also del Carmen, 1973: 1051–1052).

While Marcos' first term passed and his second term began relatively calmly, from the perspective of his relations with the Court, changing patterns of Supreme Court recruitment (see Tate, 1971: 75–161) led to his appointing a majority of the Court before the end of his first term, and to the Court being dominated by his appointees by the middle of his second. In addition, the Philippines convened, during Marcos' second term, a constitutional convention to draft a replacement for the American-influenced 1935 constitution. Finally, the level of domestic unrest in the Philippines increased in the late 1960s and early 1970s, as it did in many nations around the world. These events combined to produce a changed role for the Supreme Court under the martial law regime Marcos proclaimed in late 1972.

THE SUPREME COURT UNDER MARTIAL LAW

In discussing the Philippine Supreme Court's exercise of judicial review under Ferdinand Marcos' martial law regime, it will be useful to focus on human rights issues, since these were by any standard the most controversial issues the Court faced during that time. The story actually begins a year before the president's martial law declaration, with the Court's review of his suspension of the writ of *habeas corpus* in response to a bombing at an opposition party rally in Manila. In that case (*Lansang v. Garcia* 42 *SCRA* 448 [1971]), the Supreme Court's majority upheld the president's suspension of the writ and, probably unwittingly, provided the initial tool later used by President Marcos to justify martial law. The Court asserted its right to rule on the evidence supporting the president's judgment of the necessity of suspensions of civil rights, holding, contrary to the Marcos administration's contention, that it could inquire into the factual basis of the suspension—that such a question was justiciable. But the justices also agreed (unanimously) that the president's judgments of the facts could not be found unsatisfactory in the instant case: that they were not in a position to second guess his conclusion that a "state of rebellion" existed in the country.

From one perspective, the Court was taking a strong stand in support of its judicial review powers and its ability to protect human rights, for, in 1952, it had ruled that the president's more limited suspension of the privilege of the same writ was not justiciable (*Montenegro v. Castañeda*, 91 *Phil* 882), that it was a "political" question. A similar doctrine was also followed in a 1905 case raising the same question (*Barcelona v. Baker*, 5 *Phil* 87). Nevertheless, by not disagreeing with the president's judgment, *Lansang* laid the foundation for the declaration of martial law and all its consequences.

The truly crucial test of the Court's ability to exercise judicial review meaningfully under martial law, however, was the "ratification cases" (*Javellana v. Executive Secretary*, 50 *SCRA* 30, [1973]). The *Javellana* decision negatively legitimized the 1973 constitution, with its transitory provisions providing President Marcos with essentially absolute power for as long as he wished to have it.[11] In these cases, a sharply divided court was unable to rule against Marcos' declaration that the 1973 constitution was "in effect." Contrary to the Court's usual practice, there was no majority opinion in these cases. Instead, the Court's decision was summarized in an opinion authored by, but dissented from, by Chief Justice Roberto Concepcion, a Magsaysay appointee. This summary opinion reported the voting of the justices on the numerous questions considered by the Court in the decision. It ruled that

1. the validity of the new constitution was justiciable and that it had not been validly ratified (by a majority of six to four justices);

2. it could not authoritatively rule, for lack of a requisite majority, whether the Filipino people had acquiesced in the new constitution (four justices voted that the people had acquiesced, three ruled that they had not; the remaining three ruled that this question was beyond their ability to determine with "judicial certainty");

3. the petitioners challenging the new constitution were not entitled to an injunction against the executive (by a vote of six to four), because

4. it could not declare the new constitution *not* in force for lack of a requisite majority of six votes. Two justices voted to declare it not in effect, four declared it in effect, while the other four again lacked the judicial certainty to vote against the constitution's effectiveness.

As apparently originally written by the Chief Justice, the ruling in the ratification cases was entirely negative. But, because of fears that such a decision would be unduly divisive, a majority of the Court apparently agreed to add the phrase that became the primary justification for the new constitution and President Marcos' extended authoritarian rule: "This being the vote of the majority, there is no further obstacle to the new Constitution being considered in force and effect."[12]

Whatever its origins, the "in force and effect" phrase meant that, in future challenges to Marcos' one-man rule, there was very little legal ground on which the challengers could stand, and little basis for judicial review of the actions of the president. If the 1973 constitution was in effect, together with its transitory provisions, the president was virtually unchallengeable unless the Supreme Court was unwilling to reverse the ratification cases ruling. It never was willing to do so during Marcos' rule. Thus, while plaintiffs continued to seek their rights in the Supreme Court,[13] they met with virtually no success.

The Court relied on the ratification cases precedent and the political question doctrine to justify its refusal to grant human rights petitions or significantly challenge Marcos in other ways. As time went on, the president made it increasingly less likely that he would be challenged by the Supreme Court, using his untrammeled appointment power to name to the Court justices, who, while technically well-qualified for the higher judiciary, were very close to him personally, in their political beliefs, or both. By the late 1970s, such appointees dominated the court. Their perceptions of the political situation were quite similar to those of the president, and their personal gratitude and ties to him worked to insure decisions that were sympathetic to him and his government.

The political question doctrine was the tool most used to avoid the use of judicial review in challenges on any issue that was important to the president. By 1983 the composition of the Court was so favorable to the president that even the justiciability of the factual basis of the president's suspension of *habeas corpus*, established in the *Lansang v. Garcia* case, was revoked by a majority of the Court in the case of 14 detainees (*Garcia-Padilla v. Ponce Enrile*, 121 *SCRA* 472 [1983]). The Court had openly defaulted on its ability to consider allegations of human rights failures of the regime or to challenge the president in any other significant way. Timidity in the exercise of judicial review was the rule of the day.

The 1983 assassination on his return from exile of Benigno Aquino, Marcos' most prominent political opponent, may have made some difference in the Court's willingness to use judicial review to challenge the administration, at least in a few cases. But by and large, efforts to challenge Marcos and to restore democratic rights in the Philippines, galvanized by the Aquino assassination, now took the form of renewed media activity and mass protests. Claims of violations of rights still came to the Supreme Court. But dominated by a strong pro-Marcos majority, the Court consistently denied their validity. In the two and one-half years from Aquino's assassination until the success of the "People Power Revolution" that removed Marcos, the practical, and sometimes dangerous, exercise of the guaranteed rights of freedom of speech, press, and assembly found expression in the growth of opposition newspapers, the increasing outspokenness of the media controlled by the Catholic Church, and the growing mass demonstrations organized by previously quiescent members of the middle class and economic elite. They found little support in the Supreme Court.

THE SUPREME COURT FROM THE PEOPLE POWER REVOLUTION TO THE PRESENT

The "constitutional authoritarianism" of Ferdinand Marcos was brought to an end in February 1986 by a combination military mutiny and popular revolt. Thrust into power by virtue of her leadership of the organized opposition forces and her assumed victory in the election that Marcos had unwisely called was Corazon Aquino, widow of the slain senator, now a martyr sacred to the opposition's cause.

The Supreme Court in the Aftermath of Revolution

Aquino indicated her hostility to the incumbent Supreme Court in her initial proclamation. That document announced her expectation that she would immediately receive "courtesy resignations" from all members of the government, "beginning with" the members of the Supreme Court. Aquino pledged to remake the Supreme Court and reorganize the judiciary. She began that remaking by reappointing to the Supreme Court two justices who had been Marcos' only vocal opposition on the Court in the latter years of his rule. She continued by naming to the new Supreme Court four men who were well-known supporters of the Aquino coalition with reputations for resisting the Marcos regime. Only then did she reappoint to the Court with reduced and altered seniority three other justices of the Marcos Court who had not spoken out strongly against Marcos' rule, but were viewed as "not too close" to the dictator. Finally, she completed the Court with a combination of her supporters, anti-Marcos human rights activists, and career judges. Pointedly, Aquino did not reappoint seven eligible members of the pre-Revolution Supreme Court who were viewed as too close to Marcos.

The consequences of Aquino's remaking of the Supreme Court are interesting to consider. The remaking was probably necessary to the regime's goals and in order to break the grip of the Marcos dictatorship. It apparently restored the Supreme Court to the confidence of the administration and the population. As evidence, one might cite the editorial judgment of a Manila newspaper (*Philippine Star*, October 1, 1987):

The Supreme Court recently won top marks from respondents of a survey conducted by the Makati[14] Businessmen's Club as the most trustworthy government institution. That was an impressive turnaround, in the span of less than two years. Shortly before the February Revolution, the high tribunal's reputation had reached quite a low. . . . The Marcos revamp of the judiciary helped institutionalize deficiencies until popular perception reached the conclusion that justice was no longer attainable. . . . The Supreme Court . . . [has regained] the faith of the people. . . . Congress is still at the testing stage. The executive is being buffeted. But so long as the judiciary remains firm, the people could always be convinced that peace through lawful means is the preferential option.

The new constitution and the Aquino regime's practice have enhanced the Court's powers of judicial review and autonomy even more than before martial law. Provisions of the 1986–87 constitution provide for an extraordinary strengthening of the formal independence and power of the judiciary. The constitution grants to the judiciary, and specifically to the Supreme Court, the power to determine actual controversies involving "grave abuse of discretion" from any agency of government. There are no questions involving the actions of government agents that are outside the Court's purview; the Court now has no grounds to defer or avoid "political cases" involving other branches of government.

The judiciary is also granted fiscal autonomy; Congress may not reduce the Court's budget, and that budget must be immediately made available to the courts. The constitution sets up the Judicial and Bar Council to control appointments to the judiciary; even Supreme Court appointments must be made by the president from a list of three nominations submitted by the Judicial and Bar Council.

The Supreme Court is also given greater ability to control its workload: it is authorized to sit in up to five divisions of three justices each to process cases.[15] The Supreme Court is also granted the presiding officers of the House and Senate Electoral Tribunals, and serves as *the* Presidential Election Tribunal.

The Supreme Court has been given the constitutional power to review the factual basis of any martial law declaration, has been guaranteed freedom from administrative functions outside the work of the judiciary, and has been granted the power of appointment of all officials and employees of the judiciary. It has been guaranteed that it can control increases in its jurisdiction: there can be no increase in its jurisdiction without its agreement. The independence of judges is further guaranteed by the provision that no judge can be transferred permanently to another assignment without his or her agreement. Finally, the Supreme Court is once again granted disciplinary/supervisory powers over the judiciary.

This strengthening of the independence and policy-making power of the judiciary makes the Philippine Supreme Court perhaps the most powerful court in the world, at least from a formal legal standpoint.

Certainly this is not what might have happened. Aquino and her supporters might have been presumed to have little reason to have confidence in the ability of a supreme court to protect a population from deprivation of its essential rights or any inclination to strengthen its judicial review powers. I asked Philippine Supreme Court justices and other politically knowledgeable Filipinos why the regime chose to put so much faith and potential power in a reformed Supreme Court. They usually indicated that Aquino, her advisers, and the convention that drafted the 1986–87 constitution must have felt there was nothing wrong with the legal statements and judicial guarantees that had always been a part of Philippine tradition. The problem, they felt, was not the general willingness and ability of the judiciary to exercise judicial review in appropriate ways with vigor. The problem arose from the ambition and corruption of one man and his cronies. While they recognized that a new dictator might again arise and challenge the system they had so carefully reconstructed, they could not imagine any viable alternative to trying to strengthen the same system that had failed them under Marcos.

The remaking of the judiciary, though necessary from the Aquino regime's perspective, inevitably raises questions about the Court's independence of the regime and its ability to criticize or challenge it forthrightly. Few imply that the Aquino administration tries to dictate to the Supreme Court, as the Marcos administration allegedly did; the evidence is all to the contrary. But it may be difficult for these judges, some victims of human rights offenses under Marcos, to see the regime that restored their authority as being capable of abusing its own.

This does not mean that the new Supreme Court has not had occasions to exercise judicial review on matters of importance to the regime and to the population as a whole. The first annual report of the chief justice of the new Supreme Court enumerated a substantial list of decisions that did so (see Teehankee, 1987: 6–19). Specifically, in its first months, the Supreme Court

1. ruled that the new regime headed by Corazon Aquino and Salvador Laurel was the *de jure* government as a result of the nonjusticiable acceptance of the people of the Philippines, the exercise of control over the national territory by that government, and the acceptance of the government by the international community (*Lawyer's League for a Better Philippines et al., v. President Aquino* G.R.[16] 73748 [May 22, 1986]; *Re: Petition of Saturnino Bermudez for Declaratory Relief*, G.R. 76180 [October 24, 1986]);[17]

2. validated the removal of incumbent elected local government officials by the Aquino regime's minister of local governments (*Topacio, Jr. v. Pimental*, G.R. 73770 [April 10, 1986]; *Unido Ilocos Sur Chapter v. Pimentel*, G.R. 75963, [October 2, 1986]);

3. upheld the sequestration of the "ill gotten" assets of alleged Marcos cronies by the Presidential Commission on Good Government (*Tourist Duty-Free Shops, Inc. v. Presidential Commission on Good Government et al.*, G.R. 74392 [May 27, 1986]; *Baseco v. Presidential Commission on Good Government*, G.R. 75885 [October 28, 1986]);

4. went out of its way to remind the police and military of the necessities of due process in arrest and detention of suspected persons, even though the detainees in question already had been released by the Aquino government (*Tiotuico v. Brig. Gen. Ramontano et al.*, G.R. 76447 [November 20, 1986]);

5. reestablished formal civilian supremacy over the military, ordering transfer of a trial of civilians for the ordinary crime of murder from a military tribunal to a civil trial court (*Animas v. Minister of National Defense*, 146 *SCRA* 406 [December 19, 1986]);

6. formally abandoned and rejected a Marcos-era decision (*Benigno S. Aquino, Jr. v. Military Commission No. 2*, 63 *SCRA* 546) accepting the jurisdiction of military courts over ordinary civilian offenses (*Olaguer v. Military Commission No. 34*, 150 *SCRA* 144 [May 22, 1987]);

7. outlawed secret laws and decrees, which had been used by the Marcos regime (*Tañada v. Tuvera*, 146 *SCRA* 446 [December 29, 1986]);

8. corrected a "travesty of justice" in the Aquino murder case by reinstating the defendants on grounds the people did not receive due process (*Galman et al. v. Sandigabayan*, 144 *SCRA* 43 [September 12, 1986]). (Some argued that this decision represented a debatable blow at the right of defendants to avoid double jeopardy even while it protected those victimized by the dictator.)

This represented a strong assertion by the reformulated Supreme Court of its right to review the most significant legal policy questions facing the new government. But it was not one that brought the court into conflict with the new president or her supporters. Most Filipinos strongly supported the regime and would likely have agreed with the Court's decisions in these disputes. These cases did not test the ability of the Court to use its judicial review powers to challenge actions of the incumbent regime.

The most significant decision in which the Court did rule against the putative interests of the Aquino government in 1986–87 involved a dispute over who should be awarded the 24th and last seat in the new Philippine Senate.[18] The contestants were Augusto Sanchez, Aquino's sometime minister of labor, and Juan Ponce Enrile, Marcos' former longtime minister of defense and comaker of the military mutiny that, as a part of the People Power Revolution, brought Aquino to office. Enrile was named minister of defense, in Aquino's post-Revolution cabinet. But before the end of 1986, he had split with Aquino, been implicated in an abortive coup d'état, removed from his cabinet post, and taken up the mantle of leader of the opposition.

Enrile's three-month row with the Commission on Elections was resolved by the Supreme Court in his favor on August 12, 1986 (*Sanchez v. Commission on Elections*, 153 *SCRA* 67). The significance of the decision for the Supreme Court was not lost on Philippine journalists ((*Philippines Dispatch*, 1987: 11):

The other winner in the August 12 decision was the High Tribunal itself. Critics had wanted to gift Chief Justice Claudio Teehankee with a presidential umbrella, a symbol of the SC's seeming subservience to Malacanang.[19]

Senator Enrile himself expressed the sentiment of many: "Now I can say the Supreme Court is the real bulwark of justice and liberty in our country and that, for as long as that court remains faithful to its mission as the court of last resort, I have no doubt this country will survive."

But, What Have You Done for Us Lately: The Supreme Court and the Aquino Regime after 1987

The second anniversary of the reformulation of the Supreme Court after the February 1986 Revolution had barely passed when the Court's reputation and prestige came under attack as a result of a convoluted dispute with the Aquino government's chief antigraft prosecutor (Tanodbayan), Raul Gonzalez. Gonzalez had sought to interview four Supreme Court employees about Audit Commission charges of improper expenditures under former Chief Justice Fernando (of umbrella fame). Incumbent Chief Justice Pedro Yap refused to allow the employees to be summoned, "declaring that the court's justices could only be investigated if impeached" (*Asiaweek*, 1988: 17).

One week later the Court further infuriated Gonzalez by ruling, in a controversial constitutional interpretation, that he must cease investigating and filing complaints with the antigraft court (the Sandiganbayan) unless ordered to do so by the ombudsman established by the 1987 constitution, but not yet appointed. In effect, the Court stripped Gonzalez of all his authority. In reaction, Gonzalez not only denounced the decision to the press, but accused several Supreme Court justices of trying to pressure him by writing notes on behalf of friends and constituents. In a special session of the Court, the accused justices admitted they had written the notes to which Gonzalez referred, but denied attempting to pressure him. At the same time, the Court issued a statement deploring "the making of irresponsible charges by publicity seekers which baselessly excite public suspicion of the tribunal and impair and degrade the administration of justice" (*Manila Chronicle*, April 30, 1988: 3).

The significance of the controversy was not lost on the influential *Manila Chronicle*. While editorially urging "A word to the justices: Never write notes," the *Chronicle* also opined (May 2, 1988: 4):

A controversy involving the propriety of the justices' behavior is the last thing that should happen to the High Court, given that among the major state institutions, it enjoys relatively higher public esteem than its political counterparts, the Executive and the Congress. At this time, when political institutions are unstable, we need a Supreme Court that is beyond reproach.

Several days later, the Court moved to discipline Gonzalez, ordering him to show cause why he should not be held in contempt for airing his charges in public. To round out the quarrel, the Anti-Graft League of the Philippines and opposition leaders in the House of Representatives filed impeachment proceedings against the Supreme Court justices. Some time later, Chief Justice Yap denounced the impeachment charges in a speech to a Philippine Bar Association testimonial luncheon for the Supreme Court justices:

Never in the history of our country has the Supreme Court as a court been sought to be dragged into the mud with wild and malicious charges in an unreasoning orgy of wrath and denigration. . . . By seeking to destroy the highest tribunal in the land, they seek to destabilize the government as much as the extremists of the Right and of the Left (*Journal* [Manila] June 25, 1988: 1; see also *Malaya*, June 25, 1988: 3).

The controversy resulted from the Supreme Court's defense of its autonomous position under the separation of powers, and its interpretation of the powers of the ombudsman and Tanodbayan granted in the 1987 constitution. It involved the Supreme Court in direct conflict with an Aquino administration appointee charged with a task of presumed importance to the government, cleaning up graft and corruption. But id did not bring the Court into direct conflict with the president. She and her closest advisers took a hands-off approach "to avoid misinterpretation that she is violating the independence of the judiciary" (*Manila Chronicle*, April 30, 1988: 3), and declared the problem to be Gonzalez' but not theirs. The controversy eventually wound down, the Supreme Court justices were not impeached, and the Court's assertion of its judicial review powers against an executive official backed by an unsupportive president was successful. However, there is little doubt that, as the chief justice and the *Manila Chronicle* feared, the Court's reputation and prestige suffered.

One year later, the Supreme Court was involved in a dispute that did directly involve the preferences of President Aquino: the effort by Ferdinand Marcos and his wife and supporters to reverse Aquino's ban on his return to the Philippines. In May 1989 Marcos' lawyers asked the Supreme Court to overturn the ban as an infringement on his constitutionally guaranteed right to travel (*Manila Chronicle*, May 14, 1989: 4), and to allow him and his wife to return to defend themselves against a series of graft charges and civil suits aimed at recovering billions of dollars they allegedly stole while in office. Two months later the Supreme Court rejected Marcos' petition by a vote of 8–7. The Court rejected the contention of Aquino's Solicitor General that the question was political and beyond their jurisdiction, noting the constitutional language specifically authorizing the Court to hear such questions. But the majority argued that while the right to travel was protected by the constitution, the right to return home was not, and President Aquino's ban on Marcos' return was not a grave abuse of her discretion exercised in protection of national security: circumstances in the country justified the president's conclusion that allowing Marcos to return home would be a threat to the nation's stability.

The irony of the Court's decision in the Marcos return case was not lost on even friendly observers, including the seven dissenters. Even before the hearing, constitutional lawyer Father Joaquin Bernas—an Aquino confidant, constitutional convention delegate, president of the prestigious Ateneo de Manila University, and a regular newspaper columnist—noted the irony that the solicitor general's argument for faith in the president's judgment was "the main argument that won for Marcos victory in the defense of his exercise of executive powers" (Bernas, 1989a: 4). Afterwards, Bernas lamented that the majority's decision had performed "emasculatory surgery on the Bill of Rights" and, more, had expanded "the powers of the Presidency at the expense of the Court" (Bernas, 1989c: 4; see also Bernas, 1989b: 4 and 1989d: 4–5).

Bernas argued forcefully that the constitution contained language that would have allowed the Court's majority to reach the result of not allowing Marcos to return, while defending, not limiting, its own authority, and not expanding the implied powers of the president in a way that could be useful to future dictators (Bernas, 1989d: 4–5). Marcos' death in September 1989 led to a motion asking the Supreme Court to reconsider the question and allow the deceased's body to be returned to the country. But the Court rejected the motion and, by implication, the solution to their dilemma offered by Bernas, by the same 8–7 vote recorded on the original petition (Castro, 1989: 1, 3).

The Court's majority judgment in the Marcos return case certainly involved a vigorous exercise of judicial review. Indeed, critics of the decision regarded it as a very activist demonstration of review powers. What it was not, however, was a demonstration of temerity in sustaining the Court's power and the rights of citizens in the face of executive opposition. Whether the renewed Supreme Court can regain its historic ability to challenge powerful executives is still to be determined.

NOTES

1. Portions of this chapter follow Tate (1971) and Tate and Sittiwong (1986).

2. See, for example, Abad Santos (1966) and Concepcion (1955) for summary discussions, and Agpalo (1963), Bacuñgan (1966), Doronilla (1959), Felix (1948), Fernando and Fernando (1952), E. Fernando (1966), Gamboa and de Guzman (1963), Goco (1968), Lanting (1958), Mariano (1958), and Peck (1965) for discussions relating to specific policy areas.

3. The reasoning behind the American majority policy is illustrated, perhaps, by the following cablegram sent in 1909 by Governor-General W. Cameron Forbes to the U.S. Secretary of War Jacob W. Dickinson (cited in Samonte, 1969: 162): ''Believe that the appointment of Filipinos to the Supreme Court making the majority of the body native, would have very disastrous effect upon capital and those proposing to invest here.''

4. The relevant cases are *Government of the Philippine Islands v. Springer et al.*, 50 *Phil* 259 and *Government of the Philippine Islands v. Agoncillo et al.*, 50 *Phil* 348 (April 1, 1927) and *Springer v. Government of the Philippine Islands*, 277 *US* 189 (May 14, 1928).

5. I do *not* mean to imply that the routine dispute processing of the Philippine Supreme Court—or that of any court, for that matter—was not both socially and politically significant. I have always shared the view, recently put forward pointedly by Jacob (1991), that such activities are of great political significance, especially from the perspective of the average citizen-litigant.

6. There were apparently two motivations for the administration's desire to make transfer of judges feasible. One was the understandable reluctance of judges to be reassigned to remote provincial locations outside the ambit of the capital city, Manila. Another was to prevent judges from becoming too settled in their local communities and, possibly, therefore too much influenced by local elites. The relevant cases are *Borromeo v. Mariano* 41 *Phil.* 322 (1921) and *Concepcion v. Paredes* 42 *Phil.* 599 (1921).

7. In 1929 the Filipino leaders had tried to establish a court of appeals to help the Supreme Court with its caseload and, not coincidentally, to reduce the policy control of the American-dominated Supreme Court. They had been frustrated in their efforts by a governor-general's veto and eventually acquiesced in the American-preferred plan to expand the Supreme Court to 11 members and to allow it to sit in two divisions (see Zaide, 1956).

8. Quezon's intentions may be arguable, since reducing the size of the court limited his immediate ability to shape its work by appointing its members: only one Supreme

Court vacancy remained on the seven-member court after the retirement of the Americans remaining on the eleven-member court.

9. Hukbalahap is an abbreviation for the Tagalog words Hukbo ng Bayan Laban sa Hapon (People's Anti-Japanese Army). Shortly before Roxas' death, the Huk changed its name to Hukbong Magpalayang Bayan (People's Liberation Army) after the Hukbalahap had been declared illegal. See Grossholtz (1964: 33, 40).

10. The text of Macapagal's statement, made in a press conference of September 14, 1962, is given in Appendix R of his memoirs (Macapagal, 1968). Macapagal's side of the controversy is presented at pp. 236–245.

11. The final draft of the constitution produced by the Constitutional Convention, which was called during Marcos' second term, was completed after the president had declared martial law, and under his strong influence.

12. The only majorities in question were the majority of six that dismissed the petitions and the majority (allegedly of eight—see E. Q. Fernando, 1984: 11, although it is difficult to count the votes so as to get a total of eight) that agreed to the "in force and effect" statement interpreting the meaning of the decision. For a revealing, if not completely clear, discussion of the inclusion of the phrase in the decision report, see Brillantes, 1987: 63–64.

13. "What other choice did we have?" is the way one civil liberties activist put it in an interview with the author. Notable among the disputes the Supreme Court resolved in Marcos' favor were the "martial law cases" brought by Senator Benigno Aquino and several other of Marcos' imprisoned opponents to challenge the validity of his martial law rule, the use of military courts to try civilians, and other issues (*Aquino v. Ponce Enrile* and numerous others, 59 *SCRA* 183 [1974]; *Aquino v. Commission on Elections*, 62 *SCRA* 275 [1975]; *Aquino v. Military Commission No. 2*, 63 *SCRA* 546 [1975]).

14. Makati is the nation's financial center.

15. Since July 1987 it has chosen to sit in three divisions of five justices each. From 1973 through 1987, it had sat in two divisions of seven justices each, with the chief justice (the Court's fifteenth member) not permanently assigned to a division.

16. *General Reports* are the unpublished reports of the Court's resolutions and decisions. Most of the decisions cited by Chief Justice Teehankee in his first annual report as upholding the new regime's authority have not been published in the principal reporter of the Court's "important" decisions, the *Supreme Court Reports Annotated*.

17. Marcos supporters were no doubt impressed by the similarity between these arguments and those used by his supporters on the Court in *Javellana v. Executive Secretary* to legitimize Marcos' establishment of constitutional authoritarianism. The Chief Justice also noted that "with the overwhelming ratification of the 1987 constitution at the plebiscite held on February 2, 1987, the Filipino people unequivocally and decisively affirmed beyond any further question the above rulings of the Supreme Court" (Teehankee, 1987: 7).

18. The Philippine senators are elected from a single nationwide 24-member constituency.

19. The reference is to a much-publicized photograph of Marcos-era Chief Justice Enrique Fernando holding an umbrella over First Lady Imelda Marcos at a public ceremony. The importance of this symbol of the subservience of the Supreme Court under Fernando is suggested by the fact that it also surfaced in a retirement interview with Chief Justice Teehankee (Sicam, 1988: 18). In discussing his participation in installing Aquino in power, Teehankee is reported as insisting "nonetheless, that he has maintained

a discrete distance from the Executive as required by his post. He was never in danger of carrying an umbrella over the President's head, he quips."

REFERENCES

Abad Santos, Vicente. (1966). The role of the judiciary in policy formation. *Philippine Law Journal* 61: 567–576.

Agpalo, Remigio E. (1963). *The political process and the nationalization of the retail trade in the Philippines*. Quezon City: University of the Philippines.

Aquino, Ramon C. (1967). *A chance to die: A biography of José Abad Santos, late chief justice of the Philippines*. Quezon City: Alemar-Phoenix and José Abad Santos Memorial Society.

Araneta, Francisco, and Carroll, John J. (1968). Politics and government. *Solidarity* 3 (December): 53–71.

Asiaweek. (1987). Taking on the Supreme Court. May 27: 17–18.

Bacuñgan, Forolian A. (1966). The Supreme Court and social security. *Far Eastern Law Review* 13: 1–14.

Bernas, Joaquin G., S. J. (1989a). Will the SC make an act of faith?" *Manila Chronicle*, June 30: 4.

———. (1989b). The Supreme Court ban on Marcos, Part I. *Manila Chronical*, September 20.

———. (1989c). The Supreme Court ban on Marcos, Part II. *Manila Chronicle*, September 22.

———. (1989d). The Supreme Court ban on Marcos, Part III. *Manila Chronicle*, September 25.

Brillantes, Alex Bello, Jr. (1987). *Dictatorship and martial law: Philippine authoritarianism in 1972*. Quezon City: New Day.

Castro, Bert. (1989). High court rules final on Marcos ban. *Manila Chronicle*, October 28: 1, 3.

Concepcion, José C. (1955). The Supreme Court and political questions. *Philippine Law Journal* 30: 941–950.

Del Carmen, Rolando. (1973). Constitutionalism and the Supreme Court in a changing Philippine polity. *Asian Survey* 13: 1050–1061.

Doronilla, Amando. (1959). The Supreme Court and the Huk movement. *Manila Daily Bulletin*, 59th Annual Edition, April 3, Sec. 1: 39.

Felix, Alfonso. (1948). The income tax law and the salaries of the members of the judiciary. *Unitas* (the Faculty Journal of the University of Santo Tomas) 21 (April–June): 285–295.

Fernando, Emma Quisimbing. (1984). *Philippine constitutional law*, 1984 ed. Quezon City: Central Lawbook Publishing Co.

Fernando, Enrique M. (1966). The Supreme Court and civil liberties. *Weekly Graphic* 32, May 25: 10–12.

Fernando, Enrique M., and Fernando, Emma Q. (1952). The role of the Supreme Court as protector of civil liberties in times of emergency. *Philippine Law Journal* 27: 1–18.

Gamboa, Ma. Elena, and de Guzman, Raul P. (1963). The redistricting bill of 1961. *Philippine Journal of Public Administration* 77: 11–26.

Garcia, Isidro V. (1965). The independence of the judiciary. *Philippines Free Press* 58 (February 20): 28ff.

Goco, Raul I. (1968). Land reform and the Supreme Court. *Philippines Free Press*, (August 24): 16–18.

Grossholtz, J. (1964). *Politics in the Philippines*. Boston: Little, Brown.

Hayden, Joseph Ralston. (1942). *The Philippines: A study in national development*. New York: Macmillan.

Jacob, Herbert. (1991). Beyond legal mobilization: Finding the lost branch of government. Paper presented to the Annual Meeting of the Southern Political Science Association, Tampa, November 8.

Journal [Manila]. (1988). SC chief hits detractors. June 25: 1.

Lachica, Eduardo. (1971). *The Huks: Philippine agrarian society in revolt*. New York: Praeger.

Lanting, Juan L. (1958). The trend of court decisions affecting labor-management relations. *Lawyer's Journal* 23 (October 31): 329ff.

Lasswell, Harold D. (1958). *Politics: Who gets what, when, how*. New York: Meridian Books.

Liwag, Juan R. (1963). The Supreme Court and the rule of law. *University of the East Law Journal* 5 (January): 227–234.

Locsin, Raul. (1964). Defenders of the constitution. *Chronicle Magazine* 19 (February 8): 4ff.

Locsin, Teodoro M. (1964). Men of the year: The rule of law. *Philippines Free Press* January 4: 1, 8.

Macapagal, Diosdado. (1968). *A stone for the edifice: Memoirs of a president*. Quezon City: Mac Publishing House.

Macaraeg, Feliciano. (1963). The Supreme Court and the administration. *Mirror Magazine*, November 16: 36.

Makabenta, Yan. (1968). The Supreme Court in our changing times. *Graphic* 34 (January 17): 18–20, 61.

Malaya. (1988). SC says impeachment case meant to destabilize govt. June 25: 1.

Malcolm, George A. (1957). *American colonial careerist*. Boston: Christopher Publishing House.

Manila Chronicle. (1988). SC justices own notes deny pressure on *Tanod*, April 30: 3.

Manila Chronicle [Editorial] (1988). A word to the justices—never write notes, May 2: 4.

Manila Chronicle. (1989). SC asked to order return of Marcos, May 14: 4.

Mariano, L. C. (1958). The Supreme Court and local autonomy. *Philippine Journal of Public Administration* 2: 38–53.

Peck, Cornelius, J. (1965). Nationalistic influences on the Philippine law of citizenship. *American Journal of Comparative Law* 14.

Philippines Dispatch. (1987). They do want him in the senate, August 11–19: 1.

Philippines Free Press. (1962). Again, 55 (September 22): 1, 8.

Philippines Star [Editorial] (1987). Supreme Court—bastion of justice, October 1: 2.

Republic of the Philippines, Supreme Court. (1901–60). *Philippine Reports*. Manila: Bureau of Printing.

Samonte, Abelardo, G. (1969). The Philippine Supreme Court: A study of judicial attributes, attitudes, and decision-making. In Glendon A. Schubert and David J.

Danelski (eds.), *Comparative judicial behavior*. New York: Oxford University Press.

Sicam, Paulynn P. (1988). We have to educate judges: Paulynn P. Sicam interviews Chief Justice Claudio Teehankee. *The Chronicle on Sunday, Manila Chronicle*, April 17: 18.

Steinberg, David J. (1967). *Philippine collaboration in World War II*. Ann Arbor and Manila: University of Michigan Press and Solidaridad Publishing House.

Supreme court reports annotated [Philippines]. 1961– . Manila: Central Lawbook Supply, Inc.

Tate, C. Neal (1971). The social background, political recruitment and decision-making of the Philippine Supreme Court justices, 1901–1968. Ph.D. Diss., Tulane University.

Tate, C. Neal and Sittiwong, Panu (1986). The Supreme Court and justice in the Marcos era. *Pilipinas: A Journal of Philippine Studies* 6: 1–19.

Teehankee, Claudio. (1987). *A year of restoration, a time of renewal: 1986 annual report of the Supreme Court*. Manila: Supreme Court of the Philippines.

Tingson, Fortunato, Jr. (1955). Know your Supreme Court. *Manuel L. Quezon Law Quarterly* 4 (April).

Worcester, Dean C. (1930). *The Philippines past and present*. New York: Macmillan.

Wurfel, David (1964). The Philippines. In George McT. Kahin (ed.), *Government and politics of Southeast Asia*. Ithaca, N.Y.: Cornell University Press.

Zaide, Gregorio F. (1956). *Philippine Political and Cultural History*, 2 vols. Manila: Philippine Education Co.

9

Judicial Review and the Rule of Law: Comparing the United States and Sweden

Nils Stjernquist

The power of judicial review is written into the Swedish constitution (Instrument of Government) Chapter 11, Article 14. The Constitution of the United States has nothing to say about such a review. Yet, judicial review is a fundamental aspect of the American constitutional system, while it plays only a very minor role in Sweden. This, certainly, is a paradox.

In the United States, Chief Justice Charles Evans Hughes said (first in 1907 and again while campaigning for the presidency in 1916): "We are under the Constitution, but the Constitution is what the judges say it is" (Abraham, 1980: 343). At a conference held in Sweden in 1987 an American scholar explained that the U.S. Constitution is what people ask judges to declare. As far as Sweden is concerned such statements are never made.

Why is Sweden so contrary to the United States? And how can we understand the paradox? One answer, of course, is that the United States has a federal government while Sweden does not. But certainly there are other answers—differences in constitution and legal systems and differences in traditions. Owing to the fact that Swedish traditions are less known than the American ones in the international arena, I shall go more into detail as far as the Swedish ones are concerned. To understand the Swedish tradition we have to go far back into history.

THE ORIGINS OF SWEDISH "JUDICIAL REVIEW"

On May 19, 1654, Cromwell's ambassador to Sweden, Bulstrode Whitelock, had a discussion with the Swedish chancellor, Axel Oxenstierna. The chancellor noted that fortunately the members of the Swedish parliament, the Riksdag, did not have the right to initiate topics for debate and legislation. The Riksdag discussed only what the king wanted it to discuss. Whitelock responded, "This may be a good way to preserve your quiet, but may it not be ill for the rights and liberty of the people? For the king would hardly propose a new law for the liberty of the people which derogates from his own power." "This were an inconvenience," the chancellor replied, "if the peoples' rights and liberties were not already settled; but, by our laws, the boundaries of the king's power and of the peoples' rights are sufficiently known and established" (Koenigsberger, 1989: 59). Whatever you think about the chancellor's statements, they show something that, from the beginning, has been typical for Sweden: the Rule of Law.

In order to understand the role of judicial review in Sweden, it is necessary to understand the development of the Swedish constitutional and political system. The roots go so far back in time that historians can give us little information about the beginnings. Rimbert, ninth-century archbishop in Hamburg, wrote in his biography about his predecessor, Ansgar, the apostle of the Scandinavian countries, that "among the Swedes it is a custom that all official matters are decided more by the unanimous consent of the people than by royal decrees. In times of peace there have to take place negotiations at the *tings*. Else the decisions by the King are not valid" (Rimbert, 1930: 115).

The first Swedish written constitution for the whole country dates from the 1350s. Long before Montesquieu, it established the separation of powers between the king and the people, who assembled in meetings on different regional and local levels. A separate Supreme Court did not exist. Instead, supreme judicial power belonged for many purposes to the king.

The principle of separation of powers declined during periods of absolutism in Swedish constitutional history. However, even when absolutism dominated, the principle of the rule of law was recognized. There is a famous letter in 1682 from Charles XI, who in that same year introduced an overt system of absolutism. The king said he did not want any decision of his to be carried out that was in conflict with the law or against the rights of a citizen (Schmedeman, 1706: 749).

In the old days there was in Sweden no distinction between constitutional (or fundamental) law and other laws. All law was thought to be everlasting and unchangeable. However, in the seventeenth century fundamental law came to be seen as a separate and special category. Fundamental law, contrary to other laws, was now seen as everlasting and unchangeable (Holmberg and Stjernquist, 1988: 23).

From 1719 to 1772, during the so-called Era of Liberty, Sweden developed a constitutional system characterized by parliamentarism, with two parties competing in elections and in the Riksdag and entering or leaving the government in accordance with the winds of the electorate. During this period all power was vested in the Riksdag and also in matters of law applications could be revised by the Riksdag. The constitution for that era was established in 1720. It was seen as unchangeable in principle, but the political parties nonetheless sometimes wanted to change the fundamental law. The solution was the declaration by the

Riksdag that they did not *change* the constitution but only *improved* it by declaring its meaning.

But in 1766 the Riksdag did introduce a process for changing the fundamental law. Amendments of the fundamental law required consideration by two successive sessions of parliament, with an intervening election to the Riksdag. Amendments also required unanimous consent of all the four estates: nobility, clergy, burghers, and farmers (Metcalf, 1987: 112ff; Constitutional Documents of Sweden, 1990: 11.) My impression is that this is the first example of a special provision for Swedish constitutional amendments, and this pattern has been followed, with varying formulations, by many countries. The process for amending the fundamental law is still based on the understanding in Sweden that the constitution is a kind of treaty between the citizens and the government, so that the citizens have a right to be consulted when changing it.

After a period of absolutism, followed by disaster in the war against Napoleon and his ally the Russian czar, Sweden got a new constitution in 1809, again built on the principle of separation of powers. The founding fathers of the new constitution said they had "tried to make a constitution with an executive power, operating within distinct forms with only one decision-maker (the king) with effective instruments in executing the decisions, a legislative power, independent under the laws but not prevailing over them." The founding fathers added that "these powers should watch one another and should not be mixed." The proponents of the new constitution said they wanted to create three distinct branches of government to watch one another. This was clearly a reflection of Montesquieu's thought, but in Montesquieu's scheme executive power would have belonged to the king, legislative to the parliament, and judicial to the courts. The Swedish constitution of 1809, however, involved other divisions and functions and had its roots in Swedish constitutional history. Executive power was assigned to the king, but legislative power was divided between the king and the Riksdag. The consent of both was required. However, the power to enact economic and administrative legislation was vested in the king, while taxing and budgetary powers were placed in the Riksdag.

What about judicial power? There was in the Swedish system an old rule that allowed each citizen to seek the king's protection of his or her rights. Up to 1789, the highest court consisted of a division of the King's Council with the king himself serving as president. King Gustaf III abolished the Council in 1789, following his second revolution, and established absolutism. A new Supreme Court was formed, but with the king still serving as president. The constitution of 1809 continued this model and added the minister of justice to the Supreme Court. Given this composition, there was no place for an independent Supreme Court, and, consequently, no place for judicial review (Wedberg, 1922: 1940).

It can be mentioned that Montesquieu meant that the position of the judicial power was very weak. It was *en quelque façon nulle* (in a way not existing). But wasn't there a need for an institution or process to make certain that the ordinary laws were consistent with the constitution? The process established by the constitution of 1809 was for review *before* a law came into being, not after it was enacted. When the king in his council wanted to propose an ordinary law to the Riksdag, he had to send it to the Supreme Court for review. Conversely, before the king in his council could agree to an ordinary law proposed by the Riksdag, he was obliged to send it to the Supreme Court for review. When in 1909 the king lost his seat on the Supreme Court, the task of reviewing proposed laws was given to a Law Council, consisting of three members of the Supreme Court and one member of the Supreme Administrative Court, which had been created that same year.

Other factors also contributed to the absence of *a posteriori* judicial review in the Swedish constitution of 1809. In the Swedish legal tradition, principles of law were more important than the specific text of laws. As late as the nineteenth century, the Riksdag delegated to the king the power to prepare the text of laws. Given that tradition, it was quite natural to interpret the text of laws to produce a desired result rather than to amend the text. The practice of interpreting laws, even fundamental ones, is well-established in Swedish constitutional history. The agencies presumed competent to interpret the laws were the lawmakers themselves—that is, the king with the Riksdag, concerning fundamental and ordinary law, and the king alone, concerning administrative and economic laws (Stjernquist, 1961: 289).

This made it difficult to maintain consistency in interpretation. When uncertain about the proper interpretation, judges and civil servants had to ask their superiors. In early days Courts of Appeal had to ask the king to resolve uncertainty. When the Supreme Court was established in 1789, it was given authority over such inquiries. The constitution of 1809 had the same system. Article 19 stated that the Supreme Court should furnish interpretations in response to any inquiries made to the king by lower courts or officials regarding the meaning of the law. The constitution of 1809 made it clear that the lower courts had no power of judicial review. It was also clear that the Supreme Court was the king's court (The Constitution of Sweden, 1954: 16).

The Freedom of the Press Act of 1812 provided a good example. The Press Act is a fundamental law, but it was not enacted according to the rules for amending the constitution, which required approval by the Riksdag at two consecutive sessions. This deviation from the rules was quite unusual, but the courts never hesitated to apply the law, which continued in force until 1950.

It is interesting that the Committee on Laws at the 1828–30 session of the Riksdag declared that old laws that were obviously inconsistent with fundamental law, or with more recent ordinary laws, should not be enforced, because an ordinary law had to yield to a fundamental one and an older law to a younger one (Committee on the Laws, 1828/29: 34). Their point was much like that made by John Marshall in *Marbury v. Madison* in 1803.

The Committee on the Laws of the Riksdag returned to the problem of judicial review at its 1853–54 session, following a declaration by the ombudsman that courts were entitled to examine laws to ensure that they had been decided in the prescribed manner. The majority of the committee found that the constitution had not given the courts the general power of judicial review (Committee on the Laws, 1853/54: 4).

MODERN RECONSIDERATIONS

Beginning about 1881, constitutional scholars began to consider judicial review seriously. Christian Naumann, a professor at the University of Lund, took as his starting point Article 47 of the constitution of 1809, which provided that courts should decide cases in accordance with laws and the statutes. To Naumann that meant that the court had the duty of ascertaining what was existing law. Rules made by the king alone, but which by the constitution should have been made by the king and Riksdag together, could not be valid. However, the courts were not entitled to review laws that had been decided by the king and the Riksdag together (Naumann, 1881/83: 120–123).

Hugo Blomberg, a professor at Uppsala University, maintained, however, that the courts also were entitled to review and to set aside laws made by the king and the Riksdag together, if those laws were obviously irreconcilable with fundamental law (Blomberg, 1896: 55–84).

Professors were also at that time, as the Germans say, *Männer anderer Meinung* (men of a different opinion), and some years later Ludvid Widell, professor at Lund University, found that the only thing the courts could test was whether a law had been promulgated in the form prescribed by the constitution (Widell, 1903: 82–95).

In 1918 Professor C. A. Reuterskiöld at Uppsala University published an important paper concerning judicial review. Previously he had seen judicial review from a very restrictive point of view, but he now changed his position and concluded that the courts had a broad power of judicial review over the substance of laws. The key point for Reuterskiöld was the fact that the king, through an amendment to the constitution of 1809, had lost his seat on the Supreme Court. From that time one, the courts could be regarded as independent. Moreover, the old practice of interpreting a law in the same way as making a law and with inquiring of the Supreme Court as to the proper interpretation of laws faded away with desuetude (Reuterskiöld, 1918: 95).

Behind Reuterskiöld's argument there was another important factor. In 1917 parliamentary supremacy had been established in Sweden. That meant that the separation of powers established in the 1809 constitution had been abolished, even though the text of the constitution was unaltered. In 1918, general suffrage for both men and women was introduced on all levels. This meant that a lot of poor people now were entitled to vote and, consequently, made it necessary for the Riksdag to consider their needs more than previously. Reuterskiöld belonged to those who disapproved of democracy. His view was that both the separation and balance of powers were necessary in the country with a tradition of the rule of law. Since the king in his council was no longer able to counterbalance the Riksdag, it must be replaced, he argued, by the Supreme Court, which would act in the king's name (Reuterskiöld, 1918: 95ff). He was himself also a politician, and in opposing parliamentarism and general suffrage he resorted to Montesquieu and others who had preached the necessity of separation of powers. He could also find support in the first constitution of the French revolution from 1791, which stated: *Toute société dans laquelle la garantie des droits n'est pas assurée, ni la séparation des pouvoirs déterminée, n'a point de constitution* (A society in which the guarantee of rights is not assured, nor the separation of powers determined, does not have a constitution). This sentence may surprise today, but remember that the great French revolution was *la révolution de la bourgeoisie* and that the 1791 constitution also explicitly protected the right to property.

Reuterskiöld had his international contacts with colleagues in France and Germany. His knowledge of English law and his knowledge about the United States were more restricted, as were almost all of his Swedish colleagues at that time. Otherwise, he could have referred to the fact that separation of powers was also the cornerstone of the U.S. constitutional system. As John Adams had written in 1805, "the nation which will not adopt an equilibrium of power, must adopt despotism. There is no other Alternative" (Mills, 1956: 242). According to Reuterskiöld there must be judicial review to exercise control over the Riksdag and the government, so that both would act according to the constitution.

Those who had willingly accepted parliamentary supremacy were not able to understand Reuterskiöld's argument for the separation of powers and judicial review. Nor could his colleagues at the two other law faculties, Robert Malmgren and Nils Herlitz, agree with him. But in 1930 there was a meeting that in some way affected our perspective on judicial review. A meeting held under the auspices of the Nordic Administrative Association took place in Stockholm. The principal topic was judicial review, which had already been established in Denmark and Norway. The Danish and Norwegian members conveyed to the Swedes present a more positive attitude toward judicial review (Castberg et al., 1930: 317–384).

Another more important factor was that cases had been filed questioning the conformity with the constitution of administrative rules and of rules concerning taxes and salaries for state employees. The courts held that the rules in question were not in conflict with the constitution, but in so doing they apparently exercised judicial review, even though they did not strike down any provision of law (Westerståhl, 1941: 126–128).

Reuterskiöld's successor at Uppsala, Halvar G. F. Sundberg, continued his advocacy for judicial review. Eventually, Professor Malmgren, the author of the annotated commentaries to the Swedish 1809 constitution, agreed that rules which by their content were directly in conflict with the constitution must yield to it and that rules that had not been decided by a competent decision maker must be set aside (Malmgren, 1937: 59).

As yet there had not been a case in which an ordinary law—that is, a law made by the government (in the name of the king) and the Riksdag together—had come before a court for constitutional review. The Riksdag Committee on the Constitution stated in 1938 (p. 16) that there was no power over the government and the parliament that could set aside a law made by them together.

It is likely that this strong assertion by the Riksdag committee was influenced by the opinion of judicial review in the United States held at that time by knowledgeable observers in Sweden. For many people in the United States, Sweden was the country of the four S's: sin, sex, suicide, and socialism. For many Swedes, the United States was the Wild West, with cowboys, guns, and movie stars. But in both countries a better mutual understanding gradually came into being. In 1936, Marquis Childs published *Sweden, The Middle Way*. It portrayed Sweden as a harmonious welfare state, a consensual democracy with a politics of compromise. In Sweden, contact with Swedish immigrants in the United States and their children and grandchildren strengthened the impression of the United States as a country with great opportunities. President Franklin D. Roosevelt's New Deal employed some of the same instruments against economic depression and unemployment as the Swedish ones. We apparently had something in common. But the disapproval by the U.S. Supreme Court of some of the key programs of the New Deal and FDR's fight against the Court provided the impetus for a negative appraisal in Sweden of American judicial review.

In Swedish discussions of the time, there was an important difference between judicial review of formal procedures (to ensure that the proper steps had been taken) and review of the substance or content of legislation. Those in Sweden who wanted judicial review according to the U.S. model argued for an amendment to the Swedish constitution that would have further protected civil rights. There were in Article 16 of the 1809 constitution some provisions, emanating from medieval times, that gave a rather uncertain protection of civil rights. It is important to remember, however, that freedom of the press and the right of public access to official documents had already been established by the Freedom of the Press Act, which, as I have already noted, was a fundamental law. A declaration of rights, added to the constitution, would nonetheless have provided a broader base for judicial review. The perceived need for such a declaration was reinforced by the trampling of human rights in the 1930s and 1940s by European dictatorships.

A Royal Commission, with representatives from the four big parties, proposed in 1941 that the medieval provisions contained in the 1809 constitution be replaced with a modern declaration of rights. The issue of judicial review was then discussed but not resolved. World War II left the commission's proposals in suspense (Betänkande, 1941).

The debate on judicial review was renewed in the 1950s. Gustaf Petrén, himself a professor and judge, argued (in the spirit of Reuterskiöld and Sundberg) in favor of review, while foreign minister Östen Undén, formerly a member of the law faculty at Uppsala, maintained that judicial review was not a proper part of the constitution of 1809.

Since 1918, Sweden had been working under a system of parliamentary supremacy but with a constitution that provided for separation of powers. In 1932 the Social Democratic Party had come to power and remained in power, with a short interruption, up to 1976, sometimes in coalition with the Farmers Party and during the war together with all the three nonsocialist parties. The opposition maintained that the election system combined with the bicameral system favored the largest (the Social Democratic) party. Thus the 1809 constitution came in the focus of the political debate. In 1954 a Royal Commission was appointed, headed by former Prime Minister Rickard Sandler, and charged to modernize the old constitution. The power of judicial review was one of the issues to be considered.

EVALUATING JUDICIAL REVIEW IN SWEDEN

There are, in my view, two factors that should be decisive in appraising judicial review in Sweden. The first is that an ordinary law has to yield to a fundamental law, an inferior law to a superior one, and an old law to a younger one. These ideas were already stated by the U.S. Supreme Court in 1803 in *Marbury v. Madison* and by the Swedish Riksdag Committee on the Laws at the 1828–30 session. That follows from a cornerstone, expressed by the Swedish constitution of 1974, that no law shall be amended or repealed otherwise than by law and no fundamental law otherwise than by fundamental law. These are guiding principles that the courts, and everybody who is applying rules, have to follow.

The second factor is the obvious resistance that Swedish judges and civil servants have shown toward judicial review. Their resistance is based on the fear of becoming involved in partisan politics. The only way around this is for the conflict between ordinary and fundamental law to be *obvious and apparent*. This demand that the conflict must be obvious and apparent was underlined by Hugo Blomberg in 1896 and has been, as we shall see, repeated many times later on.

The Sandler Commission considered judicial review as part of the even more complicated problem of how to deal with civil rights and liberties, which were at that time rather well-observed in Sweden. Moreover, the United Nations had adopted a Declaration on Human Rights in 1948, and the European Council two years later adopted the European Convention on Human Rights, which Sweden ratified. West Germany had, with the Nazi regime in mind, provided in its *Bundesverfassung* a far-reaching chapter about civil rights and with *ein Verfassungesgericht*, established a constitutional court with power of judicial review. In its final report in 1963 the Sandler Commission proposed that a new constitution would have a special chapter concerning fundamental rights and freedoms (Författningsutredningen, VI, 2, 1963: 159–209).

As far as judicial review was concerned, the solution proposed by the commission was the fruit of a political compromise. The commission referred to the fact that the courts had already found they were entitled to judicial review. Noting this fact the commission stated that there was no ground for any other conclusion that the judicial review would be used restrictively. And the commission did not propose that the right to judicial review should be written into the constitution (Författningsutredningen, VI, 2, 1963: 155–156).

Sitting members of the Supreme Court maintained that the commission, according to their opinion, had accurately stated what should be considered as valid. The proposal was followed when the new constitution finally came into being in 1974. From one point of view, the solution coincided with the American model: judicial review was not written into the constitution. From another way not: the conflict must be obvious and apparent.

When the new constitution was adopted in 1974, the political parties made a compromise concerning civil rights. They should be further investigated so as to better protect them. A new commission reported in 1975 with a new proposal. At the same time the commission proposed that judicial review be written into the constitution. It should, however, be limited so that a provision in law, made by the Riksdag, or by governmental regulations, could be set aside *only if the conflict was obvious and apparent*. This proposal engendered great controversy. Sitting members of the Supreme Court maintained that if the power of judicial review was far reaching, many people would say that the courts had entered the field of politics. The new rules in the constitution concerning civil rights could lead to conflicting interpretations. For that reason they agreed that the requirement that conflicts be obvious and apparent was well founded. The Swedish Trade Union Confederation argued the judicial review would work against the principle in Article 1 of the constitution that public power in Sweden emanates from the people. The Confederation argued that judicial review should be expressly forbidden. The minister of justice responded that the first article of the constitution also provided that public power be exercised *under the law* (Regeringens Proposition 1975/76, 209: 91–95).

A third commission was appointed. It proposed in 1978, for the first time with the unanimous support of the four big political parties, that judicial review be written into the constitution. This was agreed to by the Riksdag in 1979. Chapter 11 of Article 14 of the Swedish constitution thus provides:

If a court, or any other public body, considers that a provision conflicts with a provision of a fundamental law or with a provision of any other superior statute, or that the procedure prescribed was set aside in any important respect when the provision was introduced, the provision may not be applied. However, if the provision has been approved by the Riksdag or by the Government, it may be set aside only if the fault is manifest (Constitutional Documents of Sweden, 1990: 59).

An often underlined element in the long discussion about the codification of the judicial review was that such a review would have a preventive effect and urge the lawmaker to prepare the laws better. We are then back to the main line: a review in advance of the enactment. It is interesting that at the same time the functions of the Law Council were expanded. It was explicitly said in Chapter

8, Article 18 of the constitution that the Law Council's scrutiny shall, inter alia, relate to the way in which a proposal relates to the fundamental laws and to the legal system in general. At the same time, however, it was stated that failure to obtain the opinion of the Law Council on draft legislation shall never prevent the application of law.

The Riksdag Committee on the Constitution annotated the requirement that the inaccuracy has to be obvious and apparent with the following words:

The Riksdag is according to the Constitution the most prominent lawmaker. Only the Riksdag can enact fundamental law. For that reason it is quite natural that the Riksdag is the authority which is most fit to prove if a provision is in accordance with the Constitution. The demand that the inaccuracy must be obvious and apparent means that the courts have to respect the Riksdag's application of a constitutional rule, as long as it is lying within the frames of what is a possible interpretation (Committee on the Constitution, 1978/79: 39, 13).

The provisions concerning judicial review are characterized by the cautious attitude, which the Swedish courts generally have demonstrated.

Since the 1974 constitution came into force, there have been only a few unimportant instances of judicial review in Sweden, although in political debate from time to time it has been argued that decisions made by the Riksdag or by the government are in conflict with the constitution.

CONCLUSION

Let me summarize. The way to determine whether a law conflicts with the Swedish constitution has been from the beginning, and still is in practice, to let a proposed statute be reviewed in advance of its enactment. *A posteriori* judicial review by the courts was for a very long time unknown to the Swedish system. While judicial review does follow logically from the principle that ordinary laws should not be enforced if they conflict with fundamental law, most Swedish judges continue to be careful to avoid the prospect of jumping into a political battleground. This is the reason for restricting review to obvious and apparent conflicts.

That doesn't mean that everyone in Sweden is agreed on that standard of judicial review. The Conservative Party, the Liberal Party, the Center Party, and the Swedish Employer's Confederation want to strengthen constitutional protection for the right to property. There are also some lawyers who want to broaden the field of judicial review and who want to make their colleagues more active and intrepid. As a matter of fact, in Chapter 2 of the constitution, there are wordings that can be used concerning fundamental rights and freedoms. Also a constitutional court with the German *Verfassungsgericht* as a pattern has its advocates.

Judicial review may become more relevant for Sweden owing to European cooperation. Sweden is a member of the European Council and has ratified its convention concerning human rights. When ratifying, the Swedish government declared that its law was in harmony with the convention with only one exception. However, this is not completely true. In several cases Swedish citizens have gone to Strasbourg with their complaints and in some instances the European judges have held that Swedish practices have not been in compliance with the European Convention (Corell, 1989).

More important are Sweden's relations with the European Community (EC). If Sweden is going to become a member of the EC, or in some other way become more associated with it, judicial review probably will be broadened. Brussels has decided to introduce a real common market from the beginning of 1993 with free competition and no limits for goods, services, capital, and labor. More than half of Sweden's exports go to the EC countries and for that reason Sweden should have the same kinds of rules, for most situations, as the EC countries. Brussels demands a free competition between all firms in an area and a review process executed by courts. As far as the Swedish municipalities are concerned, that will mean a total revision of the system for local appeals.

The incidence of judicial review in Sweden may become higher, but, on the whole, and with reservation for what Sweden's relations to the Common Market will bring, I believe that Sweden will continue to live with a paradox. Contrary to the United States, Sweden has judicial review written into its constitution, but it will probably continue to play a rather unimportant role. The key to understanding the paradox is this: In Sweden it is, contrary to the United States, rather easy to change the constitution. It doesn't need to be changed by amendment or by judicial interpretation. Constitutional change through political practice was accepted when parliamentary supremacy was introduced in Sweden in 1917. Even so, Sweden nominally continued under its old constitution of 1809—in terms of age second only to the U.S. Constitution—and replaced it only in 1974. The new constitution corresponds better to current reality, but judicial review has played only a very minor role in creating that reality.

REFERENCES

Note: All of the sources with the notation "in Swedish" were originally published as books, reports, or articles in Swedish journals, in Swedish. For simplicity, they have all been translated into English.

Abraham, H. J. (1980). *The Supreme Court in the governmental process*, 5th ed. Boston: Allyn & Bacon.

Betänkande. (Report). (1941). Report with suggestions for alteration of wording of Sec. 16 of the Form of Government, presented by experts summoned from within the Department of Justice. *The Official Reports of The Swedish State* 20. Stockholm (in Swedish).

Blomberg, H. (1896). Concerning the constitutional guarantees of independence of the courts. *Journal of Legal Science* (Tidskrift for Retsvidenskab) 9: 55–84 (in Swedish).

Castberg, F., Erich, R., Andersson, P., and Sundberg, H.G.F. (1930). The authority of the Courts of Law to override unconstitutional laws. *Journal of Political Science* (Statsvetenskaplig tidskrift) 33: 317–384 (in Swedish).

Childs, M. W. (1936). *Sweden, the middle way.* New Haven, Conn.: Yale University Press.

Commission on the Constitution. (1963). The Swedish Constitution. Part 2: Motives, Suggestions on form of government. *The official reports of the Swedish State* 17. Stockholm (in Swedish).

Committee on the Constitution. (1938). Appendix to the Report of the Proceedings of the Swedish Parliament at the statutory session of the Riksdag 1938. Vol. 5, 2nd sec., *Reports and notes of the standing Committee on the Constitution.* Stockholm (in Swedish).

———. (1978/79). The Riksdag 1978/79. Report of the Proceedings, Appendix. Vol. 4, *Reports and notes of the standing Committee on the Constitution.* Stockholm (in Swedish).

Committee on the Laws. (1828/29). Appendix to all the Reports of the Proceedings of the Swedish Parliament at the statutory sessions of the Riksdag the years 1828 and 1829. Vol. 7, containing *the notes and reports of the Committee on the Laws.* Stockholm (in Swedish).

———. (1853/54). Appendix to all the Reports of the Proceedings of the Swedish Parliament at the statutory sessions of the Riksdag the years 1853 and 1854. Vol. 7, *The notes and reports of the Committee on the Laws.* Stockholm (in Swedish).

The Constitution of Sweden. (1954). *Documents published by the Royal Ministry for Foreign Affairs.* New series II: 4. Stockholm.

Constitutional Documents of Sweden. (1990). *The Instrument of Government, the Riksdag Act, the Act of Succession, the Freedom of the Press Act.* Stockholm: Published by the Swedish Riksdag.

Correll, H. (1989). *Sweden and the European Court. Negotiations at the 31st Nordic meeting of jurists in Helsinki,* 2. Helsinki (in Swedish).

Holmberg, E., and Stjernquist, N. (1988). *Our Constitution,* 7th ed. Stockholm: Norstedts (in Swedish).

Koenigsberger, H. G. (1989). Riksdag, Parliament and States General in the sixteenth and seventeenth Centuries. In N. Stjernquist (ed.), *The Swedish Riksdag in an international perspective.* Stockholm: The Bank of Sweden Tercentenary Foundation.

Malmgren, R. (1937). *The Constitutional Laws of Sweden and their appurtenant statutes with explanations,* 3rd ed. Stockholm: Norstedts (in Swedish).

Metcalf, M. F. (1987). Parliamentary Sovereignty and Royal Reaction 1719–1809. In M. F. Metcalf (Ed.), *The Riksdag: A history of the Swedish parliament.* New York: St. Martin's Press.

Mills, C. W. (1956). *The power elite.* Toronto: Oxford University Press.

Naumann, C. (1881–83). *The Constitutional Laws of Sweden,* 2nd ed., vol. 3. Stockholm: Norstedts (in Swedish).

Regeringens Proposition (Bill of Government). (1975/76). The Swedish Riksdag, 1975/76. Report of the Proceedings. Appendix. Vol. 1, *The Bills of the Government.* Stockholm (in Swedish).

Reuterskiöld, C. A. (1918). The transformation of our judicial system. *Journal of Political Science* (Statsvetenskaplig tidskrift) 21: 69–97.

Rimbert. (1930). *Vita Anskarii*. Swedish translation by G. Rudberg (*The life of Ansgar*), 2nd ed. Uppsala: The publishing company of the Board of Deacons of the Swedish Church.

Schmedeman, J. (ed.). (1706). *Royal statutes, ordinances, letters and resolutions concerning judicial and executive issues*. Stockholm (in Swedish).

Stjernquist, N. (1961). Declaration of law through joint decisions. *Journal of Political Science* (Statsvetenskaplig tidskrift) 64: 289–313 (in Swedish).

Wedberg, B. (1922). *The Royal Supreme Court 1789–1844*. Stockholm: Norstedts (in Swedish).

———. (1940). *The Royal Supreme Court 1809–1844*. Stockholm: Norstedts (in Swedish).

Westerståhl, J. (1941). The question of the judicial right of the Courts of Sweden to examine laws. In *The official reports of The Swedish State* 20: 114–128. Stockholm (in Swedish).

Widell, L. (1903). Do Swedish courts have the right to test the appropriateness of laws and regulations? *Journal of Political Science* (Statsvetenskaplig tidskrift) 6: 82–95 (in Swedish).

10

The Incidence and Effect of Judicial Review Procedures Against Central Government in the United Kingdom

Maurice Sunkin

Accounts of recent developments of judicial review in England emphasize the growing use of judicial review litigation and growing activism of the judges in handling such cases. It is now almost axiomatic that judicial review is a growth area that is playing an increasingly central part in the government and politics of the United Kingdom (Woolf, 1986; Boynton, 1986; Kerry, 1986; Ackner, 1987). In this chapter I will assess this view by looking at the incidence of judicial review and the impact of judicial review litigation on central government. I will draw on my empirical studies of judicial review caseload to argue that while there has been an increase in the use of the courts to challenge governmental action, judicial review is used regularly in only a very few subject areas against a correspondingly narrow range of public agencies, by litigants advised by a small band of lawyers.[1] Despite general impressions, judicial review litigation impinges only upon a tiny fraction of governmental decision making, vast tracts of which remain free from legal challenge and resulting judicial scrutiny. However, the importance of judicial review litigation cannot be assessed by numbers alone and I will look briefly at the principal impacts of judicial review on central government.[2]

As I am using the term, judicial review refers to the process by which those aggrieved by actions of public authorities may challenge those authorities in the High Court on the grounds that they have (or will do so) abused or exceeded their legal powers. This process is generally known as the application for judicial review procedure. While there are signs that European Community law may oblige English judges to measure the legality of primary legislation against community law, as yet judicial review in the United Kingdom is predominantly concerned with the legality of administrative action and the jurisdictional powers of lower courts and tribunals.

The judicial review procedure is based on reforms introduced in the mid-1970s intended to provide a comprehensive and flexible system for challenging public bodies (Law Commission, 1976; Wade, 1988: Ch. 18; Blom-Cooper, 1982). Without dwelling on procedural details, those unfamiliar with the system should be aware of the essential characteristics of the judicial review process in England.

CHARACTERISTICS OF THE JUDICIAL REVIEW PROCESS

First, the procedure has two stages. Applicants must obtain leave (judicial permission) before making an application for review. In recent years between 25 percent and 40 percent of applications have failed at the leave stage, and for this reason alone the leave requirement is an extremely important component of the U.K. system of public law. It is also an exceptional procedure. Only in judicial review proceedings do litigants require judicial permission to litigate. The general position is that litigants are free to institute litigation and defendants are free to ask the court to dismiss the action if it is without merit. The usual justification given for the leave requirement in judicial review proceedings is that it provides judges with an efficient method of filtering out frivolous or unarguable cases. This is said to benefit applicants by providing them with an early judicial opinion as to the merits of their claim; judicial administration by preventing the courts becoming clogged by unarguable cases; and public authorities by protecting them from litigious harassment.

Leave should be granted if three criteria are satisfied: the application must be made within three months of the action being challenged, it must be arguable, and applicants must show a sufficient interest in the matter. In practice these can be very uncertain criteria. For example, the test of arguability varies widely. At one end of the spectrum certain judges may make a "quick perusal" of the papers and grant leave if they reveal what might turn out to be an arguable case. At the other extreme, leave has been refused after a day of legal argument in court. This is not the place to dwell on this issue; suffice it to say that I am not convinced that the leave filter is necessary nor that it is having a desirable effect. In particular, I am not convinced that in its present form the leave requirement effectively discriminates between the truly frivolous cases and those with some substance. In my view, there is a real risk that worthy cases may be turned away prematurely, and I would prefer to see a system that places far greater emphasis on the principle of access to courts, particularly in public law issues (Justice-All Souls, 1988: paras. 623–627).

Second, judicial review is essentially a written procedure designed to deal with legal, but not factual, disputes. Here again it contrasts with normal English procedures. For whereas discovery of documents and cross-examination of witnesses is usually automatic and regarded as central to the forensic process, this is not the case in judicial review proceedings. In judicial review procedure neither discovery nor cross-examination are available automatically and cross-examination of witnesses, in particular, is very rarely permitted. Evidence is submitted in the form of sworn affidavits and neither deponents nor witnesses are called into the witness box. This will not pose problems where the dispute is truly one of law. But there are times when judicial reluctance to allow cross-examination seriously undermines the ability of the parties to present their case as effectively as possible. It may also result in judicial decisions that are not based on the best evidence available.

The well-known decision in *Council of Civil Service Unions v. Minister for the Civil Service* (the GCHQ case) illustrates the type of problems that can arise.[3] Here the prime minister (as head of the Civil Service) acting under prerogative powers had issued an edict directing workers at the Government Communications Headquarters to relinquish their trade union membership. This action was taken without first consulting the unions. The unions challenged the legality of the edict, arguing that the failure to consult constituted a breach of the rules of natural justice and was therefore unlawful. At first instance Glidewell J. accepted this argument and found for the unions. In so doing he dismissed the government's argument that pervading interests of national security would have restricted the consultation to a point that would have rendered consultation ineffective and futile. When appealing to the Court of Appeal the government introduced a new argument. Now for the first time it was argued not that consultation would have been futile, but that consultation per se would have been disruptive and would have endangered national security. Professor Griffith (1985) has noted that this claim was supported by an assertion in Sir Robert Armstrong's affidavit. In this the secretary to the cabinet said that "to have entered such consultations would have served to bring out the vulnerability of areas of disruption to those who have shown themselves ready to organize disruption." Needless to say, the unions disputed this and would have liked to explore why, if the risks were so great, the government had not previously referred to them as its explanation for not consulting. But they were unable to call Armstrong (or the prime minister or foreign secretary for that matter) into the witness box to question him on the grounds for the claim. As Griffith emphasizes, "their evidence might have shown conclusively that their ground for failing to consult was indeed based on considerations of national security; or it might have shown that their decision was based merely on political convenience and expediency" (p. 571). But the judges were unwilling to investigate the truth of the matter and were content to find in the government's favor by relying on the unchallenged assertions contained in the affidavit evidence. This saga highlights the limitations of the judicial review process; it is also a classical example of judicial deference to the executive whenever national security is claimed as a justification for actions.

The short limitation period, the leave requirement, and the absence of automatic discovery of documents and cross-examination of witnesses combine to produce a procedure that is often less favorable to the needs of potential litigants than other court procedures. So why do litigants use judicial review and not other procedures? Down to the early 1980s it was assumed that litigants were free to go to court by whichever procedure they regarded as being in their best interests and there were indications that the procedural limitations of judicial review were causing litigants to avoid the process. By the late 1970s, however, there were indications that judges were keen to restrict this freedom to choose procedures. For example, the Court of Appeal criticized the use of Chancery proceedings in an immigration case on the basis that judicial review judges were more expert in these cases than those who sat in the Chancery Division of the High Court.[4] Soon after this, a prisoner seeking to challenge the legality of disciplinary proceedings of the Hull Prison Board of Visitors had his case struck out solely because the judicial review had not been used.[5]

This restrictive approach was later confirmed by the landmark decision of the House of Lords in *O'Reilly v. Mackman*.[6] Here again prisoners sought to challenge disciplinary decisions of a prison board of visitors. Because they were out of time for judicial review, and because they desired an opportunity to cross-examine witnesses so that the factual foundation of the board's decisions could be tested in court, they decided to use normal High Court procedures rather than judicial review. The prison authorities applied to have the actions dismissed. At first instance, Payne J. refused to do this. He said that until legislation changed things, litigants were free to choose the procedure they thought best. The Court of Appeal and the House of Lords disagreed. Giving the unanimous opinion of the House, Lord Diplock delivered one of the most important judgments in U.K. recent public law. In it he said that

it would . . . as a general rule be contrary to public policy, and as such an abuse of process of the court, to permit a person seeking to establish that a decision of a public authority infringed rights to which he was entitled to protection under public law to proceed by way of an ordinary action and by this means to evade the provisions (within the judicial review procedure) for the protection of public authorities.[7]

The result is that the judicial review procedure must be used whenever public law rights are claimed. According to Diplock, the reason is that public interest demands that public authorities enjoy the protection by judicial review's short limitation period, its leave requirement, and its absence of automatic discovery and cross-examination. The decision has been widely criticized by academic writers (Sunkin, 1983; Wade 1988: 678; Woolf, 1986; Harlow, 1980). The association of the public interest with the interests of public authorities rather than with the interests of litigants in gaining access to the courts does not bode well for those hoping for a dynamic and activist public law.

A jurisdictional distinction between public and private law was previously unknown to English law and decision in *O'Reilly v. Mackman* led to a new generation of formalistic and sterile jurisdictional controversies of the type that the reforms of the mid-1970s were intended to eradicate.

Judicial review is being molded by the judges to become a specialized procedure for resolving issues of public law. The central features of the procedure

Table 10.1
Numbers of Civil Judicial Reviews*

1981	1982	1983	1984	1985	1986	1987	1988	1989
356	515	670	703	948	1030	1335	1087	1335

* Judicial Statistics, Lord Chancellor's Department. The figures given are
for civil applications, they therefore exclude applications known to be purely
criminal. There are between 150 - 200 of these annually.

are designed to protect public authorities against the possibility of being harassed
by litigation and to enable the judges to maximize their discretion over public
law challenges. The cost of these features is borne by applicants for judicial
review who are forced to use a process that does not encourage either access to
the courts or effective discovery of facts. In short, judicial review in our system
is a procedure better suited to judicial pragmatism than activism.

THE INCIDENCE OF JUDICIAL REVIEW

General Trends

Table 10.1 shows the numbers of civil applications for leave to apply for
judicial review over the years of 1981–89 inclusive. The figures confirm a general
increase in the overall judicial review caseload that has been evident for at least
the past two decades. As readily can be seen, the caseload almost doubled
between 1981 and 1983, broadly coinciding with the judicial attempts to focus
public law litigation into the judicial review process (culminating in *O'Reilly v.
Mackman*) that were described earlier. Although the increase between 1984 and
1986 was more gradual, it peaked sharply during 1987 and declined for the first
time for at least a decade, in 1988.

These data will be used both by those who seek to emphasize the growing
importance of judicial review and by those who would emphasize its virtual
irrelevance. Sir Harry Woolf, one of the most influential public law judges, not
surprisingly falls into the former category. Commenting in 1986 (p. 222), he
said that the statistics show a "convincing picture of an increasing need to resort
to the courts for protection against alleged abuse by public bodies of their public
duties." On the other hand, even with over 1,200 civil applications annually,
"the number of cases is infinitesimal compared with the millions of decisions
taken daily by public authorities" (Harlow and Rawlings, 1984: 258; also see
Hutchinson, 1985). The reality, as I have argued elsewhere, is that data of this
sort provide an unreliable basis for generalizing about the importance of judicial
review as a whole (Sunkin, 1987). Most specifically the data do not reveal who
is using judicial review, and against which agencies, and in what subject areas.

Table 10.2
Immigration Applications*

1981	1982	1983	1984	1985	1986	1987**	1988	1989
157	215	226	266	516	409	697	359	419

Proportion of all civil applications

1981	1982	1983	1984	1985	1986	1987**	1988	1989
46%	41.5%	32%	33%	59%	43.5%	52%	33%	32%

* All figures based on known applications; the actual numbers may therefore
have been higher.

** The figures given for 1987 - 89 are drawn from the Judicial Statistics,
Lord Chancellor's Department.

If statistics are to help us, we need to look more closely at the types of applications
being made.

Who Is Using Judicial Review and in What Areas?

Applications for judicial review are extremely diverse. During any period the
courts may be asked to adjudicate the legality of the actions of a vast array of
public agencies involving issues ranging from prison discipline to education;
salmonella levels in poultry to social welfare; the licensing of sex shops to hospital
decisions not to operate on children; the funding of local government to the
provision of riot equipment to local police forces; and the granting of asylum to
tax collection. But, despite this diversity, much of the caseload consistently
focuses on a very narrow band of issues, and a great majority of the challenges
are to the decisions of a very few agencies. As Table 10.2 shows, throughout
the 1980s immigration has generated a very substantial proportion of the litigation
and, not surprisingly, the Home Office has been the most challenged central
government department.

Immigration Applications

At its peak in 1985, immigration generated nearly 60 percent of all civil
applications for review. Table 10.1 suggested that there was a steady increase
in the use of judicial review during the mid-1980s. But if the immigration cases
are excluded, we find that the nonimmigration caseload presents a far more
erratic picture. For example, contrary to expectations between 1984 and 1985,
the number of nonimmigration cases actually declined by nearly 32 percent.
While the overall figures seemed to confirm the widespread assumption that

resort to judicial review was increasing, in reality resort to judicial review was either steady or declining in many subject areas during this period.

The focusing of litigation is also evident when we look more closely at the immigration caseload. The great growth in immigration cases between 1984 and 1985, for example, coincided with the increasing use made of judicial review to challenge one type of immigration decision, namely refusals of entry. The known number of these increased from 128 in 1984 to 291 (that is, nearly half of the immigration caseload) in 1985. Moreover, in 1985, over 60 percent of the 183 entry cases were known to have been brought by those claiming to be genuine visitors (individuals who having arrived in the United Kingdom without a visa failed to persuade immigration officers that they were genuine visitors). In other words, during 1985 this one type of administrative decision generated approximately 20 percent of all civil applications for judicial review.

The ability of the court system to cope with the overall quantity of litigation is a pervasive concern of those responsible for judicial administration. Judges, of course, deny that they are influenced by such bureaucratic considerations, but there can be little doubt that such factors do impinge on their decision making and will lead, for example, to the imposition of more stringent leave criteria in certain classes of case. In *Ex parte Swati & Butt*,[8] for example, the Court of Appeal expressed its concern over the numbers of "genuine visitor" cases and took steps to stem the flow of these cases by directing judges not to grant leave to apply for judicial review unless the application revealed exceptional circumstances. The effect was immediate. As the statistics show, between 1985 and 1986 the size of the immigration caseload fell for the first time since 1981, and the number of "genuine visitor" applications fell drastically so that they no longer represent a significant group of applications. A similarly restrictive approach was taken by the House of Lords toward homelessness litigation and I will consider this later.

Before leaving immigration, there are two other matters that should be noted. During 1987 approximately 200 applications were brought seeking to challenge refusals to grant political asylum; this replaced visitor applications as the largest subject of judicial review challenge. Most of the 200 or so applications were brought by Tamils fleeing the unrest in Sri Lanka and by Kurds trying to escape torture in Turkey. At the time of this writing, only 320 of the 4,000 Kurds seeking asylum have been granted full refugee status and a very large number of applications are still being processed by the Home Office (Mills, 1990).

The second issue relates to representation. One of the striking findings of my work on judicial review caseload has been the apparent influence on the caseload of a small number of lawyers. During the first six months of 1985, for example, five firms of solicitors processed 40 percent of the immigration caseload. This implies that if we are to gain an understanding of why immigration has been such a fertile area of litigation, while vast tracts of governmental activity have been largely untouched by judicial review, we must look at how and why particular types of cases get to these lawyers and at the litigation strategies employed by them. These issues lie at the very heart of our living public law; I hope to be able to explore them in a future study.

Homelessness Applications

Our housing legislation imposes duties upon local housing authorities toward the homeless.[9] The duties arise if authorities are satisfied that applicants for housing are homeless, or are threatened with homelessness. The nature of the duties will then vary and the full duty to secure the provision of permanent accommodation arises only when applicants satisfy local housing authorities that they have a priority need and that they became homeless unintentionally. These decisions are of critical importance and will often determine whether families are housed or not. But despite their importance, the legislation does not provide for an appeal against the decisions and usually the only possible avenue of recourse is by way of judicial review (Hoath, 1990).

In *Puhlhoffer v. The London Borough of Hillingdon*,[10] a family with small children living in a single hotel room without cooking facilities applied for permanent housing from the London Borough of Hillingdon. Hillingdon refused to help on the grounds that the family had somewhere to live and therefore were not homeless within the meaning of the legislation. The Puhlhoffers applied for judicial review, but their application was ultimately rejected when the House of Lords held that homelessness was a question of fact for the authority to decide and not a matter of law for the courts. Delivering the only opinion of the House, Lord Brightman, referring to what he called the "mass of litigation" under the homelessness legislation, said that he was "troubled at the prolific use of judicial review . . . [to challenge] the performance by local authorities of their functions." He indicated that leave to apply for review should be granted only in exceptional case and he concluded by expressing "the hope that there will be a lessening in the number of challenges . . . mounted against local authorities who are endeavoring in extremely difficult circumstances, to perform their duties." In light of these comments it is interesting to look at the incidence of challenge in this area. The relevant figures are set out in Table 10.3, which shows the numbers of known homelessness applications over the period 1981–89 together with the numbers refused leave.

The figures must be looked at against the background of the overall scale of homelessness in England and Wales. There are 365 housing authorities and in 1985 there were 203,480 applications to these authorities for assistance under the legislation, and of these just over 100,000 were rejected. By 1989 the numbers of applications for help had grown to 251,850 and again approximately half of these were rejected. Over this period, then, there was an annual pool of between 100,000 and 125,000 dissatisfied claimants and their families.[11] We cannot tell from these figures how many would have wanted to pursue a grievance, nor how many had a potential basis for legal action. But it is difficult to understand how 60 or 70 applications—most of which were granted leave and were therefore

Table 10.3
Homeless Applications

1981	1982	1983	1984	1985	1986	1987	1988	1989
8	55	75	69	66	32	79	94	144

Number Known to have been refused leave

1981	1982	1983	1984	1985	1986	1987	1988	1989
-	4	4	4	6	13	13	10	-

presumably accepted as arguable by the judges—can be described as prolific. Nor is it easy to understand how this relatively small number of challenges could be seriously interfering with the work of the housing authorities in general. On the contrary, the statistics in Table 10.3 seem to imply that judicial review is actually being underused in this area. The resounding message given by the *Puhlhoffer* decision is that judicial sensitivity to the pressures facing the administration can weigh far more heavily on judges than the claims of the homeless, despite the acknowledged desperation of their plight.

Puhlhoffer may be explicable as an attempt to focus judicial resources on issues of particular importance, to the exclusion of more routine applications, however arguable these may be. But if arguable claims of illegality are excluded simply because they are routine and unexceptional, the rule of law is indeed turned on its head. This results in a situation in which judges become increasingly reluctant to handle issues as claims of illegality become more frequent. Attempts to focus on issues of strategic and public importance are understandable in light of the potential pressure of the caseload but they will continue to create tensions within the system, unless individual redress is effectively provided for elsewhere so that judicial review can become a purely public interest jurisdiction, as some have argued it should (Woolf, 1986). At present this seems unlikely in the near future. Despite the liberalizing of standing in the early 1980s[12] and the regular flow of well-publicized applications for judicial review designed to put public interest issues before the courts, to attract publicity, and act as a catalyst for protest, personal redress litigation continues to generate most of the judicial review challenges.

One sort of litigation, however, that forces the judiciary into the public interest domain, and that has played an important part in politicizing the work of the judges over the past decade, has been *between* public bodies; most notably, between central and local government. Many of these cases have been brought by Labour-controlled local councils against the central government to challenge budgetary decisions. They reflect "the aggressive use of the law" by central government to control local government, particularly local government expenditure (Leach and Stoker, 1988). The resulting "juridication of the central-local relationship (Loughlin, 1986: 193; Grant, 1989) has forced issues that would have been previously resolved by bargaining and by negotiation into the courts. The most significant recent example concerned the new community charge (poll tax), which replaced the system of rates in April 1990. Under the old rating system, authorities raised money from local residents based on the rental value of the property in which they lived. The community charge is a sum levied by authorities on all adults regardless of the value of their property, the sums levied vary between authorities depending on the needs of the authorities. After authorities had set their budgets, however, central government imposed ceilings on the level of the community charge that could be imposed. Several Labour councils unsuccessfully challenged this charge-capping on the grounds, inter alia, that its imposition was unreasonable because the criteria used were secret and discriminated against Labour councils. In dismissing the claims the courts emphasized the breadth of power that had been given by Parliament to the secretary of state and indicated a familiar deference to the executive, this time in the area of "public financial administration."

Which Central Government Departments Are Being Challenged?

My principal theme has been to argue that judicial review is a process used regularly by a small number of lawyers in a few subject areas against a correspondingly narrow band of public agencies. A graphic example of this final point is provided by the range of central government departments that are regularly challenged. During the first six months of 1985 there were 159 applications against central government, of which 149 were against the Home Office. Most of these were immigration cases, some were applications brought by prisoners. The other ten applications were against the Department of the Environment, the Department of Health and Social Security, and Department of Education and Science. A similar picture was revealed during 1987. In that year nearly half (616) the civil applications were brought against central government. Of these, over 80 percent (503) were against the Home Office. As in 1985, the vast majority of these were immigration cases. During 1988 the numbers of central government applications fell in relative terms to approximately 33 percent (354) of the civil caseload and the proportion brought against the Home Office also fell to just below 70 percent (332).

There is therefore some evidence to suggest that the numbers of central government challenges have been declining recently. This may indicate that the steps taken by central government to protect itself from challenge (discussed later) are beginning to have an effect. On the other hand, it is likely that the bulk of this decline can be accounted for by the reduction in the number of immigration applications against the Home Office in 1988 and that governmental agencies in general are being challenged more frequently. Even if this is the case, the overriding impression is that judicial review remains a process that, in quantitative terms at least, appears hardly to touch most areas of central government administration.

THE IMPACT OF JUDICIAL REVIEW ON CENTRAL GOVERNMENT

I now consider the principal impacts of judicial review litigation on central government. I do not intend to comment on the impact of individual cases on particular policies save to say that in the United Kingdom judicial review operates within a constitutional and political climate dominated by the executive, and impacts of litigation on the content of government policy are likely to be peripheral and short-lived. As Prosser (1985: 74) has commented: "successful test cases which threaten established policy, especially by increasing expenditure, will meet with quick nullification or administrative action." To discern the more enduring impacts of judicial review we have to examine the effects of litigation on the way government approaches policy implementation and manages and reacts to litigation.

The past ten years may be characterized as a period during which central government has been forced to take judicial review seriously. By the early 1980s, government had become aware that it was vulnerable to legal challenge; the then Treasury solicitor, Sir Michael Kerry (1983: 168–177), for example, complained that too many cases were being lost in the courts. According to Kerry, the reasons for this vulnerability lay in the low levels of legal awareness among civil servants and their failure to pay adequate attention to the legal implications of action, particularly at the policy planning stage. He illustrated this criticism by reference to one of the leading rate-capping cases brought by the Labour-controlled London Borough of Brent.[13] Brent had successfully challenged the secretary of state for the environment's refusal to meet council officials before setting the sum that could be raised by Brent from its rates. Apparently the department had not contemplated the possibility that councils might ask the secretary of state for a hearing or the legal consequences, should a hearing be refused. The decision came as a surprise to the department and must have been a considerable embarrassment to the responsible minister. Kerry's point was that the result might have been different had officials paid more attention to the law.

The situation in the early 1980s may be summarized as one in which law and lawyers were operating on the fringes of the administrative process. The tradition within the civil service was that civil servants were generalists and rarely were administrators (Drewry, 1981, 1986). Moreover, the role of government lawyers was primarily responsive and consisted of handling litigation that had already been instituted and providing advice when sought. Within this tradition, lawyers were encouraged to consider legal issues only where problems arose, and the prevailing pragmatism did not encourage more coherence or planning. In other words, the overall impression is of a system that was muddling through.

The 1980s have seen central government adopting a three-pronged strategy, designed to ensure that the risks of successful challenge are reduced. First, there has been an emphasis on improving the quality of legislative drafting in the hope that departmental intentions are more clearly expressed and discretionary power more effectively insulated from judicial interference. This has produced more comprehensive preclusion or ouster clauses and the more explicit allocation of subjectively worded discretionary power to ministers. Second, administrators have been encouraged to become more legally aware by improved training and the circulation by the Cabinet Office of an internal pamphlet entitled "The Judge Over Your Shoulder." The purpose of this was to summarize the basic principles of judicial review and the "precautions that could be taken" to reduce the risks of challenge (Bradley, 1987). Finally, management within departments has encouraged officials to make greater use of government lawyers in the hope that they will be able to play a more proactive role in decision making.

The theory underlying these management strategies is that the system as a whole must be equipped to anticipate and respond to legal challenge. But how will the theory be translated into practice? Will it, for example, reduce the incidence of challenge or lead to an improvement in the quality of decision making? Although, as we have seen, there was some evidence of a reduction in the numbers of challenges to central government between 1987 and 1988, it is unlikely that internal strategies will have great effect on the incidence of judicial review. Indeed, it is possible that increased legal awareness and a greater emphasis on law will stimulate a more litigous legal environment leading to more rather than fewer challenges.

The effects on the quality of decision making are also difficult to predict. The law in this area is extremely open-textured, and while officials may now be aware of the general obligations to act "fairly" and "reasonably" and to act with procedural propriety, such duties leave tremendous room for doubt and uncertainty in day-to-day decision making (Rawlings, 1986). More important is the fact that law will inevitably remain but one of a complex of multiple constraints operating upon public officials. Political, policy, and budgetary pressures will continue to force departments to take actions that are known to be susceptible to challenge. In this context, the best that departments can hope for is that they will be able to make decisions knowing the risks being incurred rather than unconsciously assuming risks of challenge. As an academic public lawyer, I will conclude with the hope that my assumptions are correct and that government will be unable to stem the flow of challenges. I prefer a system that encourages claims of government illegality to be fought out in the judicial arena to one that insulates them within the closed environment of a government department that has managed to cross its "t"'s and dot its "i"'s.

NOTES

This chapter is based on a presentation to the interim meeting of the Research Committee on Comparative Judicial Studies of the International Political Science Association, University of Victoria, May 1990.

1. For a more detailed consideration of the judicial review caseload during the years 1981–86, see Sunkin (1987). This chapter includes data on the years 1987 and 1988 that have been collected with the help of a grant from the Nuffield Foundation.

2. The comments contained in the last section of the chapter are based on a pilot study of the impact of judicial review on central government in the United Kingdom that was carried out under the auspices of the Royal Institute of Public Administration and was funded by a small grant from the Nuffield Foundation. A more extensive paper based on the study is being prepared for publication.

3. [1985] A.C. 374.

4. *Uppal v. Home Office* [1978], *The Times*, November 11.

5. *Heywood v. Hull Prison Board of Visitors* [1980] 1 W.L.R. 386.

6. [1982] 3 All E.R. 1124.

7. Ibid. at p. 1134.

8. [1986] 1 All E.R. 717.

9. Part 111 of the Housing Act 1985.

10. [1986] 1 All E.R. 467.

11. Statistics on homelessness applications to local housing authorities are from the Department of the Environment.

12. See, for example, *I.R.C. v. National Federation of the Self-Employed and Small Businesses Ltd.* [1982] A.C. 617; *R v. Hammersmith & Fulham London Borough Council, exparte People Before Profit Ltd.* (1982) 80 L.G.R. 322; *R v. Secretary of State for Social Services, exparte Child Poverty Action Group*, *The Times*, August 16, 1984; *R v. Secretary of State for the Environment exparte Rose Theatre Trust Co* [1990] 1 All E.R. 754. It should be noted, of course, that the statistics do not reveal the intention of the litigants.

13. *R v. Secretary of State for the Environment exparte Brent London Borough Council* [1982] 2 W.L.R. 693.

REFERENCES

Ackner, Lord. (1987). Judicial review-judicial creativity at its best. *The Australian Law Journal* 61: 442–451.

Blom-Cooper, L. (1982). The new face of judicial review: Administrative changes in order. *Public Law*, Summer: 250–261.

Boynton, Sir J. (1986). Judicial review of administrative decisions—A background paper. *Public Administration* 64: 147–161.

Bradley, A. W. (1987). The judge over your shoulder. *Public Law*, Winter: 485–488.

Drewry, G. (1981). Lawyers in the U.K. civil service. *Public Administration* 59: 15–46.

———. (1986). Public lawyers and public administrators: Prospects for an alliance. *Public Administration* 64: 173–188.

Grant, M. (1989). Central-local relations: The balance of power. In J. Jowell and D. Oliver (eds.), *The changing constitution*, 2nd ed. Oxford: Oxford University Press, 246–272.

Griffith, J.A.G. (1985). Judicial decision-making in public law. *Public Law*, Winter: 564–582.

Harlow, C. (1980). Public and private law: definition without distinction. *Modern Law Review* 43: 241–265.

————, and Rawlings, R. (1984). *Law and administration*. London: Weidenfeld & Nicolson.

Hoath, D. (1990). The view of the homelessness legislation: A missed opportunity. *New Law Journal* 140: 412–415.

Hutchinson, A. (1985). The rise and ruse of administrative law and scholarship. *Modern Law Review* 48: 293–324.

Justice-All Souls. (1988). *Administrative justice: Some necessary reforms*. Oxford: Oxford University Press.

Kerry, Sir M. (1983). Administrative law and the Administrator. *Management in Government* 3: 168–177.

————. (1986). Administrative law: The practical effects of developments over the past 25 years on administration in central government. *Public Administration* 64: 163–172.

Law Commission. (1976). *Report on remedies in administrative law*. London: Cmnd. 6407.

Leach, S., and Stoker, J. (1988). The transformation of central-local relations. In C. Graham and T. Prosser (eds.), *Waiving the rules: The constitution under Thatcherism*. Milton Keynes, U.K.: Open University Press.

Loughlin, M. (1986). *Local government in the modern state*. London: Sweet & Maxwell.

Mills, H. (1990). Hunger strike by Kurds over refugee status. *The Independent*, August 22.

Prosser, T. (1983). *Test cases for the poor: Legal techniques in the politics of social welfare*. London: Child Poverty Action Group.

Rawlings, H. (1986). Judicial review and the "control" of government. *Public Administration* 64: 135–145.

Sunkin, M. (1983). Judicial review: rights and discretion in public law. *Modern Law Review* 46: 645–653.

————. (1987). What is happening to applications for judicial review? *Modern Law Review* 50: 432–467.

Wade, H.W.R. (1988). *Administrative law*, 6th ed. Oxford: Oxford University Press.

Woolf, Sir H. (1986). Public law-private law: Why the divide? A personal view. *Public Law*, Summer: 220–238.

11

Judicial Review and Israel's Struggle for a Written Constitution

Martin Edelman

Right from its establishment in 1948, Israel has been an exceptional, that is to say, a different state. Consider the status of constitutionalism in Israel. Of the 159 members of the United Nations, only 5 nations do not have formal, integrated written constitutions. Israel is one of this strikingly small group (Blaustein and Franz, 1988).

Ideally, a constitution should help resolve certain fundamental political issues. It should incorporate a national consensus about a society's basic values and the structure of its government. A constitution elevates those matters above the ordinary political realm. In this sense a written constitution has both a legal and a political significance. Legally, it embodies the highest norms of the state. State organs, including the judiciary, are expected to give those norms priority in arriving at their decisions. Politically, a constitution sets parameters on public policy. As a statement of the nation's values, it helps to educate the citizenry while it simultaneously serves as a guideline for the political elite.

Israeli political leadership has not been unaware of the benefits to be derived from a written constitution. From its inception as a state, Israel has wrestled with the problem of adopting a constitution. Yet each time the political leadership has been on the brink of decisively resolving the remaining issues in contention, they have backed away. Despite the fact that both a relatively stable pattern of institutional arrangements and an adherence to democratic values have emerged, the reluctance to adopt a formal written constitution indicates that certain matters continue to be politically sensitive. Moreover, although the Israeli Supreme Court is an increasingly active policymaker, the Israeli justices do not exercise judicial review akin to their American counterparts. Without a written constitution, the Israeli justices cannot claim the authority of guardians of the fundamental law of the land.

INITIAL FAILURE TO DRAFT A CONSTITUTION

Following the terms of the 1947 United Nations Partition Resolution, the Jewish Community in Palestine established the State of Israel on May 14, 1948. Simultaneous with the Proclamation of Independence, a Provisional Government was established.

The Israeli leadership began with the belief that every modern state ought to have a written constitution. Even before the Partition Resolution, the National Council (of the Jewish Community in Palestine) had appointed a Committee on Constitutional Questions. That Committee prepared several memoranda. After the UN Resolution, the Jewish Agency (of the World Zionist Organization) had Dr. Leo Kohn prepare a draft constitution. And the proclamation of Independence stated that the Provisional Government was to remain in office "pending the setting up of duly elected bodies of the State in accordance with a Constitution to be drawn up by a Constituent Assembly" (I Laws of the State of Israel 1, 1948: 3).

Accordingly, a Constitutional Committee was appointed by the Provisional Government. It considered the previous material, particularly the Kohn draft, and published a series of booklets to guide the work of the forthcoming Constituent Assembly. In sum, the Israeli leadership gave every indication, both before and immediately after statehood, that they would promptly adopt a written constitution (Sager, 1976; Freudenheim, 1967: 1–18).

Moreover, the Israelis were concerned with establishing their state more firmly in the international community. The 1947 UN Resolution had called for democratic constitutions in both the proposed Jewish and Arab states in Palestine.[1] Yet many nations had not recognized Israel and the surrounding Arab countries had attacked the newly proclaimed Jewish state in order to destroy it. The problematic status of their state made the Israelis most anxious to comply with the terms of the UN Resolution.

Nonetheless a written constitution did not emerge. The first obstacle was the division between (Orthodox) religious and secular political parties about the role of Jewish Law (Halachah) in the new state. Orthodox Jews believe that divine commands are embodied in Halachah and that therefore this system of religious law cannot be subordinate to secular law; on the contrary, the Jewish state and its constitution had to be based upon Halachah. That seemed like a theocracy to secularists; they sought to establish a constitution whose validity was derived solely from the political and legal authority of the state.

In 1949 the secular majority was unwilling to decide this matter simply by putting it to a vote. That might have caused irreparable harm to the much-needed consensus both within Israel and among the Jewish communities in the Diaspora. After all, the country was under attack from the surrounding Arab armies. Roughly 28 percent of the Jewish population considered themselves Orthodox. A population of that magnitude can seldom be ignored in a democracy, a system of government that strives for reconciliation and consensus. And war leads any nation to emphasize unity.

Similar considerations applied to Jewish communities outside Israel, particularly in the United States. Those communities had led the struggle to obtain international recognition of the need to establish a Jewish State in Palestine. Why risk fragmenting those communities along Orthodox/non-Orthodox lines when unity was imperative? Prudence and statecraft cautioned against alienating a sizable minority at the very beginning of the new, fragile, state (Edelman, 1980).

Narrower political interests also argued against adopting a written constitution. Mapai, then the dominant political party, and its leader, David Ben-Gurion, came to see distinct advantages in a constitutionally unrestricted supreme parliament. Conversely, most of the other secular parties continued to see great virtue in a written constitution precisely because it would limit a Mapai-led coalition government (Sager, 1976; Likhovski, 1971).

In the event, Mapai and the Torah Front (the Orthodox parties) prevailed. When the Constituent Assembly was elected on January 25, 1949, it never undertook the task for which it was called into existence. Yet it was more representative than the Provisional Government, whose members were largely self-selected. The members of the Constituent Assembly derived their authority directly from the people. The Provisional Government therefore dissolved itself and transferred its powers to the newly elected Constituent Assembly. That body in turn enacted the Transition Law under which it became the First Knesset (parliament).

THE PARTIES: ISRAELI'S OPERATIVE "CONSTITUTION"

To this day, Israel functions without a formal written constitution. Its governing arrangements are an outgrowth of the decisions of the Provisional Government and the 1949 Transition Law. The stable pattern that has emerged makes it possible to describe the operative constitution: Israel is a secular republic, with a theoretically sovereign parliament (the Knesset), a politically powerful cabinet (the government), an independent secular judiciary, and a largely ceremonial president.

Under these arrangements, the key political institutions of Israel are not the formal governmental agencies but the political parties. Israel is a highly politicized society. The reasons for this go back to the Zionist movement, where many of the existing parties had their origin. Within that nationalist movement, voluntary associations were formed in order to influence the policies of the World Zionist Organization and the projected Jewish State. The latter objective was pursued by each political group creating its own network of institutions in Palestine to reflect its ideology.

Since the establishment of the state, the extragovernmental role of Israeli parties has been reduced, but it has not been eliminated. The larger parties still provide their members with a variety of ancillary services—youth movements, health insurance, recreation and vacation facilities. And some party institutions— like the kibbutzim—are still all-enveloping. Furthermore, the creation of government agencies did not entirely displace party services; many Israeli government bureaucracies show excessive partisanship. Professor Benjamin Akzin's (1955: 509) statement is still accurate: political parties in Israel "occupy a more prominent place and exercise a more pervasive influence than in any other state, with the exception of some one-party states."

It should also be noted that until May 1977 Israeli politics was dominated by Mapai and its successor, the Labor Party. For the first 29 years of statehood, and indeed throughout most of the 30-year period of the British Mandate that preceded independence, the Jewish community in Palestine was led by socialists. While the Mapai-Labor leadership group was more pragmatic than doctrinaire, and while they were never able to enact their program completely, they were ideologically disposed to a state-run society. By design, the "House of Labor" permeated all aspects of Israeli society (Medding, 1972). The governments since 1977 have been more inclined to change that pattern into a more market-oriented society. For the present, however, Israel remains a society dominated by government institutions directed by highly partisan political parties.

As might be expected in this environment, overt partisan considerations are an inseparable element in the workings of the Knesset and the government. Parliamentary parties were created to further, in that arena, the ideological goals of the Zionist groups that spawned them. Party discipline is exceptionally strong; members are expected faithfully to carry out the party's program. Despite the multiparty system, and despite the failure of any list to obtain a parliamentary majority, decisions reached by the government are rarely overturned by the Knesset (Weiss and Brichta, 1969–70). The centralized, hierarchical nature of Israeli political parties all but insures a parliamentary majority for any government proposal. As a result, Israelis expect that public policies emanating from these institutions will reflect the partisan concerns of the parties in the governing coalition.

BUILDING A CONSTITUTION PIECEMEAL: BASIC LAWS
AND THE LIMITS OF JUDICIAL AUTHORITY

Precisely because of the rampant partisanship, the idea of a written constitution would not die. The potential for arbitrary government was obvious. A written constitution, by its very nature, would regularize procedures and define governmental powers. It would help ensure that the government of the day would not simply act as it pleased. Moreover, a written constitution would undoubtedly contain a bill of rights, for that, too, has become part of modern constitutionalism. By articulating those fundamental human rights that were beyond governmental authority in most circumstances, a bill of rights would provide another hedge against arbitrary state actions. These matters transcended the interests of the minority parties; they were rooted in a concern for democracy itself.

Thus, try as he might, Ben-Gurion could not kill the idea that a democratic Israel needed a written constitution. Toward the end of 1949, Ben-Gurion's cabinet voted to postpone indefinitely the drafting of a constitution. Yet the Knesset's Constitution, Law and Justice Committee continued to consider the issue. The committee could not resolve the matter, but the question was simply too important to die in committee. The committee referred the issue to the full plenum, where it was debated at great length. Ultimately, a compromise resolution was passed. On June 13, 1950, the Knesset agreed that a constitution would be built up, chapter by chapter, upon the enactment of Basic Laws.

To date, nine Basic Laws—The Knesset (1958), Israel Land Administration (1960), The President (1974), The Government (1968), The State Economy (1976), The Armed Forces (1976), Jerusalem, the Capital of Israel (1980), The Judiciary (1984), and The State Comptroller (1988)—have been enacted. In general, the Basic Laws have codified existing practices and symbols. The relation of Basic Laws to ordinary laws is a pivotal factor in the discussion below. But that discussion requires one more piece of background information: the role of the secular courts, particularly the Supreme Court, in Israeli politics.

The courts are seen as a functional barrier—perhaps the only one—against partisan decisions. Given the rampant partisanship of their society, Israelis value the utility of independent, objective and impartial decision making. The civil judiciary is seen as the institutional repository of those values. The authority that accompanies such an assessment gives the Israeli civil judiciary, particularly the Supreme Court, considerable power. Thus the increased authority of the civil courts derives from the same factors that lay behind the continuous, if sometimes quiescent, drive for a written constitution: the perceived need to institutionalize certain fundamental values.

The civil courts have done what they could. As Jeffrey M. Albert (1969: 1247) noted,

despite the non-existence of a written constitution or bill of rights . . . the Supreme Court has begun to assert a significant constitutional function. In a number of important cases it has asserted the right to read legislation in the light of suprastatutory principles which are said to exist independently of the legislative authority. . . . Rights to hearing and cross-examination have been required in statutory proceedings that did not provide such safeguards, and administrative discretion to deny licenses, to determine election lists, to register companies, and to censor newspapers has been substantially whittled down. When statutory language is equally susceptible to either of two readings, resort to a superstatutory standard is simply a technique of deducing the legislature's intent which does not involve wide use of the court's creative power. But where a court adds requirements to a statutory scheme, as the Israeli court has done in the hearing and cross-examination cases, or when it bends language away from its ordinary meaning to conform to some superstatutory norm, as it has done in the administrative discretion cases, it has taken upon itself a much more significant function.

The Israeli civil courts have done what they can to protect basic "constitutional" values (Shapira, 1974). But there are obvious limits so long as they cannot invalidate governmental actions for being unconstitutional. In the guise of "interpreting" legislative intent, even the Supreme Court is bound by subsequent Knesset "clarification." When the courts add procedural protections—whether by filling in lacunae or by transforming words into terms of art within the legal craft—they face essentially the same limitations.

It must be remembered that in the classic debate between James I and Chief Justice Coke about whether law was to be read by "natural" reason or the "artificial reason and judgment of law" (*Fuller's Case*, 1607), the political sovereign won in the court of history (Dicey, 1885; McWhinney, 1969). The English judges may say "Parliament never intended to give authority to make such rules; they are unreasonable and ultra-vires" (*Kruse v. Johnson*, 1898). The Israeli justices may say "the Legislator well knows of the existence of the rules of natural justice" (*Altagar v. Mayor*, 1966). But in each country, in the absence of a written constitution that functions as supreme, fundamental law, court rulings will prevail only so long as the political sovereign—which in Israel is the Knesset—acquiesces.

In Israel, the authority of the civil courts and their care in imposing only the most basic, most widely accepted values of natural justice have generally precluded Knesset reversal.[2] The Knesset's noninterference with most Supreme Court judgments has been based on a perception of the justices as neutral, impartial guardians of "the law," and on the political hesitation to confront the electoral consequences that would follow from "disobeying" a court order. Yet the commentators and the justices are well aware of the fragile political and legal base of the Court's "constitutional" rulings.[3]

BASIC LAW + NATURAL JUSTICE = "FUNDAMENTAL" LAW: THE *BERGMAN* CASE

Against this background, the importance of *Bergman v. Minister of Finance* (1969) is readily apparent. There for the first time, the Israeli Supreme Court declared an act of the Knesset void for violating a Basic Law (Klein, 1971).

Dr. Aharon Bergman brought an action before the High Court of Justice to block the implementation of the (Campaign) Financing Law of 1969. Dr. Bergman's complaint was that the law unfairly discriminated against new political parties because it provided governmental funds only for those parties represented in the outgoing Knesset. Specifically, he argued that the Financing Law violated the equality required by Section 4 of the Basic Law: The Knesset.[4]

Moreover, that section expressly provided that its provisions "shall not be varied save by a majority of the members of the Knesset." In 1959 the Knesset had entrenched that provision still further.[5] The Financing Law had passed its first reading in the Knesset by a vote of 24 to 2, a fairly common division in that assembly, since it conducts its business without any mandated quorum.

Because a majority of the entire plenum would consist of not less than 61 votes, Dr. Bergman argued that the 1969 act was plainly not a valid amendment to Section 4.

In his opinion for all five justices who participated in the case, Justice Landau agreed that the Financing Law was in conflict with the equality required by Section 4 of the Basic Law: The Knesset. The absolute denial of funds to a new list constituted a major denial of equal opportunity in the democratic electoral process. Justice Landau acknowledged the absence of any provision in Israel's written law that expressly authorized the Court to construe statutes in terms of the principle of natural justice upholding the equality of all before the law. "Nevertheless, this principle that is nowhere inscribed breathes the breath of life into our whole constitutional system" (*Bergman*: 572). It was therefore right and just, Justice Landau maintained, for the High Court to use it in interpreting the law.

The Court's opinion was a skillful amalgam of the conventional and the radical. It purported to be doing nothing more than using a principle of natural justice to interpret a "border-line case," "open to two interpretations." As noted above, this had become familiar Israeli judicial practice. Actually, without so much as a single comment, the Court had decided the case on novel grounds. It had applied its natural justice approach to a Basic Law and then used that interpretation to block the implementation of the subsequently enacted Financing Law.

Normally, Israeli courts adhere to the principle of *lex posterior derogat priori*.[6] If the Knesset is the sovereign legal authority in Israel, each Knesset has the same unlimited authority as its predecessors. The duly enacted Financing Law, precisely because it was posterior in time, should have prevailed over any conflicting interpretation of an earlier law. Plainly the Supreme Court had acted on the unarticulated premise that Section 4 of the Basic Law had constitutional status and as such was superior to ordinary law.

The Court's silence left important theoretical issues unaddressed. Why were Basic Laws—which had been enacted by the same procedures as all other statutes—to be regarded as fundamental? Was their special status derived from their designations as Basic Laws? Was it derived from their lineage—the early debates about a constitution and the chapter-by-chapter compromise? Perhaps these questions give the *Bergman* decision a "constitutional" dimension it did not warrant. Perhaps the key to the opinion was simply the fact that an entrenched provision had not been observed. The justices had not attempted to resolve these issues.

As it stood, the *Bergman* opinion meant that the political leadership could only surmise the premises on which the Supreme Court justices had operated. Yet to discuss the *Bergman* case, the Israeli political elite had to enter into serious discussion about the nature of a constitution for their polity. The Israeli Supreme Court had forced the issue back on the overt political agenda.

Two days before the High Court rendered its decision in *Bergman*, the minister of justice had indicated that the time was approaching when the Knesset should complete the Israeli constitution through its chapter-by-chapter method. He indicated that his ministry was drafting Basic Laws on the Judiciary, on Human Rights, and on Legislation. Significantly, the minister indicated that the completed constitution would not be a superior, paramount law. The Justice Ministry in that Labor-led government was acting on the premise that the Knesset, like the British Parliament, was the sovereign legal authority in Israel (Klein, 1969).

In 1969 the Knesset also was operating on that theory. True, it amended the Financing Law to comply with *Bergman*. In the midst of a general election, the major political parties literally could not afford to ignore the decision. Within two weeks the Knesset found a formula for providing funds to all political parties, including the new election lists. The major Israeli political parties were simply unwilling to enter the campaign without public funds. Nor were the politicians willing to reenact the original law by an absolute majority in the Knesset. That option was seemingly left open by *Bergman*, but it would have laid the major parties open to the charge that they favored playing with a stacked deck. Yet at the same time that the law was amended to bring it into compliance with *Bergman*, the Knesset pointedly added a section reasserting its *own* legal authority to enact laws that are "valid for every legal proceeding and for every matter and purpose" (Elman, 1969: 564).

The dramatic series of events, however, did not produce any significant movement toward the completion of a constitution. After the 1969 elections, yet another Labor-led government continued to "study" the issues. No draft bill was submitted to the Constitution, Law and Justice Committee. The committee itself took no action. To be sure, then, as always, Israel's security needs required constant attention. But given the justice minister's 1969 statement, it is clear that other factors were involved. In short, the elected leadership of the nation had not yet found a way to resolve the fundamental disagreement about the place of Orthodox Judaism in the Jewish State and they continued to prefer making policy unconstrained by the norms of a higher law embedded in a judicially enforceable written constitution.

CONSTITUTIONALIZING THE BASIC LAWS: NEAR SUCCESS IN 1975–80

Then, in December 1975 the government finally introduced the draft Basic Law: Legislation. The Ministry of Justice frankly acknowledged that it was proposing a "fundamental change." The "important innovation" related to the status of Basic Laws. Under the proposal, Basic Laws were to be treated as superior to other Knesset legislation. The Supreme Court, sitting as a special Constitutional Court, was to be authorized to nullify legislation that conflicted with Basic Laws (Draft, Basic Law: Legislation, 1975).

After six years of study and much comment from Israeli and foreign experts,[7] the government, another Labor-led coalition, had reversed its predecessors' position. The government had been persuaded that to "accord some measure of recognition to the interest in stability may be countermajoritarian, but it is not undemocratic if the interests thus stabilized are themselves the fundamental interest in human freedom and equality'' (Nimmer, 1970: 1259).

Not all members of the political elite were so persuaded. The first to attack it was another leading member of the Labor Party, the speaker of the Knesset. He criticized the proposal as an unwise denigration of the Knesset's legal sovereignty. The speaker maintained that if the draft was adopted, a group of nonelected judges would function as the supreme legislator instead of the 120 members of the Knesset elected by—and politically responsible to—the people. The speaker was not alone in his opposition to the draft. Supreme Court Justice Haim Cohn—a former attorney general and minister of justice—asserted the proposal would assign an essentially political, nonjudicial function to the Court (*Jerusalem Post International Edition*, January 23, 1976).

As the draft made its way through the legislative process, the reasons for the change in the Labor Party's position began to emerge. First, a quarter of a century had made some of the original objections to a written constitution irrelevant. In 1950, some party leaders, including Ben-Gurion, had argued that the new nation was not yet fully established. Hasty action, they maintained, would necessarily mean reliance upon foreign experience whose applicability to the emerging Israel was far from clear. Plainly, 25 years later, this argument had lost its force. Israel's experience as a self-governing democracy had produced the patterns outlined above. A written constitution could now be drafted that reflected Israel's practices.

In fact, political independence for a quarter of a century worked against a continuation of the status quo. The influence of inherited English concepts was dominant in the early years of the state. But this had changed. Israeli case law and legislation had departed from British law because of the need to adapt to local conditions. Moreover, the initial acceptance of English legal concepts also changed as Israeli-educated lawyers gradually replaced the generation that had been educated under the Mandate (Shambar, 1974: 471).

Second, in the original debates, Ben-Gurion had maintained that the British experience demonstrated that a written constitution was not essential for a modern democracy. In 1975 that argument no longer persuaded the Israeli leadership. The British constitutional system rests on its own particularistic foundations of custom and traditions developed over its long history. Israel was a new nation. Its Jewish population had come, in the very recent past, from more than 40 countries. And it contained a sizable non-Jewish population. (In 1975, approximately 15 percent of Israeli citizens were non-Jewish.) An unwritten constitutional system that produces a stable and effective democratic government in Britain appeared counterproductive in Israel. The great variety of cultural backgrounds in Israel might well require a written constitution to help educate its heterogeneous population about the norms of democracy. That had certainly been the American experience and the United States was also a nation of immigrants.

Third, the Israeli elite had come to believe that although the distinction between law and politics may have analytic utility, operationally courts do inevitably make public policy. Social and economic statutes and regulations that are the hallmark of every modern society require judicial interpretation. Those interpretations have a significant impact on public policy. From this point, it was a logical step for Israelis to accept the argument that it was better for its judges to function in a context where policy factors could be openly raised and discussed. A written constitution, indicating the basic values of Israeli society, would indicate which interests, values, and rights its judges ought to incorporate into their decisions.

Fourth, the widespread concern for individual rights remained. There was a consensus among both supporters and opponents of a written constitution that the Israeli courts had provided significant protection of human rights (Symposium, 1974). But supporters of a written constitution continued to maintain that a clear articulation of basic liberties—a bill of rights—could only enhance the situation. The absence of a written constitution entails disadvantages: the distinction between law and convention becomes blurred, and the absence of clear written rules largely imposes an onus on those who want to claim rights'' (Shamgar, 1974: 47).

This concern dovetails with a factor mentioned earlier. If judicial policy making is an inevitability in the modern state, a bill of rights is highly desirable. In matters touching upon fundamental human rights, it would *require* that the Court resort to basic political precepts, moral values, and social attitudes (Shapira, 1974: 509–511).

Finally, in 1975 partisan political considerations seemed to favor the adoption of a written constitution. The 1973 national elections had once again produced a Labor-led coalition government. But in the wake of the Yom Kippur War, the Labor Party had lost ground to a center-right grouping comprised of the Herut Party and the Liberal Party (Gahal). Leaders of both those parties, especially the Liberals, had always been in the forefront in the struggle for a written constitution. Presumably the elected political leadership reflected the wishes of part of the electorate. The Labor leadership, by now sponsoring a written constitution, was making a bid for support from the ''floating vote'' in the middle of the Israeli political spectrum.

Thus by May 1976 it was generally expected that the draft Basic Law: Legislation would soon be enacted by the Knesset. Even such opponents as Justice Cohn (1976) perceived this an inevitable. Once enacted, that Basic Law would have resolved most of the questions concerning the form and nature (as opposed to substance) of the Israeli constitution.

The question—much discussed in the scholarly literature (Nimmer, 1970: 1238–1240; Rubenstein, 1968: 202–208; Likhovski, 1971)—about whether the Knesset could legitimately enact constitutional provisions would have been answered with a clear affirmative. The proposed Basic Law: Legislation explicitly authorized the Knesset to enact Basic Laws.

The proposed Basic Law: Legislation would also have resolved the ambiguous status of the six Basic Laws then existing. It explicitly conferred constitutional status on *all* provisions of all Basic Laws—those already in existence as well as those that would be enacted at a later date.

Investing the Knesset with continuing constituent power, however, might enable a temporary parliamentary majority to entrench its particular policy objectives in the constitution. To guard against that potential abuse of power and to enhance the authority of all future Basic laws, the proposed Basic Law: Legislation provided that all such laws must be enacted, at all stages of Knesset decision making, by a majority of the full plenum. And any law that was to supersede or amend a Basic Law would not only have required a numerical majority to achieve its purpose, that purpose was required to be explicitly stated. This was to ensure that the Knesset, in enacting a law that contravened a Basic Law, did so in full, conscious knowledge. Under the proposed Basic Law: Legislation there was to be no implicit repeal of a Basic Law as some had argued on behalf of the 1969 Financing Law involved in *Bergman*.

Thus the proposal before the Knesset appeared to address and resolve most of the questions concerning the form and nature of an Israeli constitution. Israel was to have a written constitution, albeit one that was not yet complete. Duly enacted Basic Laws were to be Israel's written constitution. Most important, the constitution was to be superior to ordinary legislation.

In 1976 this change seemed politically acceptable. Because of the factors noted above, the draft proceeded through the legislative process with strong support. The preliminary discussion in the plenum (the first reading) and the subsequent full and detailed discussion in the Committee on the Constitution, Law and Justice (the second reading) produced little opposition. Even the change in government in May 1977 from a Labor-led to a Likud-led coalition did not, at first, alter this perception (Edelman, 1977). By 1978, Israel appeared to be ready to formally accept the notion that it was to be governed within the limits set out in a written constitution.

THE CONTINUING FAILURE OF CONSTITUTION-WRITING

The question remains, therefore, as to why this expectation did not come about. The usual response, from all the leaders of all the major parties, was that more pressing matters required attention. First, there was the startling Likud victory in 1977. After 29 years, Likud had replaced the Labor Alignment as the governing party.[8] Then the new government was confronted with the need to make major foreign policy decisions. That sequence of events culminated in the Camp David Accords (September 1978), and the signing of the Israeli-Egyptian Peace Treaty (May 1979). While the government of Prime Minister Begin tackled those vital matters, virtually everything else of significance—including the rapidly deteriorating economy—was all but neglected. This understandable response of the political elites cannot simply be dismissed.

But even as Israel's first peace treaty with an Arab state, and the largest one to boot, became an accepted fact, no effort was made to complete the constitution. By the 1980s, it was apparent that other problems were stalling the project. These did *not* concern the proposed Basic Law: Legislation discussed above; the support that had developed throughout the prior decade remained. Rather, concern was focused on the substantive provisions of the draft Basic Law: Human and Civil Rights. Sections of that proposal threatened to wreck the governing coalition.

Israelis cannot envision a written constitution that is superior to ordinary law that does not contain a bill of rights. In fact, as we have seen, much of the impetus behind the drive for a written constitution was linked to the demand for a formal bill of rights. Israelis, therefore, were unwilling to adopt a written constitution (as envisioned by the proposed Basic Law: Legislation) until they were assured that a bill of rights would shortly be added to the existing Basic Laws.

That assurance could not be given. The draft Basic Law: Human and Civil Rights had had a complicated preliminary history (Sager, 1976: 96–99). It was finally given a first reading on August 12, 1974, and sent to the Law, Constitution and Justice Committee for detailed consideration. That committee finished its revisions in April 1978, but the Knesset never scheduled it for the necessary second and third readings.

Two political problems caused the proposed to be derailed. One was security. Israel was still technically at war with all the surrounding Arab states except Egypt and was actually at war with the Palestine Liberation Organization. The need for swift action against terrorists and subversive elements remained. For example, most of the provisions of the British Mandate's Defense (Emergency) Regulations are still in force. Those regulations permit the military authorities of Israel to restrict freedom of movement, to place persons under police supervision, and even to deport them. The High Court may order the authorities to show cause for their actions, but they are still given a strong presumption of validity; full trial rights do not prevail at these hearings (Bracha, 1978).

Balancing the security interests reflected in those regulations against the provisions of a bill of rights was repeatedly referred to as "a difficult and delicate matter" (Sager, 1976: 97). "It is clear from the long and wavering road toward a Basic Law on civil liberties that the problem of the rights of the individual in a nation at war has been one of the major impediments to a formal constitution" (Sager, 1976: 98).

In retrospect, it is apparent that the 1978–79 optimism about a forthcoming constitution was a product of the afterglow of the Camp David Accords and the peace treaty with Egypt. When those efforts did not lead to a comprehensive peace settlement, the concern for security remained Israel's highest priority. And one fallout was the inability to strike an appropriate balance between security and constitutional rights. In turn, the momentum toward adopting a written constitution was slowed.

There was yet another issue causing delay: the division between Orthodox and non-Orthodox Jews about the role of Halachah in Israel. That division, it will be recalled, was a leading factor behind the 1949 decision to forego a written constitution. The division remained. And it posed major problems for the proposed Basic Law: Human and Civil Rights. For example, Section 14 of the draft provided that "every person is entitled to the freedom of divine worship." Under the existing religious status quo, Orthodox Jewish groups have a virtual monopoly of state recognition (Edelman, 1980). Section 14, if enacted in a law of constitutional status, would have granted equal status to the Reform, Liberal, and Conservative movements within Jewry. That is why, in 1974, a spokesman for the ultra-Orthodox Agudah movement called Section 14 the most "shocking" provision in the Draft (Sager 1976: 98).

By May 1977 Agudah and the other Orthodox parties had become essential parts of the Likud-led coalition. The secular elements in that coalition, and the overwhelming secular majority in the nation, would not tolerate the exclusion of provisions like Section 14 that protected "liberty of conscience." Therefore the government was politically unable to move the draft. Any resolution of the underlying issue of the place of Halachah in the Jewish state would have brought down the Government.

Thus Likud-led governments could enact more Basic Laws but could not complete Israel's written constitution. In 1980 the Knesset enacted Basic Law: Jerusalem, the Capital of Israel. Like the six preceding Basic Laws, it reflected an abiding consensus among Jewish Israelis that a united Jerusalem would remain the capital of the state. Four years later, the second Likud government enacted Basic Law: The Judiciary. This too reflected established practice by enacting into a Basic Law the existing structures and practices of the civil court system. Significantly the 1984 Basic Law: The Judiciary did *not* vest the Supreme Court with the power of judicial review. But neither did the discussion surrounding its enactment indicate that the Supreme Court would not eventually be given that authority when the constitution-making process was completed. In 1988 Basic Law: The State Comptroller was added. Again, this confirmed existing practice; the nonpartisan comptroller had been auditing government institutions and practices for more than three decades. In short, the issue of judicial review introduced by the 1969 *Bergman* decision remained in limbo. So, too, did the basic dissensus that precluded the adoption of a written constitution.

The general elections in July 1984 produced yet another effort to provide Israel with a written constitution. The strict proportional election system enshrined in the Basic Law: The Knesset had produced a politically deadlocked parliament. Neither of the two large party groups—the center-left Labor Alignment and the center-right Likud—could command a parliamentary majority. A National Unity Government was formed. But on the central issues confronting the Israeli polity— the future of the occupied territories, the role of Orthodox Judaism in the Jewish State—the grand coalition produced a rigid immobilism.

Frustration with the electoral system, a central feature of any democracy, led a group of scholars at Tel Aviv University Law School to draft an entire constitution for Israel. There was considerable discussion of the proposal, especially its proposed modified constituency system, when it was released in 1987. By 1988, however, the discussion was eclipsed by events, especially the Palestinian uprising in the territories. The 1988 Knesset elections produced a continuation of the left-right parliamentary stalemate and another Likud-Labor coalition government. But those events did not revive discussion of the draft constitution written at the Tel Aviv University Law School.

Even the collapse of the National Unity Government in Spring 1990 did not reenergize the demand for a written constitution. During the three-month interregnum, there were massive demonstrations calling for a change in the electoral system, but the protests were *not* coupled with a demand for adopting a written constitution. The stalemate ended with Likud forming a narrow right-wing religious-bloc coalition government. The increased power of the religious parties in the new government meant another indefinite delay in adopting the Basic Law: Human and Civil Rights and completing a written constitution supporting judicial review.

LIMITED JUDICIAL REVIEW: AFFIRMING (BUT NOT EXPANDING) THE *BERGMAN* RULE

In the meantime, the Israeli Supreme Court was confronted with the consequences of its 1968 *Bergman* decision. The justices were repeatedly being asked to consider the "constitutionality" of other statutory provisions. Their initial response was to avoid utilizing the *Bergman* opinion in subsequent cases. They plainly wanted the government and the Knesset to resolve the issues of Israel's constitution and the Court's power of judicial review in a definitive manner.

As indicated earlier, this was not an unreasonable expectation for the decade of the 1970s. But as the years passed and no action was forthcoming, the Court's delaying strategy became increasingly inappropriate. *Bergman* was plainly a leading case. Either it was to be a precedent in Israeli law or the very absence of that utilization would indicate that the Court was giving it a most restrictive reading. Faced with that existential choice, the Court began to give meaning to *Bergman* by explicitly interpreting its own decision.[9]

In *Agudat Derech Eretz v. Broadcasting Authority* (1981), the Court really had no alternative. The case posed essentially the same issue as *Bergman*. Two newly formed party lists challenged an amendment to the election laws that reduced their television time relative to that of established parties. The amendment, they argued, offended the equality requirement of Section 4 of the Basic Law: The Knesset, and because it was not passed with the specified absolute majority, the amendment was unconstitutional. Once again the Supreme Court accepted the argument. It held that because Section 4 was entrenched, its provisions could only be changed by the specified majority.

The Knesset responded by passing another law. Newly formed political parties were to retain their original broadcasting time, but the allotment of the existing parties was increased. This revised version was then passed by the Knesset with the special majority at all three readings.

In *Rubinstein v. Knesset Speaker* (1982), a small Knesset party challenged an amendment to the campaign financing law. Going into the 1981 Knesset elections, the law had provided that in exchange for state funding, parties must limit their campaign expenditures. Both large parties, Labor and Likud, had exceeded those limits by wide margins. After the elections, at the behest of those parties, the Knesset retroactively increased the amounts that parties were allowed to spend; this change protected Labor and Likud from heavy fines.

Rubenstein argued that his party, too, had had extra funds that it could have utilized in the campaign, but because of the law it had not done so. The retroactive amendment, Rubinstein maintained, penalized the law-abiding and, moreover, it was inconsistent with the equality requirement of Section 4 of the Basic Law: The Knesset. Because the retroactive amendment had not been passed with the specified majority, the Court ruled it invalid.

Agudat Derech Eretz and *Rubinstein* do not by themselves resolve any of the issues raised by *Bergman*. By themselves these opinions indicate only that the Court was not going to treat *Bergman* as a dead letter. Therefore, at a minimum, the three cases in which the Israeli Supreme Court has invalidated Knesset legislation stand for the proposition that the Court has the power, which it will sometimes exercise, to invalidate Knesset legislation when it conflicts with an *entrenched* clause in a Basic Law and *if it was not enacted with the specified majority*.

Other recent cases indicate that the Supreme Court is, as yet, unwilling to extend this limited judicial review. In *Kaniel v. Minister of Justice* (1973), the High Court rejected the argument that a Basic Law, as a section of Israel's "piecemeal" constitution, could only be altered by an amendment to the Basic Law itself. A provision of ordinary legislation could work a change. In *Ressler v. Chairman of Central Elections Commission* (1977), the Court rejected a challenge that the Election Campaign Law, which allocated more broadcasting time to existing parties than to new parties, was invalid; that law had been enacted with the majority specified by Section 4. In the course of this opinion, the Court explicitly said that the difference between a Basic Law and ordinary law is purely semantic.

Thus the limited form of judicial review exercised by the Supreme Court in *Bergman*, *Agudat Derech Eretz*, and *Rubinstein* does not involve restrictions on the legislative power of the Knesset, based on some higher law, but rather based upon respect for Knesset legislation that binds the Knesset itself (Kretzmer, 1978: 117). The Supreme Court, at least until a written constitution indicates a change in political relationships within Israel, accepts the supremacy of the Knesset:

The Knesset, and it alone, is entitled to revoke a statute, in part or in totem, to amend a statute or to legislate another statute in its place. It is clear that this Court will not

interfere in such a process, which lies in the sole jurisdiction of the legislature. (*A.H.L.
v. Minister of Construction and Housing*, 1986: 629).

Justice Miriam Ben Porat, then the deputy president of the Supreme Court,
put it more bluntly:

However negative the opinion of the judiciary may be about [an] arrangement, *in the
absence of a constitution*, the Knesset possesses the authority and power to pass a
discriminatory statute, and if it has done so, there is no option but to act on it (*Cohen
v. Minister of Labor and Welfare*, 1986: 543).

In short, Israel is still functioning without a written constitution incorporating
the society's basic values and setting parameters on the acts of its political leaders.

THE STRUGGLE CONTINUES

As long as the formal adoption of a written constitution is linked to the
acceptance of a bill of rights, the current stalemate is unlikely to end. An optimist
might foresee, at some future time, an end to Israel's security problems. The
human costs of the continuing Israeli-Palestinian conflict, an emerging sense of
political realism by leaders of the two rival nationalisms, or great power intervention *might*, perhaps, prove successful.

But there is no sign whatever that Israel is approaching a resolution of the
underlying discord between Orthodox and other Jews. At best, Israelis are capable
of sustaining an uneasy, ambiguous status quo along this divide. At worst, the
religious "war" among the Jews is held in check only by the greater threat posed
by the unresolved security issues. Yet the Israelis are not about to sever their
concern for a written constitution from the issue of added protection of human
and civil rights. Individual liberty has always been at the core of the demand
for constitutional government (McIlwain, 1940).

In the more than four decades since statehood, all the obstacles to a written
constitution have not been removed. However, much progress has been made
in that direction. Nine Basic Laws have been adopted. In light of *Bergman* and
the subsequent discussions surrounding the proposed Basic Law: Legislation,
they cannot be regarded simply as ordinary statutes. If Basic Laws do not yet
clearly have overriding constitutional status, they are nonetheless fundamental
in some ill-defined sense. Each is indicative of a societal consensus on certain
governmental structures, procedures, and values. It would take a major political
effort to change a Basic Law. Most important, Israeli discussions about a written
constitution are no longer dominated by narrow partisan concerns. When Israeli
leaders think about a written constitution—which is not all that frequently—they
see the need to resolve basic political-social dilemmas.

Perhaps the Israelis have the correct priorities. They do function in a democracy
that has usually given wide recognition to civil rights even in the absence of a

written constitution. Their civil courts do take great care to protect those rights. In that situation it can certainly be argued that peace and security arrangements must come before the adoption of a formal written constitution. And certainly no constitutional bill of rights will, by itself, resolve the Orthodox/non-Orthodox dissensus.

In the absence of a written constitution, the Israeli Supreme Court continues its activist role. The justices are handing down decisions on an ever wider range of issues. In its 5749 (1988–89) term, the Court dealt with such issues as: who is a Jew under the Law of Return and thereby entitled to automatic Israeli citizenship; the Right of Reform Rabbis to perform marriages in Israel; the Right of the Knesset to exclude political parties advocating racist ideas from the ballot; and the authority of the Israeli Defense Forces to destroy houses of suspected terrorists in the occupied West Bank. Justice Barak (1989) has suggested that the very absence of judicial review enables the Court to be more activist. Unlike their American counterparts, he argues, Israeli justices need not be constrained by concerns that they are exercising an undemocratic authority since their decisions can always be overridden by a legislative majority.

Nonetheless, Israel as a relatively new and beleaguered democracy suffers from the absence of a written constitution. Political debate is wide open and robust, but it is unstructured by principles derived from a fundamental, higher set of norms. Judicial decisions may temper arbitrary, partisan, or extremist actions, but those opinions rarely educate the population in the enduring principles of constitutional democracy. Unable to base their decisions on a fundamental, higher, set of values, the justices cannot help "to stabilize and rationalize the legislative judgment, to infuse it with the glow of principle, to hold the standard aloft and visible for those who must run the race and fight the fight" (Cardozo, 1921: 93).

So the struggle for a written constitution and judicial review in Israel continues.

NOTES

1. The proposed Arab State in Palestine never materialized. Transjorden annexed the territory it had occupied during the 1948 war and transformed itself into the Kingdom of Jordan. Egypt occupied the Gaza Strip during that war and later governed it as an "administered area."

2. The Knesset has reversed Supreme Court interpretations that were not based on fundamental principles of natural justice, particularly on matters of major political concern to the government. Note, for example, the Knesset debates and actions on Supreme Court decisions touching upon the question of "Who is a Jew in the State of Israel" (Kraines, 1975).

3. "The question is not one of interpretation, but of the supremacy of the Knesset and the finality of its determination in a law duly passed by it . . . the Knesset is supreme in the enactment of laws. . . . Every law or part of a law which is passed by the Knesset must be enforced. . . . The court can only interpret the law and can question neither its

validity nor its content" (*Basul v. Minister of the Interior*, (1968) as translated by P. Elman (1969: 567).

4. "The Knesset shall be elected by general, country-wide, direct, *equal*, secret and proportional elections" (emphasis added).

5. "The majority required by this law for a change of sections 4, 44, and 45 shall be required for decisions of the plenum at *every stage* of law-making. . . . In this section 'change' means both an express or implied change" (Basic Law: The Knesset, Section 4).

6. That is, a later statute controls over a prior one if the later one expressly repeals the former or is manifestly inconsistent with the former.

7. In English, the leading study by a foreigner is Nimmer (1970), "The Uses of Judicial Review in Israel's Quest for a Constitution." In its original form, it was a report prepared by Professor Nimmer as a consultant to the Ministry of Justice.

8. The "earthquake," as the Israeli press called it, is analyzed in Penniman (1979).

9. "The more petitions there are of . . . constitutional significance that this Court deals with on the merits, the less chance there is that the Court will refrain from deciding such cases" (*Rubenstein v. Knesset Speaker*, 1982: 148).

REFERENCES

Books and Articles

Albert, J. (1969). Constitutional adjudication without a constitution: The Case of Israel. *Harvard Law Review* 82: 1245–1265.

Akzin, B. (1955). The role of parties in Israeli democracy. *Journal of Politics* 17: 507–545.

Barak, A. (1989). *Judicial discretion*. New Haven, Conn.: Yale University Press.

Blaustein, A. and Franz, G. (eds.). (1988). *The constitutions of the countries of the world*. Dobbs Ferry, N.Y.: Oceana.

Bracha, B. (1978). Restriction of personal freedom without due process of law according to the defence (emergency) regulations, 1945. *Israel Yearbook on Human Rights* 8: 296–323.

Cardozo, B. (1921). *The nature of the judicial process*. New Haven, Conn.: Yale University Press.

Cohn, H. (1976). Unpublished interview with M. Edelman, Albany, N.Y., May 3.

Dicey, A. V. (1885). *An Introduction to the study of the law of the constitution*, 10th ed. 1961. London: Macmillan.

Edelman, M. (1977). Confidential interview by author with members of Knesset, Jerusalem, June 10.

———. (1980). The rabbinical courts in the evolving political culture of Israel. *Middle Eastern Studies* 16: 145–166.

Elman, P. (1969). Comment. *Israel Law Review* 4: 565–569.

Freudenheim, Y. (1967). *Government in Israel*. Dobbs Ferry, N.Y.: Oceana.

Klein, C. (1969). Comment. *Israel Law Review* 4: 569–576.

———. (1971). A new era in Israel's constitutional law. *Israel Law Review* 6: 376–397.

Kraines, O. (1975). *The impossible dilemma*. New York: Bloch.

Kretzmer, D. (1988). Judicial review of Knesset decisions. *Tel Aviv Studies in Law* 8: 95–155.

Likhovski, E. (1971). *Israel's parliament: The Knesset*. London: Oxford University Press.

McIlwain, C. H. (1940). *Constitutionalism: Ancient and modern*. Ithaca, N.Y.: Cornell University Press.

McWhinney, E. (1969). *Judicial review in the English-speaking world*, 4th ed. Toronto: University of Toronto Press.

Medding, P. (1972). *Mapai in Israel*. Cambridge: Cambridge University Press.

Nimmer, M. (1970). The uses of judicial review in Israel's quest for a constitution. *Columbia Law Review* 70: 1217–1260.

Penniman, H. (ed.) (1979). *Israel at the polls: The Knesset elections of 1977*. Washington, D.C.: American Enterprise Institute.

Rubenstein, A. (1968). Israel's piecemeal constitution. *Scripta Hiersolymitana* 16: 201–216.

Sager, S. (1976). Israel's dilatory constitution. *American Journal of Comparative Law* 24: 88–99.

Shamgar, M. (1974). On a written constitution. *Israel Law Review* 9: 467–476.

Shapira, A. (1974). The status of fundamental individual rights in the absence of a written constitution. *Israel Law Review* 9: 497–511.

Symposium. (1974). *Israel Law Review* 9: 456–511.

Weiss, A. and Brichta, A. (1969–70). Private members bills in Israel's parliament—the Knesset. *Parliamentary Affairs* 23: 21–35.

Cases

Altagar v. Mayor 20 P.D. (1) 29 (1966).

Agudat Derech Eretz v. Broadcasting Authority, 35 P.D. (4) 1 (1981).

A.H.L. v. Minister of Construction and Housing, 38 P.D. (1) 625 (1986).

Basul v. Minister of the Interior, 19 P.D. (1) 337 (1968).

Bergman v. Minister of Finance, 23 P.D. (1) 693 (1969). [An English translation by P. Elman can be found in *Israel Law Review* 4: (1969) 559–565; it is used for all translations here.]

Cohen v. Minister of Labor and Welfare, 41 P.D. 540 (1986).

Fuller's Case, 12 Coke's Reports 64 (1607).

Kaniel v. Minister of Justice, 27 P.D. (1) 794 (1973).

Kruse v. Johnson, 2 Queen's Bench 91 (1898).

Ressler v. Chairman of Central Elections Commission, 31 P.D. (2) 556 (1977).

Rubinstein v. Knesset Speaker, 27 P.D. (3) 141 (1982).

Part IV

Logic and the Exercise of Judicial Review in Policy Making

12

Original Intent, Strict Construction, and Judicial Review: A Framework for Comparative Analysis

Donald W. Jackson

This chapter represents an effort to devise a two-part framework for the comparative analysis of judicial review. The first part has to do with the specificity or ambiguity of constitutional language, the intentions of the constitutional framers, and the role of precedent in judicial review. The second part involves distinctions between majoritarian and nonmajoritarian institutions and policies and examines the quality of representative democracy in extrajudicial institutions. With the expectation that the nature and scope of judicial review will vary from one system to another, a comparative framework must allow for all pertinent distinctions. In its present stage, this framework is chiefly built on persistent questions about judicial review in the United States. Nonetheless, the eventual goal is to achieve a framework of such generality that it will be possible to categorize and assess any given set of conditions under which judicial review might obtain. Other concepts utilized have involved distinctions between *a priori* abstract review (in France, for example) and *a posteriori* concrete review (the United States offers but one example, see Chapter 4 by Alec Stone). Kitchin's Chapter 5 proposed a four-part table into which judicial systems can be sorted according to their independence/dependence or according to the advisory/coercive qualities of their decisions.

The framework presented here is most appropriate for those systems in which institutionally independent courts with coercive powers exercise judicial review in concrete cases. The United States is a prominent example, but it is by no means the only member of that class. Canada and Germany offer other suitable examples. The framework examines the interpretive tasks faced by courts in such systems in the context of their relations with other domestic political institutions. Such an examination requires that we evaluate the actual political characteristics and practices both of courts and of the domestic institutions to which courts are related.

PREDICATES FOR A FRAMEWORK

Why develop such a framework? While few would argue that the level of everyday political rhetoric in the United States is often sophisticated, subtle, or sensitive, public debates over the role of the U.S. Supreme Court in our society—specifically over power of judicial review and over the "activism" or "restraint" of justices of the Court—may rank especially low in their quality. For example, whatever one may think of the outcome of the U.S. Senate's vote on the nomination of Judge Robert Bork, the public campaigns for and against the judge and the questions and comments in the Senate Judiciary Committee's hearings often bore little relationship to the real complexities and difficulties that lurk in a justice's decision about the appropriate exercise of the power of judicial review. One purpose of an analytic framework such as the one proposed here is to demonstrate the complexities that are often inevitable in the exercise of judicial review. Another purpose is to show that there are only some very limited circumstances in which concepts like "original intent" and "judicial restraint" are tenable, even if one accepts without reservation the normative position that they ought to apply.[1] We will see that, even within the context of concrete review conducted by independent courts with coercive power, variations in the nature of constitutional language, in the intentions of the framers, in the application of precedent, and in the positions of judges who hold the power of judicial review—all these relative to the legitimate authority of other decision makers—involve a complex set of permutations. I should note that Bradley Canon's (1982) "Framework for the Analysis of Judicial Activism" has much in common with the framework developed independently here.[2]

Beginning with *Marbury v. Madison*, Chief Justice John Marshall declared the power of judicial review to preserve the principles of limited government established in a written constitution. The U.S. Constitution as "superior paramount law" had to be protected against challenge by "ordinary legislative acts" passed by "ordinary means." He found that the power of judicial review was inescapable because it was "emphatically the province and duty of the judicial department to say what the law is." The assumption of that duty was, of course, not a matter of strict logical determination, and Marshall admitted, even then, that such duty entailed the necessity to "expound and interpret" the law.

Chief Justice William Rehnquist, while agreeing almost entirely with John Marshall's justification in *Marbury*, concedes that constitutional language sometimes does not provide a clear and unambiguous mandate for judicial decision. Using the "notion of a living Constitution," he has offered a distinction between two meanings.[3] The first version of a "living Constitution," he wrote in 1976, involves the recognition that

the framers of the Constitution wisely spoke in general language and left to succeeding generations the task of applying that language to the unceasingly changing environment in which they would live. Those who framed, adopted and ratified the Civil War amendments to the Constitution likewise used what have been aptly described as "majestic generalities" in composing the fourteenth amendment. Merely because a particular activity may not have existed when the Constitution was adopted, or because the framers could not have conceived of a particular method of transacting affairs, cannot mean that general language in the Constitution may not be applied to such a course of conduct (McDowell, 1981: 70).

The second meaning he found in a brief that had been filed in a U.S. District Court on behalf of certain state prisoners:

We are asking a great deal of the Court because other branches of government have abdicated their responsibility. . . . Prisoners are like other "discrete and insular" minorities for whom the Court must spread its protective umbrella because no other branch of government will do so. . . . This Court, as the measure of the modern conception of human dignity, must declare that the [named prison] and all it represents offends the Constitution of the United States and will not be tolerated (McDowell, 1981: 70).

Rehnquist called this meaning a living Constitution "with a vengeance." He decried such appeals for judicial intervention by invoking majoritarian democratic norms. Judges, having no constituency to which they are accountable, are antidemocratic and antimajoritarian in their exercise of judicial review—a reality that, according to Rehnquist, requires some special justification in a "self-governing representative democracy." As stated, his theoretical point may be unexceptionable, but it does seem to be contingent on the assumption that representative democracy is *in fact* working consistent with some normative theory of representation. His argument on behalf of representative democracy is also quite inconsistent with what Madison expressed (in *Federalist* 10) as his purposes in drafting the Constitution. Madison's purposes had as much to do with constraining majoritarian representation as with promoting it.

Whatever the difficulties, taking Chief Justice Rehnquist (and others of his views) at his word—that representative government, founded on the will of the people, ought to prevail—what should judges do if, for example, representative democracy fails, or even if it does not exist in a particular society? By failure I mean that the actual policy decisions made by representative institutions, such as the U.S. Congress or American state legislatures, may *not* be consistent with *any* reading of the "will of the people" directly or indirectly expressed. Sometimes decisions may instead rest on the successful lobbying efforts of a tiny but well-funded and well-organized minority. Sometimes the power of a single influential legislator may produce a particular policy outcome. The point is that the facile assumption that all laws passed by ostensible representative institutions are legitimate because they are based on the "will of the people" is often well off the mark. An even stronger case may be made for judicial intervention if a society has no representative institutions at all, or if an institution is a mere facade, as the Supreme Soviet was most of the time (until recently) in the Soviet Union. There is much that can be said about the problems inherent in implementing and maintaining representative institutions whose decisions are contingent, directly or indirectly, on majority preferences (Jackson and Maughan, 1978: Ch.10), but here it is only necessary to suggest the difficulties.

Rehnquist also elaborates his preference for representative democracy by arguing that the flexibility of the "living Constitution" was contained in the "general language by which national authority was granted to Congress and the Presidency" rather than in the constitutional limitations that were placed on both federal and state governments. He concludes that even Republican Congressmen Stevens and Bingham, both instrumental in framing the Fourteenth Amendment, would not have countenanced the uses to which that amendment has since been put. The only way in which moral judgments ought to become public policy, he argues, is when they are "embodied into positive law" by a majority of our elected representatives (McDowell, 1981: 77). This is almost the same point that is made by European critics of judicial review. Especially in parliamentary systems, the exercise of judicial review by judges who have no democratic foundation for the exercise of their powers is seen as being in direct conflict with "parliamentary supremacy"—that is, that popular elected parliamentarians have a mandate to govern, while judges do not (Landfried, 1988). Of course, parliamentary supremacy, absent some means of constitutional constraint, will serve to legitimate *any* act of a parliament. While Rehnquist's criticism of judicial activism in the United States on similar grounds is rational and moderate, others press the argument somewhat further.

PROPOSITIONS FOR A FRAMEWORK OF JUDICIAL REVIEW

Edwin Meese is a good example. As a leading disciple of "original intent," here is his assessment of his critics:

Our own time has its own fashions and passions. In recent decades, many have come to view the Constitution—more accurately, part of the Constitution, provisions of the Bill of Rights and the 14th Amendment—as a charter for judicial activism on behalf of various constituencies. Those who hold this view often have lacked demonstrable textual or historical support for their conclusions. Instead, they have "grounded" their rulings in appeals to social theories, to moral philosophies or personal notions of human dignity, or to "penumbras," somehow emanating ghost-like from various provisions—identified and not identified—in the Bill of Rights (Meese, 1986; Levine and Smith, 1988: 56).[4]

His solution? Follow some simple rules:

1. Where the language of the Constitution is specific, it must be obeyed.

2. Where there is a demonstrable consensus among the framers and ratifiers on a principle stated or implied in the Constitution, it should be followed.

3. Where there is ambiguity as to precise meaning or implication, it should be interpreted so as not to contradict the text of the Constitution.[5]

The only element he seems to have neglected is the role of precedent and the principle of *stare decisis* within our legal tradition. Possibly that omission stems from his belief that many of the decisions involving the Bill of Rights or the Fourteenth Amendment over the past 35 years or so are departures from a correct understanding of "original intent" and ought to be reversed. To be fair, *stare decisis*, from almost any perspective, is less important in constitutional cases than in the Common Law (Carter, 1979: 182–83). Still, a long line of precedents that sustain a particular constitutional interpretation must, at least, be considered. The repudiation of precedent seems to demand some sort of explicit justification. Thus we can add a fourth proposition to the list of those above, by qualifying the role of precedent to be consistent with Meese's other propositions:

4. Where a long line of consistent precedent is consonant with propositions 1–3 in sustaining a particular interpretation, it should be followed, or if modified to meet unforeseen conditions, the modifications should not contradict the text of the Constitution.

It would seem to follow that when precedent represents a clear departure from original intent, *stare decisis* should be ignored and such departures should freely be repudiated.

This elaboration of Meese's "original intent" position is presented for the purpose of specifying a set of propositions, which will allow us to identify the variables that might be involved in the exercise of the power of judicial review by judges according to his norms. If we take Meese at his word and attempt to give full credit to his ideas, can we identify the circumstances under which they would dictate a particular outcome? Here is a tentative list of variables:

THE FORMAL COMPONENTS OF A FRAMEWORK

1. The Nature of the Constitutional Language
   a. clear and umambiguous
   b. susceptible to different meanings
   c. ambiguous
   d. implications, rather than express
   e. conflicting provisions
   f. unforeseen applications of words
   g. "extra-constitutional" language

2. The Intent of Framers and Ratifiers
   a. express and consistent intent
   b. conflicting or ambiguous intent
   c. no express intent

3. The Nature of Precedent
   a. consistent precedent:
      (1) how many?

    (2) when?
    (3) by whom?
  b. inconsistent precedent (for each line):
    (1) how many?
    (2) when?
    (3) by whom?
  c. no precedent

Given these three variables, it is relatively easy to specify the permutations that are possible. For example, Meese's argument about original intent would be strongest in the instance of: *clear and unambiguous constitutional language, supported by the express and consistent intent of the framers, and sustained by a continuing long line of consistent precedents from the most appropriate court of last resort.* His position would then apparently demand a single outcome. Fair enough, but how many of the permutations are like that? For example, here is another possibility: *ambiguous constitutional language, with ambiguous and conflicting statements of intent by various key framers, and continuing conflicting lines of precedents from intermediate appellate courts or from previous Supreme Court decisions.* Of these two examples, which is closer to the actual work of the U.S. Supreme Court in interpreting the meaning of the due process clause of the Fourteenth Amendment?

Both the writing and the reading of all the possible permutations are tedious work. The complete specification is set out in the Appendix to this chapter. The only sort of summary that is possible here is to note that, using only the first four language categories set out in variable 1 above (clear and unambiguous language, language susceptible to different meanings, ambiguous language, and implication), roughly 38 decision-making permutations can be identified, and only in about 14 of them is a single judicial outcome specifically determinable, even if we were to implement, without question, norms that would require a judge to follow the plain meaning (when possible), original intent (when possible), or consistent precedent (when available). In more than 60 percent of the permutations, it is not possible to determine a particular outcome. Even that percentage is misleading, for it is based on each permutation being equally likely. While there is no basis for a precise estimate of the probability of each permutation, in many instances of constitutional interpretation by the U.S. Supreme Court, ambiguous language or implication, ambiguous or uncertain intent, and inconsistent or contradictory precedents are more likely than not. It is also important to keep in mind that the estimates of the above alternatives do not begin to take into account conflicting constitutional provisions, applications of constitutional language to unforeseen circumstances, or the possibility of extra-constitutional language or values having achieved constitutional status through authoritative precedent.

We have yet to deal with Chief Justice Rehnquist's (and others') preference for representative democracy over judicial policymaking, but it should be possible to specify the alternatives there also. Rehnquist presumably would agree that not all decisions in a constitutional democracy with limited government are supposed to be majoritarian. First Amendment rights, for example, are supposed to be beyond the will of ordinary majorities, although they may be amended by extraordinary majorities. Previously I suggested as well that Rehnquist's preference for representative democracy presumed that the representative institutions of a system were working according to plan. If we take these notions and put them in order, they provide the following alternatives for answering questions regarding who should decide:

OUTLINE OF THE FRAMEWORK

I. For policy decisions that are seen as appropriately majoritarian (not First Amendment rights, for example):

   A. When there are representative democratic alternatives (that is, when there are representative institutions that are working consistent with some application of representative theory)

      1. Who should implement majority preferences?

         *a. Judges: NO

         *b. Others (especially legislators): YES

      2. Who should decide *even against* majority preferences?

         a. Judges: NO (in theory majority preferences ought to prevail here)

         b. Others: USUALLY NOT (it is necessary to take into account the fact that even representatives may sometimes choose to vote against majority preferences—where they possess some special or superior knowledge, for example).

   B. When there are only nonrepresentative alternatives (that is, when there are no representative institutions, or when it can be shown that the decisions made by a representative institution are not at all consistent with majority preferences, for whatever reason)

      1. Who should implement majority preferences?

         *a. Judges: MAYBE

         b. Others: YES

      2. Who should decide *even against* majority preferences?

         a. Judges: NO

         b. Others: USUALLY NOT

II. Policy decision that are *not* appropriately majoritarian (for example, decisions about First Amendment Rights):

   A. When there are representative democratic alternatives

      a. Who should implement majority preferences?

         a. Judges: NO

    b. Others: NO

  2. Who should decide *even against* majority preferences?

    *a. Judges: YES

    *b. Others: MAYBE (but others are usually charged with that responsibility)

 B. When there are only nonrepresentative alternatives

  1. Who should implement majority preferences?

    a. Judges: NO

    b. Others: NO

  2. Who should decide *even against* majority preferences?

    *a. Judges: YES

    *b. Others: MAYBE

Again, the complete specification of each of the alternatives appears in the Appendix. The most interesting alternatives are in I.A.1.a. and I.A.1.b., in I.B.1.a., and in II.A.2.a. and II.A.2.b. and II.B.2.a. and II.B.2.b. (each of these is denoted with an asterisk above).

APPLYING THE FRAMEWORK

Certain political decisions (I.A.1.a. and I.A.1.b.) are supposed to be made by representative institutions, acting properly in their representative capacities. Such decisions are consistent with Rehnquist's expressed preference for representative democracy, but with an important qualification. On issues on which representative democracy is supposed to prevail, legislators or parliamentarians (or by whatever name, those who are the standard-bearers of representative democracy) are the most appropriate decision makers. That is so *if* one accepts the normative principles of representative democracy and *if* legislators do in fact seek to act consistent with their understanding of their representative duty. Judges usually have no such representative role or duty, though it is possible (in principle) to define a representative role for popularly elected judges.

When representative institutions do not exist or do not fulfill their representative duty (I.B.1.a.), we encounter situations that contradict Rehnquist's avowed preference for representative democracy. If in fact there are no representative democratic alternatives (if representative government has broken down for some reason, or if it is nonexistent) then judges may have as good a foundation as any other decision maker for attempting to implement policies that are favored by a majority of people in a society. Indeed, the instances of successful representative democracies in the world have been few in number, and even those that are supposed in theory to be representative frequently are not in fact. It is difficult to demonstrate that the Congress of the United States consistently enacts laws that are favored by a majority of the American people or that its decisions are always consistent with any plausible interpretation of representative theory. There are many reasons why laws turn out otherwise, perhaps the most important one being that power in Congress is usually not held proportionately to the preferences of the American people (Jackson and Maughan, 1978: Ch.10). In the British House of Commons, power is held by a small cadre of party leaders who control a majority of the House, but whose power is not necessarily contingent on the preferences of a majority of British voters. Even after recent reforms, neither the Congress of People's Deputies nor the Supreme Soviet in the (former) USSR could claim legitimacy stemming strictly from majoritarian preferences. Military juntas, dictatorships of all sorts, and most newly formed revolutionary regimes are even more vulnerable to criticism from the perspective of representative democracy. More often than not, the claim that judges ought not to act because they lack a majoritarian base is one that can be made with equal justice against other political actors and institutions just as well.

Many policy judgments are not supposed to be based on majority preferences. All judgments on questions arising under the U.S. Bill of Rights are like that. Under II.A.2.a. & b., we find situations in which U.S. judges are called upon to exercise the role identified by John Marshall of preserving constitutional principles, *even against majority preferences*. The 5–4 U.S. Supreme Court decisions in the recent flag desecration cases (*Texas v. Johnson*, 1989; *U.S. v. Eichman*, 1990) offer a good example of a conflict between First Amendment principles and overwhelming (though possibly transitory) popular preferences. While other decision makers, even those with a majoritarian representative base, also have a duty to uphold constitutional principles, it is easier for them to succumb to short-term passions, and it is not "emphatically their duty to say what the law is."

When there are *no* decision makers with a representative base, but questions arising under nonmajoritarian principles like those enunciated in the U.S. Bill of Rights are raised (as in II.B.2), other decision makers *might* appropriately uphold constitutional principles. Nonetheless, as John Marshall wrote, "it is peculiarly the province" of judges in our system to declare the meaning of the Constitution.

The most important point is that Rehnquist's argument for judicial deference to representative democracy or European arguments in favor of parliamentary supremacy hold only under certain circumstances. Once again we cannot assume that each of the alternatives we have outlined is equally likely (or equally important). Moreover, fairness dictates that we acknowledge the propriety of Chief Justice Rehnquist's concern about the unwarranted intrusion of judges into situations in which elected representatives, acting in fulfillment of their duties, are supposed to make policy decisions (this includes all of those instances under I.A.). When judges act with contempt for properly functioning representative institutions concerning policy decisions that are supposed to be made consistent with some sort of representative majority rule, Rehnquist is correct in concluding that such judicial intervention *is* inappropriate.

On the other hand, recently retired Justice William Brennan (1988: 61) rejected Edwin Meese's original intent position as a form of "facile historicism," given the fact that "typically, all that can be gleaned is that the Framers themselves did not agree about the application or meaning of particular constitutional provisions, and hid their differences in cloaks of generality." Brennan acknowledges Rehnquist's representative democratic theory to be more sophisticated, but he argues that it does not do justice to the Bill of Rights, which "declare(s) certain values to be transcendent, beyond the reach of temporary majorities" (p. 62). Brennan explores the implications of the Bill of Rights at some length. However, he does not consider the theoretical possibility that the institutions that are supposed to be responsive to majority preferences may not, in fact, act consistent with the norms of representative democracy.

It is not the purpose of this chapter to take a normative position between contending schools of constitutional interpretation. There is plenty of that in the literature already. A good example is a recent article by Leslie Goldstein (1987: 391), which expresses the view that those who are "extra-textualist" "promote . . . the development of a political system distressingly similar to the rule by a bevy of Platonic Guardians' once condemned by Learned Hand." This chapter offers instead a search for a comparative framework for analyzing when such normative positions (from whatever point of view) could *possibly* hold, taken at their full value. A search for such a comparative framework may be substantially enhanced by the perspectives on judicial review in systems other than the United States that are presented in this volume.

NOTES

1. As noted historian Eric Foner has recently written (1988: 256), "whether courts *should* be bound by the 'original intent' . . . is a political, not historical question."

2. Canon utilizes six dimensions:

1. Majoritarianism—the degree to which policies adopted through democratic processes are judicially negated.

2. Interpretive Stability—the degree to which earlier court decisions, doctrines, or interpretations are altered.

3. Interpretive Fidelity—the degree to which constitutional provisions are interpreted contrary to the clear intentions of their drafters or the clear implications of the language used.

4. Substance-Democratic Process Distinction—the degree to which judicial decisions make substantive policy rather than affect the preservation of the democratic process.

5. Specificity of Policy—the degree to which a judicial decision establishes policy itself as opposed to leaving discretion to other agencies or individuals.

6. Availability of Alternate Policy Maker—the degree to which a judicial decision supersedes serious consideration of the same problem by other governmental agencies (Canon, 1982: 386–387).

3. I first found these excerpts from Rehnquist's article in an edited version appearing in Murphy and Pritchett's *Courts, Judges and Politics* (1986). They are also reprinted in McDowell's *Taking the Constitution Seriously* (1981). Rehnquist's argument is familiar to many U.S. students and scholars.

4. Meese's article is reprinted in Levine and Smith's *Civil Liberties and Civil Rights Debated* (1988).

5. These propositions are paraphrased from Meese's article. His third proposition, despite his best intentions, leaves a great deal of latitude for broad construction.

REFERENCES

Brennan, W. J. (1988). The Constitution of the United States: contemporary ratification. In H. L. Levine and J. L. Smith (eds.), *Civil liberties and civil rights debated*. Englewood Cliffs, N.J.: Prentice-Hall.

Canon, B. C. (1982). A framework for the analysis of judicial activism. In S. C. Halpern and C. M. Lamb (eds.), *Supreme Court activism and restraint*. Lexington, Mass.: Lexington Books, 385–419.

Carter, L. H. (1979). *Reason in law*. Boston: Little, Brown.

Foner, E. (1988). *Reconstruction: America's unfinished revolution, 1863–1877*. New York: Harper and Row.

Goldstein, L. F. (1987). Judicial review and democratic theory: Guardian democracy vs. representative democracy. *Western Political Quarterly* 40 *(3)*: 391–412.

Jackson, D. W., and Maughan, R. B. (1978). *An introduction to political analysis*. Santa Monica, Calif.: Goodyear.

Landfried, C. (ed.). (1988). *Constitutional review and legislation: An international comparison*. Baden Baden: Nomos Verlag.

Levine, H. B., and Smith, J. E. (1988). *Civil liberties and civil rights debated*. Englewood Cliffs, N.J.: Prentice-Hall.

Marbury v. Madison, 1 Cranch 137 (1803).

McDowell, G. (ed.) (1981). *Taking the constitution seriously: Essays on the constitution and constitutional law*. Dubuque, Ia.: Kendall/Hunt.

Meese, E., III (1986). The battle for the constitution: The Attorney General replies to his critics. In H. M. Levine and J. E. Smith (eds.), *Civil liberties and civil rights debated*. Englewood Cliffs, N.J.: Prentice-Hall.

Murphy, W. F., and Pritchett, C. H. (1986). *Courts, judges, & politics: An introduction to the judicial process*, 4th ed. New York: Random House.

Rehnquist, W. H. (1981). The notion of a living constitution. In G. McDowell (ed.), *Taking the constitution seriously: Essays on the constitution and constitutional law*. Dubuque, Ia.: Kendall/Hunt.

Texas v. Johnson 491 U.S. 397, 109 S. Ct. 2533 (1989).

U.S. v. Eichman—U.S.—, 110 S. Ct. 2404 (1990).

APPENDIX

PART ONE: TO RELATE THE POWER OF JUDICIAL REVIEW (AND OF JUDICIAL RESTRAINT) TO THE CONTEXT OF INTERPRETATION

I. CLEAR AND UNAMBIGUOUS CONSTITUTIONAL LANGUAGE

A. CLEAR AND UNAMBIGUOUS CONSTITUTIONAL LANGUAGE SUPPORTED BY EXPRESS AND CONSISTENT FRAMERS' INTENT

1. Are the words a judge is supposed to apply clear and unambiguous per se? Is the clear meaning consistent with express and consistent framers' intent?

2. Have there been any previous interpretations of the constitutional provision?

If not, a judge would have little discretion and should apply the provision according to its clear meaning, which is sustained by the intent of the framers.

3. If there have been previous interpretations of the constitutional provision, have they been consistent with the clear meaning and with one another?

    a. If so, how many precedents have there been?

    b. If so, when were the precedents decided?

    c. By which court(s) were they decided?

If previous interpretations have been consistent with the clear meaning and with one another, a judge would have little discretion and should apply the provision according to precedent. The judge's discretion would decline with the increase in the number and recency of consistent precedents decided by an appropriate court of last resort.

If previous interpretations have been consistent with each other, but appear to be inconsistent with the clear meaning of the constitutional provision, the judge is forced to choose between consistent precedent and clear meaning. There appears to be no single basis for choosing between these alternatives. Presumably, one basis would be assessing the consequences of choosing to follow precedents or clear meaning. The number of precedents, their recency and source also might be taken into account. Those who espouse an original intent position would choose the clear meaning which, in this instance, is consistent with original intent.

Likewise, if previous interpretations have been inconsistent with one another, some of them being consistent with clear meaning and others not, no single answer seems to be dictated. A judge might choose to go with clear meaning and with those precedents that are consistent with that meaning, especially when they are sustained by original intent. Alternatively, the judge might look at the numbers and dates of the precedents. If many recent precedents are consistent with clear meaning, that would be a rather strong basis for choosing that line of precedents. If, however, many recent precedents are inconsistent with clear meaning, a judge might be required to assess the reasons given in precedents for the recent interpretation. Whatever the choice, no single answer is absolutely dictated.

B. CLEAR AND UNAMBIGUOUS CONSTITUTIONAL LANGUAGE BUT WITH A CONTRARY, EXPRESS AND CONSISTENT FRAMERS' INTENT

1. Are the words the judge is supposed to apply clear and unambiguous per se, but the apparent clear meaning is *not* consistent with the express and consistent framers' intent?

2. Have there been any previous interpretations of the provision?

If not, the judge is forced to choose between what appears to be the clear meaning and the express and consistent intent of the framers. In the absence of precedents to the contrary, the judge probably should interpret the language so that it will be consistent with the express and consistent intent of the framers. Even this alternative is not clear-cut. Where a great deal of time has passed between the drafting of the language and the immediate issue before the court, a judge might choose to go with the clear meaning.

3. If there have been previous interpretations of the provision, have they been consistent with each other?

    a. How many precedents have there been?

    b. When were the precedents decided?

    c. By which court(s) were they decided?

If there are many consistent recent precedents that are consistent with the clear meaning of the language, then the judge has clear meaning and precedent favoring one interpretation. If, on the other hand, there are many consistent recent precedents that are consistent with the framers' intent, then the judge has history and precedent favoring that interpretation. Frequent and recent precedents by an appropriate court of last resort would represent a fairly strong basis for interpretation in either instance.

If previous interpretations have not been consistent with each other, again the judge would want to know how many precedents there had been on each side, when they were decided and by whom. In choosing between clear meaning, converse but consistent framers' intent, history, and inconsistent precedents in varying numbers and dates from appropriate courts, a judge would have no clear-cut basis for decision.

C. CLEAR AND UNAMBIGUOUS CONSTITUTIONAL LANGUAGE IN THE ABSENCE OF EXPRESS OR CONSISTENT FRAMERS' INTENT

1. Are the words the judge is supposed to apply clear and unambiguous per se, but the clear meaning is not sustained or controverted by express or consistent framers' intent? (The record of the framers' intent may be conflicting, ambiguous, or silent.)

2. Have there been any previous interpretations of the provision?

If not, a judge ordinarily should apply the provision according to its clear meaning.

3. If there have been previous interpretations of the provision, have they been consistent with clear meaning and with one another?

    a. If so, how many precedents have there been?

    b. If so, when were the precedents decided?

    c. By which court(s) were they decided?

If previous interpretations have been consistent with clear meaning and with one another, the judge would have little discretion and should apply the provision according to precedent. The judge's discretion would decline with an increase in the number and recency of consistent precedents by an appropriate court of last resort.

If previous interpretations have been consistent with each other, but appear to be inconsistent with the clear meaning of the provision, the judge is forced to choose between clear meaning and consistent precedent. There appears to be no single basis for choosing between these alternatives. Presumably, one basis would be assessing the consequences of choosing to follow precedents or clear meaning. The number of precedents, their recency, and their source, also might be taken into account.

If previous interpretations have not been consistent with each other, again the judge would want to know how many precedents there had been on each side, the dates when they were decided, and their source.

In choosing between clear meaning (given nonexistent or ambiguous framers' intent) and inconsistent precedents in varying numbers, dates, and sources, while the judge might weigh numbers and recency of precedents as a guide, there is no clear-cut basis for choosing.

II. CONSTITUTIONAL LANGUAGE THAT IS REASONABLY SUSCEPTIBLE TO DIFFERENT MEANINGS, BUT THE ALTERNATIVE MEANINGS THEMSELVES ARE CLEAR AND UNAMBIGUOUS.

A. ONE ALTERNATIVE MEANING IS SUPPORTED BY EXPRESS AND CONSISTENT FRAMERS' INTENT

1. Are the words the judge is supposed to apply susceptible to one alternative meaning that is supported by express and consistent framers' intent?

2. Have there been any previous interpretations of the language?

If not, the judge should choose the alternative meaning that is supported by express and consistent framers' intent. Even this choice, which would seem clear-cut, may become problematic when much time has passed since the framers' intent was expressed, especially where there are some clearly undesirable consequences of choosing that alternative now.

3. If there have been previous interpretations of the provision, have they been consistently supportive of the alternative supported by the framers' intent?

    a. If so, how many precedents have there been?
    b. If so, when were the precedents decided?
    c. By which court(s) were they decided?

If previous interpretations have been consistently supportive of the alternative meaning sustained by the framers' intent, the judge would have little discretion and should apply the provision according to precedent. The judge's discretion would decline with an increase in the number and recency of consistent precedents by an appropriate court of last resort.

4. Have previous precedents been consistently supportive of an alternative meaning other than that supported by the framers' intent?

a. If so, how many precedents have there been?

b. If so, when were the precedents decided?

c. By which court(s) were they decided?

If previous precedents have been consistently supportive of an alternative other than that supported by framers' intent, the judge is forced to choose between consistent precedent and framers' intent. There appears to be no single basis for choosing between these alternatives. Presumably, one basis would be assessing the consequences of choosing to follow precedent or framers' intent. The number and recency of precedents and their source might also be taken into account.

5. Have previous precedents been inconsistent with one another?

a. If so, how many precedents have there been for each alternative?

b. If so, when were the precedents decided?

c. By which court(s) were they decided?

When previous interpretations have been inconsistent, some of them being consistent with framers' intent and some not, no single answer is dictated. While some judges might choose to go with framers' intent, as sustained by certain precedents, others might choose to follow an alternative line of precedent, especially where there are many recent precedents that favor an alternative not sustained by the framers' intent.

B. ALTERNATIVE MEANINGS ARE SUPPORTED BY CONFLICTING EXPRESSIONS OF THE INTENT OF THE FRAMERS

1. Are the words the judge is supposed to apply susceptible to alternative meanings, more than one of which is supported by selected statements of intent by framers?

2. Have there been any previous interpretations of the language?

If not, the judge has no clear basis for choosing among the alternative meanings. The judge may attempt to assess the greater weight of one view sustained by certain framers relative to others, or the judge may be persuaded by the position taken by a particularly influential framer.

3. If there have been previous interpretations of the provision, have they been consistent with one another?

a. If so, how many precedents have there been?

b. If so, when were the precedents decided?

c. By which court(s) were they decided?

If previous precedents have been consistent with a particular alternative meaning, then precedent offers the judge a fairly secure guide, especially if there are many secure precedents on the subject.

If previous precedents have not been consistently in favor of a particular interpretation, then the judge has no clear basis for deciding between alternatives. The judge may assess the greater weight of precedent or choose to be guided by a particularly persuasive line of authority.

C. ALTERNATIVE MEANINGS WITH NO FRAMERS' INTENT

1. Are the words the judge is supposed to apply susceptible to alternatively meanings, while the record is silent as to the intent of the framers?

2. Have there been any previous interpretations of the language?

If not, the judge has no clear basis for choosing between alternatives.

3. If there have been previous interpretations of the provision, have they been consistently supportive of a particular alternative?

    a. If so, how many precedents have there been?

    b. If so, when were the precedents decided?

    c. By which court(s) were they decided?

If previous interpretations have been consistently supportive of a particular alternative, the judge would have a secure guide in simply following precedent, especially where there is a strong line of precedents, including recent ones.

When previous precedents have not been consistent, then the judge has no clear basis for choosing among alternatives, other than by attempting to assess the greater weight of precedent, to take a line consistently supported by more recent decisions, or an alternative that seems particularly persuasive.

III. AMBIGUOUS CONSTITUTIONAL LANGUAGE

A. AMBIGUOUS CONSTITUTIONAL LANGUAGE CLARIFIED BY EXPRESS AND CONSISTENT INTENT OF THE FRAMERS

1. While the words seem to be ambiguous, are they clarified by the clear and umambiguous intent of the framers?

2. Have there been any previous interpretations of the provision?

If not, the judge would ordinarily interpret the language consistent with the framers' intent. Even so, if a great deal of time has passed since the enactment of the provision, the judge may choose an interpretation on some other grounds.

3. If there have been previous interpretations of the provision, have they been consistent with one another and with the intent of the framers?

    a. If so, how many precedents have there been?

    b. If so, when were the precedents decided?

    c. By which court(s) were they decided?

If they have been consistent with each other and with the intent of the framers, the judge would have little discretion and ordinarily should apply the provision according to precedent. The judge's discretion would decline with an increase in the number, recency and authoritative source of consistent precedents.

If prior interpretations have been inconsistent, some of them being consistent with the intent of the framers and others not, no single answer seems to be dictated. A judge might choose to go with the intent of the framers and the line of precedents consistent with that history. But a judge might also look at the number, recency, and sources of precedents. If many recent precedents decline to follow the intent of the framers, a judge might choose to go with that line, if persuaded by its reasoning.

B. AMBIGUOUS CONSTITUTIONAL LANGUAGE WITH AMBIGUOUS FRAMERS' INTENT

1. Are the words a judge is supposed to apply ambiguous and is the record of the framers' intent ambiguous as well?

2. Have there been any previous interpretations of the provision?

If not, a judge has little to go on. A judge may choose to follow the meaning suggested by a particularly influential framer, such as its draftsman or principle proponent, or a judge may attempt to assess the greater weight of opinion.

3. If there have been previous interpretations of the provision, have they been consistent with one another?

    a. If so, how many precedents have there been?

    b. If so, when were the precedents decided?

    c. By which court(s) were they decided?

    If previous precedents have been consistent with a particular interpretation, then precedent offers the judge a fairly secure guide, especially if there are many consistent recent precedents from authoritative sources on the subject.

    If previous precedents have not been consistently in favor of a particular interpretation, then the judge once again has very little to go on.

C. AMBIGUOUS CONSTITUTIONAL LANGUAGE WITH NO FRAMERS' INTENT

1. Are the words themselves ambiguous and is the record silent as to the intent of the framers?

2. Have there been any previous interpretations of the provision?

If not, the judge is entirely without guidance.

3. If there have been previous interpretations of the provision, have they been consistent?

    a. If so, how many precedents have there been?

    b. If so, when were the precedents decided?

    c. By which court(s) were they decided?

If previous precedents have been consistently in favor of a particular interpretation, then the judge once again has a fairly secure guide in precedent, even more so as the number of consistent recent precedents by appropriate courts increases.

If previous precedents have not been consistently in favor of a particular interpretation, then the judge once again has little to go on. That will especially be the case when recent precedents appear to be quite inconsistent.

IV. IMPLICATION, RATHER THAN EXPRESS CONSTITUTIONAL LANGUAGE

A. IMPLICATION SUSTAINED BY THE INTENT OF FRAMERS

1. Does the provision exist only by implication, even though that implication is sustained by the express and consistent intent of the framers?

2. Have there been any previous interpretations of this language?

If not, a judge would have to rely on the intent of the framers alone.

3. If there have been previous interpretations of the language, have they been consistent with each other and with the intent of the framers?

    a. If so, how many precedents have there been?

    b. If so, when were the precedents decided?

    c. By which court(s) were they decided?

If previous interpretations have been consistent with the framers' intent and with one another, the judge would have a fairly secure guide for decision. That would especially be true as the number of recent consistent decisions by appropriate courts increases.

If previous interpretations have been consistent with each other, but contrary to the intent of the framers, a judge is forced to choose once again between precedent and framers' intent. The number, source, and recency of precedents might be persuasive.

Likewise, if previous interpretations have been inconsistent, a judge will be forced to choose between conflicting precedents. A judge may do so based on the number, source, and recency of one line of precedent relative to another, on his/her assessment of the consequences of one line relative to another, or a judge may choose to follow the framers' intent.

B. IMPLICATION WITH AMBIGUOUS INTENT OR NO FRAMERS' INTENT

1. Does the language arise only by implication, while there is no unambiguous history to sustain it?

2. Has there been any previous interpretation of the language?

If not, the judge is almost at the zenith of acting alone. The judge has no explicit provision, no legislative history, and no precedent to guide him or her. The judge's only source is the sense that the implication is appropriate, given the language that raises the implication.

3. If there have been previous interpretations of the provision, have they been consistent?

    a. If so, how many precedents have there been?

    b. If so, when were the precedents decided?

    c. By which court(s) were they decided?

If previous interpretations have been consistent, the judge can rely on precedent. The judge's reliance is strengthened as the number of recent authoritative precedents increases.

If previous interpretations have not been consistent, then the judge may assess precedent according to number, source, and recency, or the judge may claim to be persuaded by the logic of one line, rather than another. Still, the judge would be pretty much without guidance in choosing one interpretation over another.

V. CONFLICTS BETWEEN PROVISIONS

It is worth remembering that under I–IV above, it is always possible that two or more constitutional provisions may be in logical or practical conflict. Noted

American constitutional examples include the ever-present possibility of conflict between free exercise and establishment clause principles of the First Amendment and the necessity sometimes of reconciling conflicts between the free press and fair trial provisions within the Bill of Rights. Again, a judge may or may not be able to rely on the intent of framers or on precedent in resolving such problems. Each of the alternatives specified in I–IV above in principle could be possible in reconciling conflicting provisions.

VI. UNFORESEEN CIRCUMSTANCES

However clear and unambiguous original constitutional language may have been, however consistently it was sustained by consistent framers' intent, however often and consistently it may have been sustained by precedent, unforeseen circumstances may arise. An example would be the application of Fourth Amendment search and seizure language to modern electronic eavesdropping. Judges may be required to adapt language and interpretations to fit such circumstances. Of course, judges may attempt to develop applications that seem consistent with the overall purposes of the provision, and once there is precedent for that adaptation, subsequent judges will have precedent to sustain them. Nonetheless "original intent" of the framers can never be applied precisely to entirely unforeseen circumstances.

VII. EXTRACONSTITUTIONAL PROVISIONS, RIGHTS, OR VALUES

Such provisions might have their source in international law, natural law, social tradition, other societies, or even the judge's personal values. While they would have no explicit foundation in the constitutional text the judge is called upon to apply, it is possible that traditions or precedents could be found for certain of them. To the extent that the judge can rely on precedent, she/he would have some justification for a decision. If there is no such precedent, then the judge's position would be at its weakest. Of all of the alternatives considered in this part, this one is the most questionable. It would appear to fit under paragraph I.A.1.b. of PART TWO.

PART TWO: TO RELATE THE POWER OF JUDICIAL REVIEW TO THE NATURE AND CONTEXT OF OTHER DECISION-MAKING ALTERNATIVES

I. POLICY DECISIONS THAT ARE APPROPRIATELY MAJORITARIAN
  A. WHEN THERE ARE DEMOCRATIC DECISION-MAKING ALTERNATIVES:
    1. Who should make decisions consistent with majority preferences?
    *[1]a. Judges: NO. On policy decisions that are supposed to be contingent on majority preferences, where majoritarian/democratic decision makers act consistent with the country's majority preferences, judges should have no policy-making role.
    *b. Other decision makers (especially legislators): YES. Democratically

---

[1]The * denotes a particularly important instance.

elected decision makers acting on subjects that are supposed to be subject to majority preferences, in a manner consistent with those preferences, should have the policy-making role.

2. Who should make decisions inconsistent with majority preferences?

a. Judges: NO. Judges should not use the power of judicial review to pronounce policies inconsistent with majority preferences, on matters on which majority preferences are supposed to prevail.
b. Other decisionmakers: USUALLY NOT. Democratically based policy-makers, in theory, would be in much the same position as judges. They also ought not to vote inconsistent with majority preferences on subjects on which the majority will is supposed to prevail. Of course, democratically elected executives or legislators often *do* act on grounds other than majoritarian preferences.

B. WHEN THERE ARE ONLY NONDEMOCRATIC DECISION-MAKING ALTERNATIVES:

1. Who should make decisions consistent with majority preferences?

*a. Judges: MAYBE. Where there is no reason to believe that other decision makers will act consistent with majority preferences, judges would have about as strong a base as any other nondemocratic decision-maker for enacting majority-based preferences.
b. Other decision makers: YES. As above, other decision makers would be in the same position as judges. From a majoritarian/democratic viewpoint, they ought to enact majority-based preferences.

2. Who should make decisions inconsistent with majority preferences?

a. Judges: NO. Again, judges would be in the same position as other nondemocratic decision makers. They have no right to enact policy not favored by the majority when majority preferences ought to prevail.
b. Other decision makers: NO. They are in much the same position as judges.

II. POLICY DECISIONS THAT ARE NOT APPROPRIATELY MAJORITARIAN

A. WHEN THERE ARE DEMOCRATIC DECISION-MAKING ALTERNATIVES

1. Who should make decisions consistent with majority preferences?

a. Judges: NO. When decisions are *not* supposed to be based on majority preferences, judges, through the power of judicial review, are supposed to make policy judgements consistent with constitutional provisions, *not* with the majority preferences.

b. Other decisionmakers: NO. They also are supposed to uphold constitutional principles. Given their popular majoritarian/democratic base, they may, of course, be tempted to vote for highly popular provisions.

2. Who should make decisions inconsistent with majority preferences?

*a. Judges: YES. Again, this particularly is the province of judges, to make constitutional decisions, even against majority preferences, when necessary.

*b. Other decision makers: MAYBE. While majoritarian/democratically elected policymakers have an obligation to uphold constitutional principles, making principled constitutional decisions is not their special province. Of course, if it appears that judges have reneged on their responsibility to uphold constitutional principles, then it may be essential for other decision makers to enter this arena, to the extent that is possible through legislative or executive powers.

B. WHEN THERE ARE ONLY NONDEMOCRATIC DECISION-MAKING ALTERNATIVES

1. Who should make decisions consistent with majority preferences?

a. Judges: NO. This is the same as II.A.1.a.

b. Other decision makers: NO. The same as II.A.1.b.

2. Who should make decisions inconsistent with majority preferences?

*a. Judges: YES. As in II.A.2.a this is the special province of judges through their power of judicial review.

*b. Other decision makers: MAYBE. Like judges they would have an obligation to uphold constitutional principles, but they may not have the independent position, training, or experience most appropriate to the exercise of constitutional review.

Selected Bibliography on Comparative Judicial Review

Abraham, H. J. (1980). *The supreme court in the governmental process*, 5th ed. Boston: Allyn & Bacon.

————. (1986). *The judicial process: An introductory analysis of the courts of the United States, England and France*, 5th ed. New York: Oxford University Press.

Agresto, J. (1984). *The supreme court and constitutional democracy*. Ithaca: N.Y.: Cornell University Press.

Antieu, C. J. (1985). *Adjudicating constitutional issues*. London: Oceana Publications.

Aquino, R. C. (1967). *A chance to die: A biography of José Abad Santos, late chief justice of the Philippines*. Quezon City: Alemar-Phoenix and José Abad Santos Memorial Society.

Barak, A. (1989). *Judicial discretion*. New Haven, Conn.: Yale University Press.

Baxi, U. (1985). *Courage, craft and contention: The Indian Supreme Court in the eighties*. Bombay: Tripathi.

Beard, C. A. (1962). *The supreme court and the constitution*, rev. ed. Englewood Cliffs, N.J.: Prentice Hall.

Becker, T. L. (1970). *Comparative judicial politics: The political functioning of courts*. Chicago: Rand McNally.

Berger, R. (1969). *Congress v. the Supreme Court*. Cambridge, Mass.: Harvard University Press.

————. (1977). *Government by judiciary*. Cambridge, Mass.: Harvard University Press.

————. (1987). *Federalism: The founders' design*. Norman: University of Oklahoma Press.

Black, C. L., Jr. (1957). *Old and new ways in judicial review*. Bowdoin, Me.: Bowdoin College Press.

————. (1960). *The people and the court: Judicial review in a democracy*. New York: Macmillan.

Blaustein, A. and Franz, G. (eds.). (1988). *The constitutions of the countries of the world*. Dobbs Ferry, N.Y.: Oceana.

Bork, R. H. (1990). *The tempting of America: The political seduction of the law*. New York: The Free Press.

Brewer Carias, A. (1989). *Judicial review in comparative law*. Cambridge: Cambridge University Press.

Cahn, E. (ed.). (1971). *Supreme court and supreme law*. New York: Simon and Schuster.

Calasso, F. (1985). *L'unita giuridica dell 'Europa* (Juridical unity in Europe). Manelli: Rubbettino Editore.

Cappelletti, M. (1971). *Judicial review in a contemporary world*. New York: Macmillan.

———. (1989). *The judicial process in comparative perspective*. Oxford: Oxford University Press.

Cappelletti, M., and Cohen, W. (eds.) (1979). *The modern systems of judicial review: Comparative constitutional law*. New York: Bobbs-Merrill.

Cappelletti, M., and Golay, D. (1981). Judicial review, transnational and federal: Its impact on integration. Florence: EUI Working Paper No. 4, European University Institute.

Cardozo, B. (1921). *The nature of the judicial process*. New Haven, Conn.: Yale University Press.

Carter, L. H. (1979). *Reason in law*. Boston: Little, Brown.

Cooper, P. J. (1988). *Hard judicial choices*. New York: Oxford University Press.

Corwin, E. S. (1914). *The doctrine of judicial review*. Princeton, N.J.: Princeton University Press.

———. (1930). *The establishment of judicial review*. Princeton, N.J.: Princeton University Press.

Cox, A. (1976). *The role of the Supreme Court in American government*. New York: Oxford University Press.

Dahl, R. (1957). Decision-making in a democracy: The Supreme Court as a national policy-maker. *Journal of Public Law* 6 (2): 279–295.

———. (1967). *Pluralist democracy in the U.S.* New York: Rand McNally.

de Smith, S. A. (1973). *Judicial review of administrative action*, 3rd ed. London: Stevens.

Dean, H. (1966). *Judicial review and democracy*. New York: Random House.

Dhavan, R. (1978). *The Supreme Court under strain: The challenge of arrests*. Bombay: Tripathi.

———. (1986). *Litigation explosion in India*. Bombay: Tripathi.

Dicey, A. (1885). *An Introduction to the study of the law of the constitution*, 10th ed., 1961. London: Macmillan.

Dimond, P. R. (1989). *The supreme court and judicial choice: The role of provisional review in a democracy*. Ann Arbor: University of Michigan Press.

Dudeja, V. L. (1988). *Judicial review in India*. New Delhi: Radiant Publishers.

Duguit, L. (1923). *Traite du droit constitutionnel* (Treatise on constitutional law). Paris: Sirey.

Eaton, W. (1988). *Who killed the Constitution?: The judges vs. the law*. Washington, D.C.: Regnery Gateway.

Ehrmann, H. W. (1976). *Comparative legal cultures*. Englewood Cliffs, N.J.: Prentice-Hall.

Eisenmann, C. (1986). *La justice constitutionnelle et la haute cour constitutionnelle d'Autriche* (Constitutional justice and the high constitutional court of Austria). Paris/Aix en Provence: Economica/PUAM.

Elliot, W.E.Y. (1974). *The rise of a guardian democracy*. Cambridge, Mass.: Harvard University Press.

Ely, J. H. (1980). *Democracy and distrust: A theory of judicial review*. Cambridge, Mass.: Harvard University Press.

Emery, C. T., and Smythe, B. (1986). *Judicial review: Legal limits of official power*. London: Sweet & Maxwell.

Falzone, V., Palermo, F., and Cosentino, F. (1976) *La Costituzione della Repubblica Italiana* (The constitution of the Italian Republic). Milan: Arnoldo Mondadori Editore.

Farrand, M. J. (1966). *The records of the federal convention of 1787*. New Haven, Conn.: Yale University Press.

Favoreu, L. (1986). *Le cours constitutionnelles* (Constitutional courts). Paris: Presses Universitaires de France.

Fernando, E. Q. (1984). *Philippine constitutional law*. Quezon City: Central Lawbook Publishing Co.

Fisher, L. (1988). *Constitutional dialogues: Interpretation as a political process*. Princeton:, N.J.: Princeton University Press.

Fix-Zamudio, H. (1986). *Los tribunales constitucionales y los derechos humanos* (Constitutional tribunals and human rights). Mexico, D.F.: Universidade Nacional Autonoma de Mexico.

Forte, D. F. (ed.) (1972). *The Supreme Court in American politics: Judicial activism vs. judicial restraint*. New York: D. C. Heath.

Freudenheim, Y. (1967). *Government in Israel*. Dobbs Ferry, N.Y.: Oceana.

Friedrich, C. J. (1963). *The philosophy of law in historical perspective*, 2nd ed. Chicago: University of Chicago Press.

Galanter, M. (1984). *Competing equalities: Law and the backward classes in India*. Berkeley: University of California Press.

Galligan, B. (1987). *Politics of the high court: A study of the judicial branch of government in Australia*. St. Lucia: University of Queensland Press.

Gordon, R.J.F. (1985). *Judicial review: Law and procedure*. London: Sweet & Maxwell.

Griffiths, J.A.G. (1985). *The politics of the judiciary*, 3rd ed. London: Fontana Press.

Haines, C. G. (1977). *The American doctrine of judicial supremacy*, 2nd ed. New York: Macmillan.

Hall, K. L. (1991). *The Supreme Court and judicial review in American history*. Washington, D.C.: American Historical Association.

Halpern, S. C., and Lamb, C. M. (eds.) (1982). *Supreme Court activism and restraint*. Lexington, Mass.: Lexington Books.

Hamilton, A., Jay, J., and Madison, J. (1969). (orig. pub. 1788). *The federalist or the new constitution*. New York: Modern Library.

Hand, L. *The Bill of Rights*. Cambridge, Mass.: Harvard University Press.

Harlow, C., and Rawlings, R. (1984). *Foundations of power: John Marshall, 1801–15, history of the Supreme Court of the United States*. New York: Macmillan.

Hogg, P. W. (1988). *Meech Lake constitutional accord annotated*. Toronto: Carswell.

Holmes, O. W. (1920). *Collected legal papers*. New York: Harcourt Brace.

Hynemann, C. S. (1963). *The Supreme Court on trial*. New York: Atherton.

Ioffe, O. S. and Maggs, P. B. (1983). *Soviet law in theory and practice*. London: Oceana.

Ishimine, K. (1974). A comparative study of judicial review under the American and Japanese constitutional law. J.S.D. Dissertation, Cornell University.

Johnston, R. E. (1970). *The effect of judicial review in federal-state relations in Australia, Canada and the United States.* Cambridge: Cambridge University Press.

Jolowicz, J. A. (1980). *The judicial protection of fundamental rights under English law.* Devanter, the Netherlands: Kluwer.

Jowell, J. L., and Oliver, D. (eds.) (1988). *New directions in judicial review.* London: Stevens.

Keynes, E. (1989). *The court vs. congress: prayer, busing and abortion.* Durham, N.C.: Duke University Press.

Kogan, N. (1983). *A political history of Italy.* New York: Praeger.

Kommers, D. P. (1976). *Judicial politics in West Germany.* Beverly Hills, Calif.: Sage Publications.

———. (1989). *The constitutional jurisprudence of the Federal Republic of Germany.* Durham, N.C.: Duke University Press.

Kraines, O. (1975). *The impossible dilemma.* New York: Bloch.

Lambert, E. (1922). *Le gouvernement des juges et al lutte contre la legislation sociale aux Etats-Unis* (The government of judges and the struggle against social legislation in the United States). Paris: Giard.

Landfried, C. (ed.) (1988). *Constitutional review and legislation: An international comparison.* Baden-Baden: Nomos Verlag.

LaPalombara, J. (1987). *Democracy Italian style.* New Haven, Conn.: Yale University Press.

Laurenzano, E. (1983). *Corte costituzionale e parlamento* (Constitutional Court and Parliament). Rome: Bulzoni Editori.

Levine, H. L., and Smith, J. E. (eds.) (1986). *Civil liberties and civil rights debated.* Englewood Cliffs, N.J.: Prentice-Hall.

Liebesney, H. J. (1981). *Foreign legal systems: A comparative analysis.* Washington, D.C.: George Washington University Press.

Likhovski, E. (1971). *Israel's parliament: The Knesset.* London: Oxford University Press.

Martines, T. (1986). *Diritto costituzionale* (Constitutional law). Milan: Guiffre Editore.

Mandel, M. (1989). *The charter of rights and the legalization of politics in Canada.* Toronto: Wall & Thompson.

Mason, A. T. (1962). *The supreme court: Palladium of freedom.* Ann Arbor: University of Michigan Press.

McCloskey, R. G. (1960). *The American Supreme Court.* Chicago: University of Chicago Press.

McDowell, G. (ed.) (1981). *Taking the constitution seriously: Essays on the constitution and constitutional law.* Dubuque, Ia.: Kendall/Hunt.

McIlwain, C. H. (1940). *Constitutionalism: Ancient and modern.* Ithaca, N. Y.: Cornell University Press.

McWhinney, E. (1969). *Judicial review in the English-speaking world,* 4th ed. Toronto: University of Toronto Press.

———. (1986). *Supreme courts and judicial law making: Constitutional tribunals and constitutional review.* Dordrecht: M. Nijhoff.

Medding, P. (1972). *Mapai in Israel.* Cambridge: Cambridge University Press.

Metcalf, M. F. (ed.) (1987). *The Riksdag: A history of the Swedish Parliament.* New York: St. Martin's Press.

Miller, A. S. (1985). *Politics, democracy and the Supreme Court: Essays on the frontier of constitutional theory.* Westport, Conn.: Greenwood Press.

Milne, D. (1982). *The new Canadian constitution*. Toronto: James Lorimer.

Mirchandani, G. C. (1977). *Subverting the constitution in India*. Columbia, MO: South Asia Books.

Misra, S. (1984). *Fundamental rights and the supreme court: reasonableness and restrictions*. New Delhi: Deep & Deep.

Monahan, P. (1987). *Politics and the constitution: The charter, federalism and the Supreme Court of Canada*. Toronto: Carswell/Methuen.

Murphy, W. F., and Pritchett, C. H. (1986). *Courts, judges & politics: An introduction to the judicial process*, 4th ed. New York: Random House.

Nagel, R. F. (1989). *Constitutional cultures: the mentality and consequences of judicial review*. Berkeley: University of California Press.

Naito, Y. (1961). *A history of the reform of the judiciary after the end of the war: Compiled by an official who was involved in the process* (in Japanese), 5 vols. Tokyo: Legal Training and Research Institute.

Negri, G. (1984). *Il quadro costituzionale: Tempi e istitui della liberta* (The fourth constitution: Times and institutes of liberty). Milan: Guiffre Editore.

Neumann, F. (1964). *The democratic and the authoritarian state*. New York: Free Press.

Nwabueze, B. O. (1977). *Judicialism in commonwealth Africa: The role of the courts in government*. London: Hurst.

O'Brien, D. (1986). *Storm center: The Supreme Court in American politics*. New York: W. W. Norton.

Paez, Velandia, D. (1985). *El control de la constitucionalidad en los estados latinoamericanos y fundamentalmente en la Republica de Columbia* (Control of constitutionality in the Latin American states and fundamentally in the Republic of Columbia). Bogota: Editorical de la Revista "Derecho Colombiano."

Pallotta, G. (1985). *Dizionario della politica Italiana* (Dictionary of Italian politics). Rome: Newton Comptom Editore.

Pannick, D. (1982). *Judicial review of the death penalty*. London: Duckworth.

Penniman, H. (ed.) (1979). *Israel at the polls: The Knesset elections of 1977*. Washington, D.C.: American Enterprise Institute.

Perry, M. J. (1982). *The constitution, the courts and human rights: an inquiry into the legitimacy of constitutional policy making by the judiciary*. New Haven, Conn.: Yale University Press.

Poletti, R. (1985). *Controle da constitucionalidadae das leis* (Control of the constitutionality of laws). Rio de Janeiro: Forense.

Renteln, A. D. (1990). *International human rights: Universalism versus relativism*. Newbury Park, Calif.: Sage Publications.

Rodota, C. (1986). *La Corte Costituzionale: Come e chi garantisce il pieno della nostra costituzione* (The Constitutional Court: How and why it fully guarantees our constitution). Bari: Riuniti Editore.

Romanow, R., Whyte, J., and Leeson, H. (1984). *Canada notwithstanding: The making of the constitution, 1976–1982*. Toronto: Carswell.

Rudolph, L. I., and Rudolph, S. H. (1987). *In pursuit of lakshmi*. Chicago: University of Chicago Press.

Russell, P. H., Knopff, R., and Morton, T. (1989). *Federalism and the charter: Leading constitutional decisions, a new edition*, Ottawa: Carleton University Press.

Sato, T. (1962). *A history of the drafting of the Japanese Constitution* (in Japanese), 2 vols. Tokyo: Yuhikaku.

Scott, F. R. (1959). *Civil liberties and Canadian federalism*. Toronto: University of Toronto Press.

Siegan, B. H. (1987). *The Supreme Court's constitution: An inquiry into judicial review and its impact on society*. New Brunswick, N.J.: Transaction Books.

Simons, W. B. (ed.) (1984). *The Soviet codes of law*. The Hague: Martinus Nijhoff.

Smith, Gordon F. (1978). *The Soviet procuracy and the supervision of administration*. Alphen aan den Rijn, the Netherlands: Sitjthoff & Noordhoff.

Snowiss, S. (1990). *Judicial review and the law of the Constitution*. New Haven, Conn.: Yale University Press.

Sorace, A., Battaglina, A. O., and Ruffilli, R. (1983). *Diritto publico* (Public right). Florence: Le Monnier.

Sosin, J. M. (1989). *The aristocracry of the long robe: The origins of judicial review in America*. Westport, Conn.: Greenwood Press.

Spotts, F., and Weiser, T. (1986). *Italy: A difficult democracy*. Cambridge: Cambridge University Press.

Stone, A. (1992). *The birth of judicial politics in France: The Constitutional Council in comparative perspective*. New York: Oxford University Press.

Strayer, B. (1983). *The Canadian constitution and the courts: The function and scope of judicial review*. Toronto: Butterworths.

Tarnopolksy, W. (1975). *The Canadian Bill of Rights*. Toronto: Carswell.

Volcansek, J. L. and LaFon, J. L. (1987). *Judicial selection: The cross-evolution of French and American practices*. Westport, Conn.: Greenwood Press.

Von Beyme, K. (1983). *The political system of the Federal Republic of Germany*. Aldershot, UK: Gower.

Wadem, H.W.R. (1988). *Administrative law*, 6th ed. Oxford: Oxford University Press.

Wechsler, H. (1959). Toward neutral principles of constitutional law. *Harvard Law Review* 73: 1–35.

Wellington, H. H. (1990). *Interpreting the constitution: The Supreme Court and the process of adjudication*. New Haven, Conn.: Yale University Press.

Wolfe, C. (1991). *Judicial activism: Bulwark of freedom or precarious security?* Pacific Grove, Calif.: Brooks Cole.

Name Index

Subject Index

About the Contributors

CARL BAAR is Professor of Politics at Brock University in St. Catharines, Ontario. He has served as a Russell Sage Fellow at Yale Law School and as the Jackson Lecturer at the U.S. National Judicial College. He has published extensively and has served as a consultant on the administration of the courts in Canada, the United States, and Australia. A former editor of *The Justice System Journal*, his recent interests include the administration of justice in India.

DAVID J. DANELSKI is the Mary Lou and George Boone Centennial Professor at Stanford University and also serves as the Director of Stanford in Washington. He has been a Guggenheim Fellow, a Japan Foundation Fellow, and a Fellow at the Center for Advanced Study in the Behavioral Sciences. He has published a number of studies on the American and Japanese Supreme Courts.

MARTIN EDELMAN is Associate Professor of Political Science at the Rockefeller College of Public Affairs of the State University of New York at Albany. He is the author of *Democratic Theories and the Constitution* and of many articles dealing with various aspects of American constitutional law and Israeli politics. In 1987 Professor Edelman taught the first course on Israeli politics in the People's Republic of China at Peking University. He has also been a visiting professor at the University of Liverpool and at Tel Aviv University.

DONALD W. JACKSON is the Herman Brown Professor of Political Science at Texas Christian University. He has served as Judicial Fellow at the Supreme Court of the United States. His teaching and research interests cover a range of topics on American and comparative judicial processes. His current interests include the protection of human rights in domestic and international law.

WILLIAM KITCHIN is Associate Professor of Political Science at Loyola College in Maryland. His teaching and research interests include Soviet law, Soviet criminal processes, and American constitutional law.

PETER H. RUSSELL is Professor of Political Science at the University of Toronto, where he has also served as the Principal of Innis College and as the Director of Graduate Studies in the Department of Political Science. He formerly served as the Director of Research for the McDonald Royal Commission on the Royal Canadian Mounted Police, and recently completed a term as president of the Canadian Law and Society Association. He has also served as president of the Canadian Political Science Association. His research includes extensive work on judicial and constitutional politics, most recently *the Judiciary in Canada: The Third Branch of Government.*

NILS STJERNQUIST is Professor Emeritus of the Department of Political Science at Lund University in Sweden, where he also formerly served as Vice-Chancellor. He has served on the staff of various governmental commissions, including the commission that drafted the Swedish constitution of 1974. He has published extensively in both English and Swedish on Swedish constitutional law, and on Swedish government, politics and public administration.

ALEC STONE is Assistant Professor of Political Science at the University of California, Irvine. He has published articles on the French Constitutional Council in journals and edited volumes, and his doctoral dissertation, *The Birth of Judicial Politics in France: The Constitutional Council in Comparative Perspective*, published by Oxford University Press in 1992. His current project is a book on the sources and dynamics of judicial-political confrontation in France, Germany, Spain, and the United States.

MAURICE SUNKIN, Barrister (Middle Temple), is Lecturer in Law at the University of Essex. He has also taught at the London School of Economics and at University College, London. His principal publications have been in the field of U.K. public law.

C. NEAL TATE is Regents' Professor of Political Science at the University of North Texas. He is also the current Chair of the Research Committee on Comparative Judicial Studies of the International Political Science Association. He has published extensively on the courts of the Philippines and the United States. His current research is on the long-term behavior of several national courts and their judges, including the supreme courts of Canada, Great Britain, the Philippines, and the United States.

MARY L. VOLCANSEK is Professor of Political Science at Florida International University and also serves as a member of the faculty of the FSU Study Center in Florence, Italy. Her most recent book is a comparison of judicial selection in France and the United States. Her teaching and research interests center on comparative judicial politics and on Western European politics, including her current focus on Italy.